Franchisees as Consumers

Jenny Buchan

# Franchisees as Consumers

## Benchmarks, Perspectives and Consequences

Springer

Jenny Buchan
Australian School of Business
University of New South Wales
Kensington, New South Wales, Australia

ISBN 978-1-4614-5613-1 ISBN 978-1-4614-5614-8 (eBook)
DOI 10.1007/978-1-4614-5614-8
Springer New York Heidelberg Dordrecht London

Library of Congress Control Number: 2012949561



Printed on acid-free paper

Springer is part of Springer Science+Business Media (www.springer.com)

# Acknowledgments

Many people and events led to the writing of this book. I acknowledge my clients whose experiences during my years of legal practice in fields of retail leasing and franchising sowed a seed that is now bearing fruit. I thank franchisees who generously shared their experiences of franchising; they are the subjects whose voices are often not heard.

Professionally, I have been encouraged and inspired by academic colleagues who each arrived in my life at exactly the right moment. Key figures are Professors Rosalind Mason, Paul Omar and Alan Carsrud; Associate Professor Christopher Symes; Professor Stephen Corones; Dr. Bill Dixon; Dr. Michael Schaper; and Associate Professor Elizabeth Spencer. The Rt. Hon. Sir Edmund (Ted) W. Thomas is an ongoing inspiration. He thoughtfully critiqued my draft PhD dissertation that formed the basis of this book. Professor Patrick Kaufmann suggested that the best way to tell this story is in a white paper or a book. Dr. Norris Krueger, Jr., introduced me to the Springer team, and from then on there would be a book. I also thank Associate Professor Rozenn Perrigot, who hosted me at The University of Rennes while I was writing; Dr. Lindi Renier Todd and Moritz Draheim.

I appreciate the financial support provided by CPA Australia, the Institute of Chartered Accountants Australia and the Australian School of Business at UNSW.

Above all, I thank my father, George Hitchcock, for believing that girls can achieve anything; my mother, Jo Hitchcock, for encouraging me never to shy away from hard options; my husband, Graham; and my children, Ian and Tamsin, for believing in me and graciously putting up with my absences while I wrote this book.

Jenny Buchan

# Contents

# Chapter 1
# Introduction

**Abstract** In this chapter, the economic importance of franchising is set out. The franchise, franchisor, franchisee, franchise network and franchise system are introduced and defined. The unresolved challenges that confront regulators of franchising are presented. Franchisees are clearly vulnerable at numerous junctures which are introduced in this chapter. Broadly, the causes are asymmetry, the nature of the franchise agreement as a standard form yet relational contract, and the absence of corporate governance mechanisms between franchisor and its franchisees. Weaknesses in the franchise model are brought into starkest relief if the franchisor becomes insolvent.

Twenty-first century franchisors operate in ways that rival the complexity of sophisticated multinationals. Now, neither contract laws nor the regulatory checks and balances that are designed to regulate a two-party transaction calibrate the franchisor/franchisee relationship adequately. In nature, ecosystems are most complex at the boundaries of multiple habitats. Franchising exemplifies this in the legal world. At the intersections of small business, consumer protection, competition and corporate affairs, it presents unique challenges for legal policy makers. Business format franchising (franchising) as a business model arrived on the legal scene after the law around many of the roles franchisees now assume was settled. Because of its global reach, any dubious practices in franchising can quickly become pandemic. Denied effective mitigation mechanisms, franchisees are vulnerable.

Franchising is complex and it impacts millions of people globally. Complexity is no reason to shy off understanding the franchise business model and its legal implications. The more we understand the nuances of the relationship between franchisors, their support networks and franchisees, the more we understand why franchising does not fit neatly into established rules of contracts, laws of employment, laws regulating corporations and laws enacted to protect consumers – to name the most obvious. The first question when considering any problem from a legal perspective is: Can the problem be addressed within the existing law? It is timely to review what

J. Buchan, *Franchisees as Consumers: Benchmarks, Perspectives and Consequences*,
DOI 10.1007/978-1-4614-5614-8_1, © Springer Science+Business Media New York 2013

we now know about how the law accommodates franchising and to identify whether, and if so where, new approaches are required.

A first challenge is compensating for asymmetry in franchising. Franchising entrenches the franchisor as the party with more power, and the asymmetry of the relationship exposes franchisees to often lawful but nonetheless damaging behaviour by their franchisors. Regulators have adopted a number of mechanisms to address asymmetry, but most if not all are based on outdated assumptions about the franchisor/franchisee relationship. These assumptions include that franchisors operate independent of other actors in their network, that franchisors do not franchise unless they have proven their business is profitable, that franchisees can protect their own interests and failure to do so is their own fault, that franchisees only need protection before entering the relationship or in limited situations during it and that franchisors' businesses do not fail. Asymmetry is a recurring theme through this book and is specifically addressed in Chap. 6.

A second challenge is the franchise agreement itself which is drafted by the franchisor to protect its interests. The franchisor's commitments are worded as discretions and provide franchisees with little purchase in a breach of contract dispute. The agreement appears complete, but is not. It is an important platform for the relationship between franchisees and franchisors and their relationships with third parties. It risks being treated as complete and accorded sanctity in the courts. Whilst the franchise agreement is discussed in detail in Chap. 5, it recurs throughout this book.

A third challenge is that in formulating corporate governance policies and procedures franchisors and their administrators omit franchisees. As a consequence, decisions can be made that reap a significant reward for the franchisor, or put the franchise system at risk, without regard for the franchisees.

All three challenges are brought into stark relief when a franchisor becomes insolvent. The rights franchisees are afforded exist in their contracts with the franchisor and, where there is mandatory franchise regulation, under the regulation. Both franchise agreements and regulation designed to protect franchisees from exploitation by franchisors are based on the shaky premise that the franchisor will remain solvent.

The initial impetus to write this book came from the realisation that an alarming number of franchisors fail, leaving franchisees struggling for appropriate recognition in the insolvency process. Providing a way for franchisees to protect their significant investments from the consequences of franchisor failure is a serious and unmet issue for policy makers with material economic impacts (externalities) on franchisees. Chapter 8 explores franchisor failure, focussing on the franchisees' experiences. Although contract law appears to be the logical home for questions about franchisees' rights, consumer protection, corporate governance (addressed in Chap. 7) and business failure, laws are increasingly important areas where contracts leave franchisees vulnerable.

In a situation such as franchising where participation is desirable for the economy, but where one party is clearly vulnerable, policy makers aim to level the playing field. This justifies a legislative response. There is little point in raising problems without also proposing approaches to resolving them. Any response should be calibrated by reference to appropriate theory and benchmarks. Accordingly Chap. 9 canvasses consumer protection theory, consumer protection benchmarks and solutions to the problems revealed by a franchisor's failure. In Chap. 10, some concluding thoughts are offered. Whilst this book centres on Australia, the same challenges resonate with franchise stakeholders everywhere.

## The Importance of Business Format Franchising

Franchising has become a significant part of the global commercial landscape. By 2010, franchises operated in about two-thirds of the approximately 192 countries in the world[1] and made a significant contribution to GDP, employment and the retail economy. Franchising has been used to expand businesses of all kinds. It is a well-recognised means for former employees to make a successful transition to self-employment. Believing they are investing in a proven business concept, they invest confidently. Many accept without question the 'intuitively reasoned and theoretically supported expectation by each party in a franchise that profit can be achieved at greater levels or with more certainty (ergo, less risk) through a franchise relationship than as an independent start-up'.[2] Franchisors, franchisor industry representative bodies, advisers, lenders and many academics support the story that before any franchise is offered for sale, the underlying concept has been proven. In Australia, for example, the industry association the Franchise Council of Australia ('FCA') portrays franchising as 'an extremely successful and rapidly growing aspect of Australia's small business sector'.[3] This is despite the fact that the FCA-funded biannual Franchising Australia Survey reports that the number of franchisors in Australia declined by 75 from 1,100 in 2008 to 1,025 in 2010. These failed franchisors affected between 2,200 and 5,700 small businesses operating as franchisees and put at risk some $1.6 billion worth of franchisee investments.[4] What the net loss figure of 75 masks is that over this period new franchisors will have entered the market, thus making the actual loss through failure well over 75. This pattern is repeated in other countries. However, '[t]he notion that a system is proven simply because it exists ignores the possibility that it may have been on life support from the outset'.[5]

[1] Elizabeth Crawford Spencer *The Regulation of Franchising in the New Global Economy*, (Edward Elgar Publishing Ltd 2010)

[2] Stephen Spinelli, 'Franchises Without Borders' 18 (1) *Business Strategy Review*, 50 at 51

[3] http://www.franchise.org.au/what-is-franchising-.html Accessed 21 March 2012

[4] Calculated using known total numbers of franchisor and average numbers of franchisees and dollars invested per franchisee (56 + 88)40x$275,000 = $1,584,000,000

[5] Jason Gherke, 10 April 2012, Why franchisors fail: Lessons from the Titanic. Smartcompany.com Accessed 12 April 2012

The mantra of the success of franchising is also maintained by lenders. Australia's Commonwealth Bank ('CBA'),[6] for example, identifies pros and cons of franchising and asserts that

> Franchises have a better record of survival than other small business start-ups
>
> The franchisee has a proven formula, established product or service, brand recognition and reputation, reducing risk of failure.[7]

The CBA counters the above with the ambiguously worded caution that

> If your business goes under, so might you. Many people risk their home and a lot of money to own a business and that may be lost if the franchise business doesn't work.[8]

The CBA information highlights another of the challenges facing stakeholders in the franchise sector – the inconsistency of terminology. When referring to 'the franchise', it is unclear whether the CBA means franchisor or franchisee, which brings us to the question of the terms used to describe aspects of franchising.

## Definitions

In the space of three lines above, the CBA uses the words 'franchises', 'franchisee' and 'franchise business'. Lawyers, journalists and academics researching franchising also interchange all of the terms: franchise with franchisor and franchiser, and franchise with franchisor or franchisee or franchise owner, often without clarification. The absence of consistency emphasises the fact that any attempt to conclusively define a business model, where each feature may be adapted to suit the specific objectives of each franchisor, is problematic. Both franchisors and franchisees may mimic aspects of big business and small to medium enterprises ('SMEs'). Either may be national operators or small enterprises. Franchising is complicated.

There are three commonly recognised types of franchised business. In product franchising, a distributor acts as an outlet for a manufacturer's or supplier's products within a specific market. In processing or manufacturing franchising, the franchisor provides an essential ingredient or know-how. The franchisee contracts with the franchisor to meet agreed criteria, but otherwise runs its business as it chooses. This book focuses on the third type, business format franchising ('franchising'),

---

[6] 'The Commonwealth Bank brand is the most recognised brand in the Australian financial services industry.... In terms of scale, the Group [that includes Colonial First State, ComSec and Bankwest] has the largest customer base of any Australian bank ...' at http://www.commbank.com.au/about-us/our-company/overview/default.aspx Accessed 21 March 2012.

[7] http://www.commbank.com.au/business/betterbusiness/buying-a-business/buying-a-franchise Accessed 19 March 2012

[8] http://www.commbank.com.au/business/betterbusiness/buying-a-business/buying-a-franchise.aspx Accessed 6 June 2012

that is sometimes described as system franchising.[9] In the USA in 2007, when compared with the product franchise model, '[n]early 20 times as many establishments operated under the business format model, [it] provided more than five times as many jobs,... generated nearly four times the payroll, produced more than four times as much output [and] contributed more than four times as much to GDP'.[10] Through franchising, a franchisor entrepreneur can expand a branded business very rapidly and uniformly, creating a distribution channel that harnesses the energy, equity, capital, access to debt funding and the local knowledge of individual owner-operators, the franchisees. Franchising provides an entry point to business ownership for both franchisors and franchisees. In effect, a franchisor contracts workforce and capital components to the franchisees of the system.

On examining franchising from a labour market perspective, Alan Felstead called for the definition of franchising to be 'sharpened up'.[11] Felstead characterises franchising by reference to intellectual property and contractual rights to use that property. To him it is 'the franchisor's ownership of a name, an idea, a secret process or a product; the issuing of a contract permitting a franchisee to use it; regulations on the way it is used and payments made by the franchisee for its use'.[12] James Curran and John Stanworth, writing from a small business and entrepreneurship perspective, describe franchising as

> an organization with a market tested business package centred on a product or service, entering into a continuing contractual relationship with franchisees, typically self-financed and independently owner-managed small firms operating under the franchisor's trade name to produce and/or market goods or services according to a format specified by the franchisor.[13]

Franchising can also be explained by reference to the way the tasks are divided between the franchisor and its franchisees. To legal academic Veronica Taylor, franchising is a way of organising a workforce 'where the techniques of mass-production are mastered and replicated across time and space by successfully separating conceptual work by a small core of managers and planners [franchisors] from the performance of standardised work tasks by a largely unskilled contingent of easily replicable workers'.[14]

Franchisors often portray franchising as a 'partnership'. It is not a partnership recognised by the law. For instance, there is no room in a franchise for legally defining partnership principles like joint and several liability. While franchising does contain

---

[9] Trade Practices Act Review Committee Report to the Minister for Business and Consumer Affairs, August 1976, Australian Government Publishing Service, Canberra, 36. (Swanson Report)

[10] PWC, The Economic Impact of Franchised Businesses, Volume III, Results for 2007. http://www.buildingopportunity.com/download/Part1.pdf Accessed 10 April 2012

[11] Alan Felstead, *The Corporate Paradox: Power and Control in the Business Franchise.* (Routledge, London, England, 1993) 45

[12] Alan Felstead, *The Corporate Paradox: Power and Control in the Business Franchise.* (Routledge, London, England, 1993) 58

[13] James Curran and John Stanworth, 1983 'Franchising in the modern economy – towards a theoretical understanding' *International Small Business Journal* 2(1):8–26

[14] Veronica L Taylor, 'Contracts with the Lot: Franchises, Good Faith and Contract Regulation' (1997) New Zealand Law Review, 459 at 461 citing Cox R, *Production, Poser and World Order: Social Forces in the Making of History* (Columbia University Press, 1987) 328

elements of other legal relationships such as agency, joint venture, investment, employment and supplier/consumer, none of these labels fully encapsulate it. American franchise lawyer Andrew Selden supports Stephen Spinelli's view that the franchise relationship is a 'strategic alliance between autonomous partners bounded by contract'.[15] As a South African Court concluded, franchising is 'neither an employment relationship nor an independent contracting relationship. It…combines elements of integration and delegation, control and independence and is…a multifaceted vertical structure that paves the way for endless relational and commitment problems'.[16] This ambiguity means that it requires a fresh look through the legal lens.

The *franchise* is the grant of the right to use the franchisor's brand granted by a franchisor to a franchisee, as documented in the franchise agreement. The term 'franchise' is defined in Sect. 9 of Australia's *Corporations Act 2001* (Cth) as meaning 'an arrangement under which a person earns profits or income by exploiting a right, conferred by the owner of the right, to use a trade mark or design or other intellectual property or the goodwill attached to it in connection with the supply of goods or services'. The franchise is a form of ownership akin to a ground lease, being ownership of a right for a set period of time subject to the rights and restrictions in the contract and the interpretation placed on those rights and restrictions by the franchisor.

The *franchisor*, also referred to as 'franchiser', builds and operates two levels of business. The first, it retains, is significantly different from the second. The franchisor's first business is to develop a brand, figure out how to maintain quality and make strategic decisions about how and where to locate new outlets, how to maximise the brand in the market, who to enter joint ventures with and ultimately how to exit. The second is the franchise, the product of the first. In addition to funding growth in the usual ways available to a stand-alone business (shareholder equity or debt, or merging with another business), a franchisor is also able to finance growth by selling to franchisees the blueprint to its second business, the franchise.

In Australia, a franchisor is defined broadly by regulation as including:

(a) A person who grants a franchise
(b) A person who otherwise participates in a franchise as a franchisor
(c) A subfranchisor in its relationship with a subfranchisee
(d) A master franchisee in a master franchise system
(e) A master franchisee in its relationship with a franchisee[17]

Under this definition, a national master licensee of a brand whose franchisor is overseas could be categorised as both franchisor and franchisee. There is, for the

[15] Andrew C Selden 'Beyond the Law and Contracts: Strategies for Effective Franchise Relationship Self-Management' in Elizabeth C Spencer (ed) *Relational Rights and Responsibilities: Perspectives on Contractual Arrangements in Franchising*, 160

[16] *Cacun Trading No 24 CC & Others v Seven-Eleven Corporation SA (Pty) Ltd* unreported case no 18/IR/Dec 99 in Tanya Woker, 'Franchising – The Need for Legislation' (2005) 17 *South African Mercantile Law Journal* 49, 51

[17] *Trade Practices (Industry Codes – Franchising) Regulations 1998* Statutory Rules 1998 No 162 as amended made under the *Trade Practices Act 1974* (Cth), Section 3(1)

purposes of this book, only one franchisor in each franchise system; the franchisor is the entity that has the sole right to use the defining aspects of the brand and to grant rights to master franchisees, subfranchisees and franchisees to establish and run franchises. Its characteristics will be explored in Chap. 2.

A *franchisee*, (sometimes called a franchise holder or franchise owner[18]) is defined in Australian regulation as including:

(a) A person to whom a franchise is granted
(b) A person who otherwise participates in a franchise as a franchisee
(c) A subfranchisor in its relationship with a franchisor
(d) A subfranchisee in its relationship with a subfranchisor[19]

In Chap. 4, we meet the franchisees. They perform the roles performed by many well-understood players in a non-franchised business. They replace employees and financiers. Franchisees enter a contractual relationship with their franchisor, whereby control is vested in the franchisor and ownership with the franchisee. Having bought a franchise, the franchisee's business is about building the brand locally and delivering the franchised service or products to the market whilst adhering to the franchise agreement and following the franchise system.

Franchisees are variously identified as consumers (South Africa in the *Consumer Protection Act*, 2010), business consumers (Australia in the *Competition and Consumer Act 2010* (Cth) Schedule 2, The Australian Consumer Law, Part 2-2), entrepreneurs, a business entity whose owners are in some industries entitled to join a trade union (Japan), employees (some court cases), and even specifically as not employees (Georgia, USA). The key contract, the franchise agreement, is non-negotiable; the business opportunity is sold to the franchisee as a pre-packaged formatted opportunity. In most cases, the franchisee is unable to 'test drive' the business before committing to the purchase. Franchisees are consumers of a business from a franchisor supplier that holds far more information than the franchisee can ever discover or accurately evaluate, and therefore more power. The franchisee as consumer is a recurrent theme in this book.

The *franchise network* is the overarching organisation within which the franchisor is nested. It excludes franchisees. Consequently, the definitions of franchising put forward by Felstead, Taylor, Stanworth and Curran and Selden above, which focus on the franchisor and franchisee and aspects of their relationship with each other and the brand, zero in on too narrow a field. Today's franchisor is likely to operate within an expansive network containing numerous legal entities. For example, Australia's Kleenmaid franchisees contracted with a franchisor nested within a group of 14 proprietary corporations that was integrally connected with a second corporate group comprising seven proprietary corporations and three trusts;

---

[18] Marko Grünhagen and Robert A. Mittelstaedt, 'Entrepreneurs or Investors: Do Multi-unit Franchisees Have Different Philosophical Orientations?' *Journal of Small Business Management* 2005 43(3), pp. 207–225

[19] *Trade Practices (Industry Codes – Franchising) Regulations 1998* Statutory Rules 1998 No 162 as amended made under the *Trade Practices Act 1974* (Cth), Section 3(1)

Australia's Traveland franchisor was part of a group of 40 entities including a listed public international airline-owning company. There may be more than one corporate group, the network may include trusts, and it is likely to operate in several jurisdictions. Whilst the franchise agreement is still the contract that connects franchisors to franchisees, franchisees may need to deal with other entities related or not related to the franchisor to secure premises, stock, and access to intellectual property. The nuances of premises and intellectual property rights, and how these play out if the franchisor becomes insolvent, are examined in Chaps. 3 and 8.

Entities within the network owe no directors' duties or other specific corporate governance responsibilities to the franchisees that are nevertheless dependent on them. The franchise network comprises the franchisor and all of its related entities but not the franchisees. Entities that own or control the franchisor, but with which the franchisee has no recognised legal relationship, may have a major impact on the franchisees' businesses. However, once the franchisor is located within the franchise network, it may no longer be in control of the direction the franchise system takes. This suggestion will be expanded on in Chap. 3. Separation of ownership from control occurs at franchisor/franchisee level and also at franchisor/franchise network level. The franchise network in its entirety is rarely the subject of research and is not the subject of franchise regulation. Aspects of the network fall into a legal vacuum between contract law, antitrust, corporations and consumer protection law, and corporate governance.

The *franchise system* describes a smaller group of entities than the franchise network. The franchise system is defined in Australian regulation as including 'a business system in which a franchisor grants a franchise to a franchisee'.[20] In this book, the franchise system is the franchisor and those of its franchisees operating under one brand. Where a franchisor has expanded overseas, the franchise system includes national master franchisees as well as local single or multiunit franchisees.

## Conclusion

Players in the franchise system, and their relationship to each other, are the traditional concern of franchise policy and research. This focus short-changes franchisees as it draws attention away from the complex network of legal entities within which the franchise system operates. A great challenge in regulating franchising and in applying the appropriate legal standards to the stakeholders in a franchise network is that beyond a common interest in making a profit, the interests of the players are often not aligned. Regardless of the network, or system they form part of, both franchisors and franchisees have different objectives and different responsibilities, take different risks and have different growth and exit strategies available

[20] *Trade Practices (Industry Codes – Franchising) Regulations 1998* Statutory Rules 1998 No 162 as amended made under the *Trade Practices Act 1974* (Cth), Section 3(1)

to them. In some endeavours, they compete head-on, with the franchisor in a conflict of interest situation with its franchisees; in others, their relationship is symbiotic. A consequence of the separation of ownership from control is that franchisees face major threats over which they currently have no control and no legal rights.

If we were to reposition franchisees within the law as a specific class of consumers, then this would prepare us to consider their needs and the absence of rights in a more realistic light. By then applying appropriate consumer protection benchmarks to the franchisee, now cast as a consumer, we can evaluate the appropriateness of the current laws protecting franchisees and identify gaps in policy and law. The franchisee as consumer is explored in Sect. 4.2. We start with the franchisor because it occupies the key position in the franchise network.

# Chapter 2
# The Franchisor

**Abstract** The role, identity, qualifications and characteristics of franchisors is discussed in this chapter. The impact of franchising on the economy of a nation is identified by reference to Australia, France, New Zealand, the United Kingdom and the United States. Franchisors are compared to SMEs and franchisees. Their roles as suppliers operate at two levels: supplier of the franchise system and also of stock and plant. In the second supplier role franchisors' ability to create monopolies is explored. Possible approaches franchisors adopt to managing risk are also identified.

Franchisors 'hold substantial power in the franchising relationship'.[1] To emulate Ray Croc of McDonald's 'in achieving manufacturing uniformity without stifling the individual creativity of its operators through excessive regimentation'[2] is an enduring test for franchisors and requires wise use of that substantial power. Typically, the franchisor controls the franchise's strategy, its look and feel, and sources and negotiates with suppliers to the system, and sets and enforces standards in exchange for franchisees making payments, signing contracts and creating and operating a near clone of the franchisor's prototype. Franchisors choose which functions they themselves will perform, which functions will be performed by franchisees and which functions will be performed by third parties.

After identifying a business opportunity, ideally operating a pilot business to refine the concept, and then fine-tuning the business, the franchisor drafts a franchise agreement, and where required it prepares a disclosure document.[3] The content of this disclosure document varies with jurisdictional requirements. The franchisor also documents all operational aspects of the franchised business, then recruits and appoints franchisees. Advertisements to attract franchisees appear under headings like 'your guide to living the dream'.[4] Franchisors acknowledge the

[1] Do the numbers stack up? Lesley Parker, November 2, 2011, Sydney Morning Herald quoting ACCC Chairperson, Rod Sims. http://www.smh.com.au/small-business/franchising/do-the-numbers-stack-up-20111102-1muio.html#ixzz1fqKnikkU

[2] John F Love *McDonald's: Behind the Arches*, (Bantam Books, 1986) 115

[3] According to Spencer, 20 of the 30 countries with franchise-specific legislation have regulated by means of disclosure requirements. Elizabeth Crawford Spencer, *The Regulation of Franchising in the New Global Economy* (Edward Elgar, 2010) 218

[4] Daily Telegraph, 16 March 2012

J. Buchan, *Franchisees as Consumers: Benchmarks, Perspectives and Consequences*,
DOI 10.1007/978-1-4614-5614-8_2, 

hard work that goes into building any business and promise that through choosing to put in the hard work via franchising a franchisee will be well supported. For example, Australian bookseller franchisor, Dymocks, says owning a business 'can be a bit like walking a high wire, but with Dymocks you know you have a safety net below you'.[5] Over time the franchisor refines the franchise system and updates the operations manuals. The franchisors require franchisees to respond to the commercial environment and comply with the evolving system.

The franchisor establishes a business that performs many functions. It is possible for the franchisor entity itself to conduct all functions that support the franchisees. The only role that is not open to a franchisor is 'franchisee'. However, many franchisors conduct a retail-level outlet along the same lines as a franchisee-owned outlet. This provides an opportunity for franchisors to market-test products, new technology or ideas, to benchmark expectations about stock levels and other ratios and test operational instructions before placing instructions into franchisee-bound operating manuals.

As demonstrated in Table 2.1, franchising is a business model to which each franchisor brings its own nuanced interpretation. There are notable differences between established and new franchisors. Policy makers should not see either franchisors or franchisees as all being small to medium enterprises ('SMEs'). Regardless of the level of maturity of the franchise, the franchisor is the point of connection between the franchise network and the franchise system. Table 2.1 that follows identifies some points of difference between what is recognised as a typical SME and franchisors and franchisees.

An examination of Table 2.1 reveals that numerous differences exist between franchisors and franchisees. Whilst either may be categorised as an SME, some franchisors and even some master franchisees and franchisees are large corporations, while others are travelling along the same learning curve as any newly formed independent business.

In terms of impact on the economy, there are few datasets that permit comparison of the numbers of franchisors, franchisees and their impact. Australia, France[6] and the United Kingdom[7] generate current longitudinal data and New Zealand has now conducted its second survey of its franchisors. We know there were '828,138 franchised business establishments in the United States in 2007'[8] but not the number of franchisors. In New Zealand, an estimated 423 franchisors were operating in 2010 with 23,600 franchised units trading under their brands. The best available comparative longitudinal figures for the franchise sectors are drawn from Australia and France and shown in Figs. 2.1, 2.2 and 2.3 below.

[5] Advertisement on http://www.franchisebusiness.com.au/c/Dymocks

[6] France's Banque Populaire collaborates with the French Franchise Federation to produce annual surveys of franchising in France. The survey is now in its eighth year and can be accessed at http://franchise-fff.com/presse/les-communiques-de-presse-de-la-fff/240-enquete-annuelle-sur-la-franchise.html

[7] The NatWest bank combines with British Franchise Association to conduct an annual survey of franchising in the UK. Highlights are available online at http://www.natwest.com/business/services/market-expertise/franchising/natwest-bfa-survey.ashx#1

[8] This was a figure calculated before the Global Financial Crisis bit deep. It includes product and business format franchises and franchisor-owned and franchisee-owned outlets. Of these, xxx were business format franchises and 14% of those were owned by the franchisor, 86% by franchisees. http://www.buildingopportunity.com/impact/overview.aspx Accessed 10 April 2012

**Table 2.1** Competitive dynamics: typical characteristic of SMEs, established franchisors, new franchisors and franchisees (Adapted from table in Schaper, MT 2010, 'Competition Law, Enforcement and the Australian Small Business Sector' Small Enterprise Research 17(1) pp. 7–18)

| SME | Typical established franchisor | Typical new franchisor | Typical franchisee |
|---|---|---|---|
| Geographically constrained | Not geographically constrained. Wide footprint, including multi-jurisdictional | One franchisor-owned pilot, plus franchisees in close geographical proximity | One or two outlets, but some own dozens of outlets in several brands |
| Limited product and service range | Product and service range may include selling franchises in one or more franchise systems, importing/manufacturing stock to sell to franchisees, owning/leasing franchisees' premises, training franchisees, managing system's marketing fund, managing system's superannuation company | Product or service range is limited, focussing on one franchise brand | Dictated by franchisor and further limited by terms of premises lease |
| Limited market share | Compete vigorously to attract franchisees | Compete vigorously to attract franchisees | Dependent on franchisor |
| | May have sizeable share of product or service market | Limited market share | Potential for abuse of this power by franchisor |
| | Create a monopoly through supply arrangements with franchisees | | -May be dependent on one supplier, the franchisor |
| One or two key customers | Two types of customer: franchisees buying franchises; customers buying products or services from franchisor-owned outlets or direct from franchisor, either face to face or online | Two types of customer: franchisees buying franchises; customers buying products or services from franchisor-owned outlets or direct from franchisor | One level of customer:<br>Customers buying products or services from franchisee |
| High levels of business failure | Limited inconclusive data<br>Business failure levels cannot be dismissed | No evidence to suggest that younger or more established franchisor fail at a higher rate | In theory, the franchisees should be less susceptible to failure than a stand-alone small business |
| Greater compliance costs | The bigger the franchise network becomes, the proportionally lower the compliance cost – franchisor has improved economies of scale<br>Some compliance burden is shifted to franchisees | Proportionately high because have not yet achieved economies of scale | High; compliance with franchisors rules, landlord's requirements and ongoing statutory compliance |

(continued)

**Table 2.1** (continued)

| SME | Typical established franchisor | Typical new franchisor | Typical franchisee |
|---|---|---|---|
| Imperfect information and information asymmetry | Sophisticated operator: | Limited; ad hoc | Limited; ad hoc |
| | Can access information easily, controls information dissemination to franchisees, has full information about its franchisees | Information asymmetry in relation to the market, but has full information about its franchisees | Severe information asymmetry re-franchisor and ability to pay for advisers to match franchisor's advisers but can access information on public databases and blogs |
| Less access to established suppliers | Easy, sophisticated, sought out by established suppliers, significant purchasing power | Better than franchisees but limited power until established | Being a franchisee opens doors to established suppliers BUT unable to freely negotiate |
| Usually unincorporated | Public corporations, groups of entities comprising public and proprietary corporations, trusts, few stand-alone proprietary corporations, partnerships or sole traders. Some owned by venture capitalists | Proprietary corporations, trusts, few partnerships or sole traders | |
| | Directors' assets sheltered | Directors' assets sheltered | |
| Limited financial resources | Significant ability to access finance, including thorough public listing | Often limited finances. Ability to access equity finance through appointing franchisees | Uses most of financial resources and borrowing capacity to buy franchise, thereafter limited financial resources until strongly established |
| Limited access to skilled advice | Established franchisors are advised by multi-jurisdictional law and accountings firms and have in-house advisers | May use large firms or small or brokers to help set up | Seek advice (if at all) from small firms. Once established, they use advisers only when they are in trouble. Mirror typical SMEs |

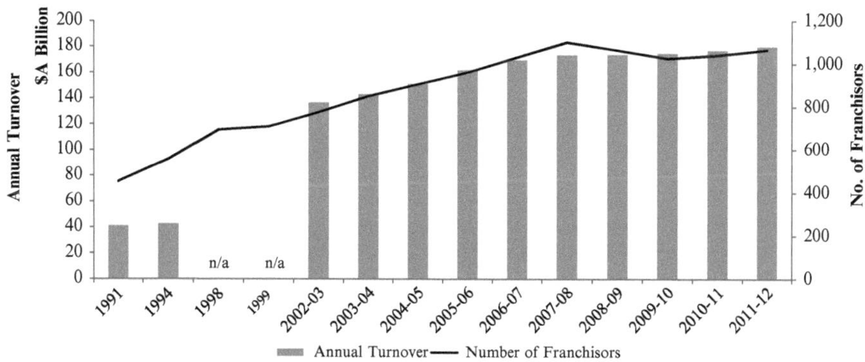


**Fig. 2.1** Number of franchisors and annual turnover of Australian franchise sector

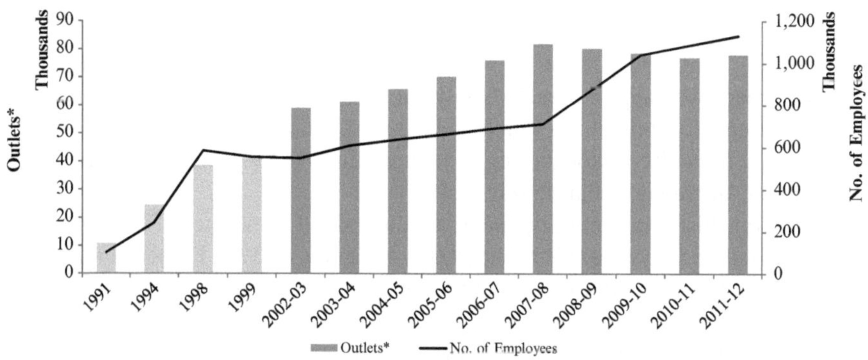


* Business format franchisee operated outlets 1991 - 1991. All outlets including franchisor operated incl. automotive services 2002 - 2012

**Fig. 2.2** Numbers of franchisor- and franchisee-run outlets and employees in Australia. (Sources of data: 1991, Franchising Task Force Final Report (Beddall report), R Fitzgerald; Department of Industry, Science and Technology Franchising Sector Survey results 1994, Australian Bureau of Statistics; 1998 and 1999; Lorelle Frazer and Scott Weaven, Franchising Australia 2002, Commonwealth Bank Franchising Survey, Griffith University; Lorelle Frazer and Scott Weaven, Franchising Australia 2004, Griffith University; for data 2002–2012, IBISworld Report X0002 Franchising in Australia May 2012)

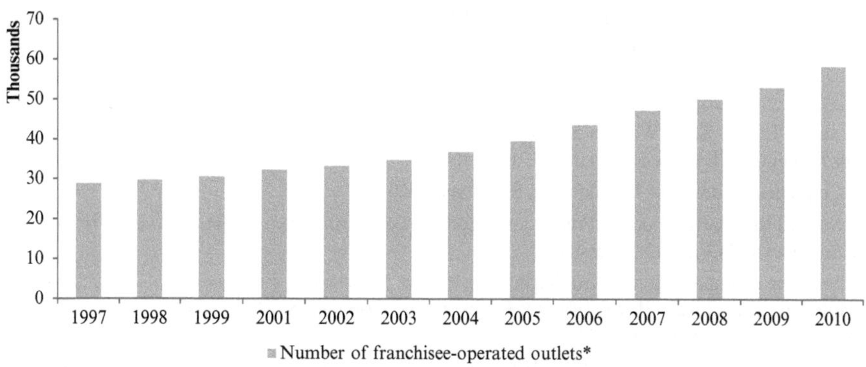


**Fig. 2.3** Numbers of franchisee-run outlets in France (*These figures represent the number of franchise outlets, not the number of franchisees)

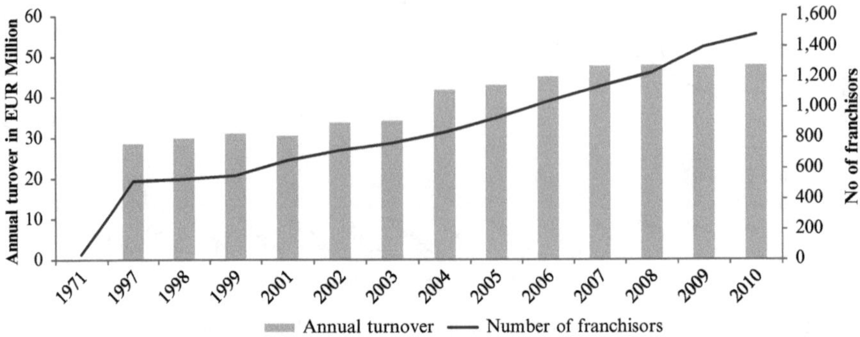


**Fig. 2.4** Number of franchisors and annual turnover of French franchise sector

By 2009, franchising provided work for 690,000 employees, and the franchise sector turned over approximately $60 billion in Australia. The 2010 figures for France are equally compelling with franchising providing work for 335,000 employees and the franchise sector turning over more than 47,89 billion euros (or nearly $60 billion Australian dollars)* (Fig. 2.4).

Each franchisor has between one and thousands of franchisees. The proportion of franchisors to franchisees is about 1:60 in Australia,[9] 1:39 in France[10] and 1:55 in New Zealand.[11] These ratios assume that one franchisee operates one outlet. It is however common for franchisees to own and operate numerous franchised units and to be known as a multiunit operator.[12] Less often, one franchisee also operates more than one brand, an approach known as co-branding which helps a franchisee diversify risk and maximise the use of its management team. An extreme example of a 'franchisee with the lot' is multiunit, co-branding operator Sun Holdings LLC, a US company founded in 1997 by Mr Perales. Sun Holdings has created a network of companies that 'operate 167 Burger King® restaurants, 72 Popeye's franchises, 33 Golden Corral, 46 CiCi's, 4 del Taco and 5 Denny's restaurants'.[13]

Becoming a franchisor or a franchisee is to accept the responsibility of running a business. Despite the level of managerial experience required to fulfil either role well, there are no specific pre-entry education requirements for franchisors. Both the formally educated and those with little formal education become franchisors. In Australia, 69% of franchisors had prior business start-up experience before entering

[9] Lorelle Frazer, Scott Weaven and Kelli Bodey *Franchising Australia 2010*, Asia Pacific Centre for Franchising Excellence, Griffith University

[10] Enquette Annuelle sur la Franchise, Résultats, 2010

[11] Susan Flint-Hartle, Lorelle Frazer, and Scott Weaven *Franchising New Zealand 2010*, Massey University and Griffith University

[12] See, for example, Marko Grünhagen and Robert Mittelstaedt Entrepreneurs or Investors: Do Multi-unit Franchisees Have Different Philosophical Orientations? (2005) 43(3) *Journal of Small Business Management* 207–225

[13] April 16, 2012, Business Wire, 'Burger King® Franchisee Guillermo Perales Acquires 96 Restaurants in Central Florida: Becomes Largest Minority Franchisee in the US' http://businesswire.com/news/home/20120416006453

their current business.[14] This means almost a third of Australian franchisors had no prior experience starting a business before they started their franchise. Their first franchisees are, in effect, their 'guinea pigs'. Of the franchisors operating in Australia in 2010, '30 per cent [had] completed secondary education [i.e. high school], 30 per cent [had] attained a technical or trade qualification and 26 per cent'[15] had a university degree. To put these figures in context, of the whole population of business owners in Australia, 49% list their highest academic qualification as completing secondary school, 46% complete a trade qualification and 23% possess an undergraduate university degree.[16] These statistics suggest that an entrepreneurial flair rather than a formal education is the foundation from which many franchise businesses begin.

Some franchisors operate the franchise through corporations, others through trusts and some through a combination of corporations and trusts. Australian data categorises 70% of 'franchisor' entities in Australia as proprietary corporations, 14% public corporations and 10% trusts.[17] Where a franchisor is owned by a public corporation, the company's published reports may or may not contain meaningful discrete information about the franchise division. Franchisees need to conduct pre-purchase due diligence. If the franchisor is set up as a trust, it is impossible for a third party, including a franchisee, to obtain information about the true identity of the franchisor from the public record. For example, in *Australian Competition and Consumer Commission v. Chaste Corporation Pty Ltd,* [18] Lander J observed:

> Chaste was entirely controlled by the fourth respondent, Mr Foster and the second respondent, Mr Webb, and those two gentlemen, through the [trusts] which they controlled,... would receive respectively 75per cent and 25 per cent of the profits. As far as a bystander [including a franchisee] was concerned, Chaste was entirely controlled by Mr Webb. No bystander could have known that there were agreements in place...which gave control of Chaste to Mr Foster.[19]

Having looked at the franchisor in general terms, let us now delve into its role as a supplier and the opportunities this affords.

---

[14] Frazer, Weaven, Bodey, *Franchising Australia 2010*, 118

[15] Frazer, Weaven, Bodey, *Franchising Australia 2010*, 116–117

[16] Frazer, Weaven, Bodey, *Franchising Australia 2010*, p. 116–117 figures drawn from Australian Bureau of Statistics 'Counts of Australian Business Operators 2006-7' Catalogue number 8175.0

[17] Lorelle Frazer, Scott Weaven, Owen Wright, Franchising Australia 2006 (Griffith University, 2006), 34

[18] *Australian Competition and Consumer Commission v. Chaste Corporation Pty Ltd (In Liquidation) (ACN 089 837 329), Braddon Ralph Webb, Orlawood Pty Ltd (ACN 059 294 334), Peter Clarence Foster, Sean Petrie Allen Cousins, Kevin Anthony McMullan, Alan Kenneth Cooper, Stephen D'alton,* Qud 252 of 2001

[19] *Australian Competition and Consumer Commission v. Chaste Corporation Pty Ltd (In Liquidation) (ACN 089 837 329), Braddon Ralph Webb, Orlawood Pty Ltd (ACN 059 294 334), Peter Clarence Foster, Sean Petrie Allen Cousins, Kevin Anthony McMullan, Alan Kenneth Cooper, Stephen D'alton,* Qud 252 of 2001 [22], [24]. For a discussion with conman Peter Foster see http://www.abc.net.au/sundayprofile/stories/2578118.htm.

## Franchisor as Supplier

One of the franchisor's roles is to establish a network of reliable suppliers who will supply everything a franchisee needs to establish and run its business.[20] A well-established franchisor has significant negotiating power with suppliers, from landlords through to suppliers of stock. This is very valuable for novice franchisees. The franchisor's 'weight' can open doors and secure deals that a stand-alone new business entrant could not achieve.

Whereas open market monopolies are closely regulated to protect consumers from the impact of anti-competitive conduct, this level of scrutiny does not occur in franchising. A franchisor creates, through the franchise network, a monopoly where the franchisee-consumers are contract bound to deal with the monopolist, the franchisor supplier, on terms set by the franchisor. So long as the law identifies 'the market' in traditional ways, the franchisor will not be seen as a monopolist and will escape rigorous regulatory scrutiny in anti-trust matters. This is particularly the case in relation to anti-competitive conduct whose legitimacy is measured by reference to impact on the ultimate consumer. Observations by Lisa Bruttel and Simeon Schudy that '[w]hen evaluating the competitiveness of a market, cartel authorities assume that subsidiary companies with the same parent do not compete with each other or their parent…antitrust law in the European Union presumes that firms belonging to the same owner always act in the owner's interest'[21] are equally valid in Australia. It could be asserted with confidence that a presumption to this effect exists when cartel authorities are evaluating the anti-competitive potential of otherwise prohibited conduct within franchise systems. On a closer look, the franchisees may be operating within a monopoly in relation to all supplies the franchisor controls. They do not have a choice to deal with other suppliers even if they could secure more favourable terms elsewhere.

There is thus little to prevent franchisors from using their pivotal role in the supply chain to operate like monopolists vis-à-vis their franchisees. Stephen Corones notes that through their supplier arrangements '[f]ranchise agreements may fall within the ambit of [competition/anti-trust legislation] if they involve horizontal or vertical anti-competitive conduct'.[22] This is the prohibited anti-competitive conduct that competition/anti-trust regulators are familiar with. In Australia, franchisors may secure the consent of the regulator, the Australian Competition and Consumer Commission (ACCC), to engage in conduct that if it were not shown to be in the

---

[20] It should be noted that where a franchisee needs supplies of highly perishable stock like fruit to make fresh squeezed juice with the franchisees may be required to source their own local suppliers of this item

[21] Lisa Bruttel and Simeon Schudy 'Competition within Firms' (2012) 8 *Journal of Competition Law and Economics*, 167

[22] Stephen G Corones, *Competition Law in Australia* (5th ed, Thomson Reuters, 2010), 618

public interest would otherwise be in breach of the competition legislation. Andrew Selden observes that 'many [franchise] agreements carefully establish the franchisor's role as the greatest competitive threat to its own franchisees by reserving plenary authority to the franchisor to establish additional locations in close proximity to the franchised unit and to distribute same-branded goods and services through other channels of distribution'.[23]

An example which elucidates some of these issues is that of the bread-baking franchise network Bakers Delight Holdings Ltd ('BDH'). Franchisees are required to order products from entities unrelated to BDH as is described in the notification to the ACCC.[24] Despite several franchisees making submissions in opposition, the ACCC accepted the franchisor's submissions that 'the public benefits likely to arise out of the proposed arrangements between [the franchisor] and its franchisees would outweigh any public detriment'.[25] For example, one franchisee submitted that BDH

> have been known to use their relationship with the supplier to terminate franchise agreements, breach privacy and call in debts normally at the detriment of the franchisee. Doing so can prevent the small business operator from obtaining another supplier and continue trading. The public receives no benefit from the franchisee being forced to purchase from Bakers Delights nominated suppliers, however Bakers Delight Holdings gains a lot, including commissions.[26]

Consequently, BDH can legally require its franchisees to deal with specific suppliers. In making its decisions, the ACCC provides franchisees and other stakeholders with the opportunity to object on a confidential basis to the proposed legitimisation of the anti-competitive conduct. The process is public to the extent that notification applications and objections to the proposed consent are posed on the ACCC's website. In the absence of a confidential process enabling franchisees to express legitimate tying or other anti-competitive conduct to the competition regulator, franchisors would always have the upper hand. They could find ways to punish franchisees who object to product supply arrangements that may be anticompetitive. For example,

> approved suppliers of ingredients, packaging and equipment contribute 2% of their sales to Bakers Delight franchisees to the Conference and Development Fund which is administered and controlled by the Franchisor.…BDH use these funds for conferences where the approved suppliers attend to market their excellent service to us but non approved suppliers are locked out. Therefore we are not given the opportunity to assess other potential suppliers during these conferences. The Conference and Development fund is also used in a punitive

[23] Andrew C Selden 'Beyond the Law and Contracts: Strategies for Effective Franchise Relationship Self-Management' in Elizabeth C Spencer (ed) *Relational Rights and Responsibilities: perspectives on Contractual Arrangements in Franchising*, (Bond University Press, 2011) 161

[24] Notification N92536 under s 47 Trade Practices Act 1974 (Cth) < http://www.accc.gov.au/content/index.phtml/itemId/750777/fromItemId/729985> Accessed 17 June 2010

[25] Letter Deacons to Australian Competition and Consumer Commission 23 June 2006. At http://www.accc.gov.au/content/index.phtml/itemId/750777/fromItemId/729985/display/notification

[26] Letter 21 April 2007 Narelle Walter to ACCC re Third line forcing notification N92536 lodged by Bakers Delight Holdings Ltd http://www.accc.gov.au/content/index.phtml/itemId/750777/fromItemId/729985/display/submission

manner…in October 2006 BDH invoiced Franchisees that source ingredients outside the approved suppliers to pay for their cost of attending the conference to the value of lost revenue to the Conference and Development Fund relative to the 2% not paid by the suppliers.…Those Franchisees who had advised BDH of their intent not to attend were threatened with a breach of their Franchise Agreement.[27]

Doug Frazey accepts the 'captive market' role of franchisees as a 'structural inevitability of franchising [where] the franchisee may depend on the franchisor not only for materials essential to the business, which the franchisee can often only purchase through the franchisor, but also for premises and finance'.[28] This structural inevitability is also structural inequality and it provides scope for abuse.

## Franchisor's Approaches to Managing Risk

A franchisor/franchisee relationship can be expressed as separating decision functions, which rest with the franchisor, from risk-bearing borne by franchisees.[29] Franchisors structure the franchise network to protect core assets like intellectual property and limit their personal exposure to loss. Within the franchise network, the separation is achieved through the franchise agreement and the segregation of functions among numerous independent franchisor-related and franchisee entities.

The agreement is the primary regulatory mechanism for the franchise relationship. It defines, preserves and protects the franchisor's interests and embeds power and risk imbalance in the relationship. These contracts expose franchisees to significant risk. For instance, before being allowed to sign the contract, franchisees are usually required to disclose every detail of their personal finances to the franchisor. This is to reassure the franchisor that the franchisee is able to afford the business. Conversely, the franchisor is able to withhold information about all aspects of its businesses except what has to be disclosed to meet statutory requirements. Through this asymmetry of financial information, for example, the franchisee takes on the risk that the franchisor may be insolvent. It relies on the franchisors' word.[30]

---

[27] Letter 25 April 2007 Paul Costanzo to ACCC re Third line forcing notification N92536 lodged by Bakers Delight Holdings Ltd. http://www.accc.gov.au/content/index.phtml/itemId/750777/fromItemId/729985/display/submission. Costanzo's company, franchisee PAKAMALA PTY LTD, was registered on 6 August 2004 and commenced trading as Bakers Delight Ulladulla in September 2004. It is now (2012) in external administration

[28] Doug Frazey, 'Case Note: When 'Good Cause' Goes Bad: Minnesota Restricts Protection for Dealers under HUMEDA – River Valley Truck Ctr., Inc V. Interstate Cos' (2006–2007) 33(2) *William Mitchell Law Review* 711, 728 quoting ABA Antitrust Section: Monograph No 17, Franchise Protection: Laws Against Termination and the Establishment of Additional Franchises 19 (1990). We see the extent to which the franchisee may rely on the franchisor for access to premises in Chap. 2

[29] See EF Fama and MC Jensen, 'Separation of Ownership and Control' (1983) XXVI(2) *Journal of Law and Economics* 301, 304 who do not include franchise networks in the spectrum of organizations discussed

[30] Franchisors are not always solvent when they sign franchise agreements. Franchisors' insolvency is discussed in detail in Chap. 8

Appropriately, franchisors give themselves the right to maintain the reputation of the franchised brand via the agreement. McDonald's is reported to have a 'morals' clause in its franchise agreements, granting itself the discretion to terminate the contract if 'a franchisee engages in conduct reflecting poorly on McDonald's or brings McDonald's into disrepute'.[31]

Business owners are aware of the opportunity to divest legal and financial responsibility that accompanies a move into franchising. Take, for example, public company telecommunication services provider, Commander Communications Limited, for which 'the effect of franchising will be an increase in sales, movement of costs from fixed to variable and a reduction in direct labour costs with an increase in commissions'.[32] All did not go to plan for Commander Communications. Having had an annual turnover of $A1billion in revenue and 1,200 employees,[33] by August 2008, the franchisor Commander Communications Limited and its 46 related entities were under external administration.[34] Commander Communications' motivation to franchise is consistent with the motivation of franchisors that responded to the question 'why did you choose a franchise model?'[35] in the 2010 Franchising Australia Survey. Perhaps not unexpectedly as this survey was conducted as the Global Financial Crisis impacted the availability of credit, the most commonly stated response was that 'franchisees provided capital for expansion'.[36]

The logic employed by Commander Communications is not lost on US-based franchisors. For example, in commenting on the potential impact of the *Californian Fair Franchising Bill*, Canadian lawyer Michael Webster noted that global franchisor United Parcel Service Company (UPS) creates franchisees who are effectively employees who pay for the right to work by buying a franchise. The company's revenue is generated from shipping packages. Traditionally UPS 'had a series of depots and unmanned drop-off boxes to process returns…[but] some packages must be returned from where they were shipped to'.[37] This left UPS with the choice of employing more staff and creating more UPS-operated depots or appointing franchisees. It resolved the problem by acquiring

[31] *Shelley Lynn v. Keith Handley, Ivernia, Inc., McDonald's USA, LLC*, Does 1–10 Complaint and Demand for Jury Trial, CV12-02140 Filed Central District of California, March 14, 2012, para 103

[32] Jacqui Walker, Small Business Does it Tough … Hardie Trio Quit … Economists Tip Wages to Firm … Gloria Jean's Tax Trouble … Domino's Setback … Small Biz Stats … Commander to Franchise … Economic Roundup' (2007) Smartcompany <http://www.smartcompany.com.au/retail/small-business-does-it-tough-hardie-trio-quit-economists-tip-wages-to-firm-gloria-jean-s-tax-trouble-domino-s-setback-small-biz-stats-commander-to-franchise-economic-roundup.html> Accessed 17 September 2009

[33] Tony Boyd, 'Employees from collapsed telco Commander Communications hit out at receivers' Smartcompany.com.au 25 March 2009

[34] Ferrier Hodgson, Administrators appointed

[35] Frazer, Weaven and Bodey *Franchising Australia 2010*, 123

[36] *Franchising Australia 2010*, Griffith University. 47% of franchisors, closely followed by 45% who chose franchising to achieve rapid market penetration

[37] Michael Webster, 'Fair Franchising Bill Will Create Jobs for California' on Bluemaumau.org.au (17 April 2012) http://www.bluemaumau.org/fair_franchising_bill_will_create_jobs_california

an existing franchise system, [MBE] out of bankruptcy. [UPS] changed the franchise agreement, giving the franchisor more control,… put their signage in front and the public now believes that they are dealing with UPS employees. UPS achieved its business goals: they effectively turned these [former MBE] franchisees into employees who will not be a payroll expense.[38]

Clearly, from the UPS example and that of the Australian bakery franchisor Pie Face, franchisors are aware of fiscal benefits of replacing staff with franchisees. For Pie Face, a deciding factor in favour of franchising is

the cost of employing staff in Australia. Having a company-owned network of stores is just so expensive, and too expensive to own all our stores with payroll tax, and so on. That's obviously part of the reason we've moved to a franchise system.[39]

In addition to controlling their exposure to payroll tax and staff superannuation liabilities by replacing employees with franchisees, franchisors can choose how the money will flow between themselves and their franchisees. The traditional pathway is for a franchisee's customers to buy the product or service from the franchisee and to pay the franchisee. The franchisee then banks the money into its own account and pays a royalty, marketing contribution and possibly premises rental and stock invoices to the franchisor. In some cases, however, franchisors choose to route the money flow in the opposite direction; from the franchisee's customers to franchisor, with the franchisor having a contractual obligation to pay its franchisees a commission. For example, the commission system was adopted by former gym franchisor Beach House Group that required its franchisees to agree to use the services of the franchisor's related entity, Skinsama Debt Collections Pty Ltd, to manage and collect the franchisees' customers 'membership payments by way of direct debit'.[40] This reverse money flow provides a franchisor with first call on 100% of the franchisees' earnings but increases the vulnerability of franchisees that then depend on their franchisor for their income. The consequences of this are pursued in Chap. 8.

Franchisors also shed or manage risk through the legal relationships created with the owners of intellectual property. The franchisor is typically not the owner of the trademarks that it licences franchisees to use. Retail leases and trademarks are expanded on in Chaps. 3 and 8.

A franchisor's ability to manage risk is again demonstrated when the franchisor wishes to exit its role. In Australia, only 50% of the franchisors surveyed replied that they were the founder of the original business.[41] In New Zealand,[42] fewer than

[38] Michael Webster, 'Fair Franchising Bill Will Create Jobs for California' on Bluemaumau.org.au (17 April 2012) http://www.bluemaumau.org/fair_franchising_bill_will_create_jobs_california

[39] Patrick Stafford quoting Homschek in A Bigger Slice of the Pie (2009) SmartCompany <http://www.smartcompany.com.au/food-and-beverages/20090821-a-bigger-slice-of-the-pie.html> on 22 September 2009

[40] Letter Mills Oakley to ACCC re Exclusive dealing Notification N92650 dated 20 September 2006 filed on the Australian Competition and Consumer Commission website

[41] Frazer, Weaven and Bodey *Franchising Australia 2010*, 112

[42] Susan Flint-Hartle, Lorelle Frazer and Scott Weaven *Franchising New Zealand 2010*, 108

45% of franchisors were the founder of their system. Although in France,[43] by way of contrast, 84% of franchise networks are still owned by the original directors, this still means at least 236 French franchise systems had a new franchisor by 2010. Just as the only certainties in life are birth, death and taxes, so for franchisors an event that needs to be addressed sooner or later is 'how do I get out of this thing?' Formulating and executing an exit strategy is an aspect of corporate governance explored in Chap. 7.

The question then needs to be asked whether and how the interests of the franchisees should be taken into account. Before examining this, I will place the franchisor and franchisee into the context of the franchise network.

[43] Enquette Annuelle sur la franchise, Résultats, 2010, 1. 'des réseaux matures (l'enseigne a 20 ans, le réseau 11 en moyenne); de grosses PME très majoritairement détenues par leurs dirigeants d'origine, qui ont choisi la franchise pour accélérer leur développement, mais aussi parce qu'ils ont confiance en les qualities intrinsèques de la franchise : effet réseau, services aux franchises'.

# Chapter 3
# The Franchise Network: Legal Fabric of a Global Player

**Abstract** The twenty-first-century franchisor may operate within a complex corporate structure. The franchisor is often no longer the entity that sets the agenda for the franchise network. Increasingly public corporations and venture capitalists own franchise networks. The possible forms of franchise network and the consequences of this complexity for both franchisors and franchisees are explored here. Emphasis is on the ways franchisors manage their trademarks and the retail premises their franchisees occupy.

> [o]nly by examining the inter-connections between firms can one fully appreciate that the ability to exercise control over production may stretch beyond a firm's legal borders.[1]

By examining the interaction between franchisor-owned firms and the law, one can appreciate the consequences of adverse events that involve the franchisor. In the early days of franchising, the legal structure of the franchisor's network was simple. Two or three legal entities were involved: a franchisor, maybe an importing or manufacturing company and a separate entity that owned intellectual property assets. For example, there were only two entities in the Tastee Freez[2] soft serve ice-cream franchise that originated in the USA before it expanded into Australia soon after World War II. This is the structure franchise regulation addresses.

Times have changed. Whilst the key players in a franchise network are still the franchisor and its franchisees, twenty-first-century franchisors operate within a highly interconnected web of relationships which they do not necessarily control. The franchise model has become increasingly complex. The complexity magnifies as the franchisor expands to other jurisdictions, or is sold to a larger entity, or transfers specific functions to related entities. Franchise networks are now complex webs

[1] Felstead A, *The Corporate Paradox: Power and Control in the Business Franchise* (Routledge, London, England, 1993) 30

[2] *Aston v. Harlee Manufacturing Co* ('Tastee Freez') (1960) 103 CLR 391

J. Buchan, *Franchisees as Consumers: Benchmarks, Perspectives and Consequences*,
DOI 10.1007/978-1-4614-5614-8_3, 

of interdependent companies and 'a nexus for a set of contracting relationships among individuals'.[3]

Increasingly the franchisor entity is not at the top of the food chain. A franchisor may be one of a number of businesses operated under the umbrella of a public company or a venture capitalist. According to Frazer,[4] the franchisor itself was a public company in 40 of the 1,025 franchise brands operating in Australia in 2010. Commander Communications Limited referred to in Sect. 1.2 is an example. To Jensen and Meckling, '[d]iversification on the part of owner-managers [directors of the franchisor] can be explained by risk aversion and optimal portfolio selection'.[5] Hence, a listed company such as Yum!Brands will own a suite of franchised brands.[6] Venture capitalists owned and operated three separate franchised retail bookseller chains consolidated under REDgroup Retail Pty Ltd ('REDgroup') before its demise in 2011. We see this pattern repeated in the holding company structure called Retail Zoo under which US private equity company Riverside has plans to 'acquire a few leading brands … and create a portfolio of four or five different brands'[7] including Boost Juice.

A franchisor is not static.[8] It may be bought by a venture capitalist or may list after franchisees sign on. Neither the future configuration of the corporate group surrounding the franchisor nor the direction in which the franchisor will develop can be apparent to its franchisees *ex ante*. This subsequently means that the franchisees are operating within a different commercial and legal environment to the one they performed due diligence on. Consequences of their franchisor's future directions are impossible for franchisees to map.

Franchisees contract with a franchisor that is often thinly capitalised. Business entities that form part of the franchisor's group of entities but do not carry the title 'franchisor' do not have to make disclosure to prospective franchisees (except possibly in relation to intellectual property rights). For a franchisee, signing the franchise agreement after receiving disclosure of the franchisor entity, but none of the other entities in the network, is comparable to getting married before meeting any family, friends or business associates of one's spouse – you should get away with it – but there could be some unwelcome revelations as the relationship progresses. The poor management or failure of any of these related entities can have an adverse effect on the franchisor and its franchisees. This is graphically illustrated by the consequences of management decisions of Australia's then publicly listed Ansett Airlines in 2002. Ansett owned a travel agency, Traveland. When Ansett failed, the

[3] Michael C Jensen and William H Meckling, 'Theory of the Firm: Managerial Behavior, Agency Costs and Ownership Structure' (1976) 3(4) *Journal of Financial Economics* 305, 311

[4] Lorelle Frazer, unreported 2010 data

[5] Michael C Jensen and William H Meckling, 'Theory of the Firm: Managerial Behavior, Agency Costs and Ownership Structure' (1976) 3(4) *Journal of Financial Economics* 305, 349

[6] http://www.yum.com/company/franchising.asp

[7] Tracy Lee, Smoothie chain is in for a boost, The Australian, 29 January 2011

[8] For example, see John Gordon Why Burger King Went Public Again, http://www.bluemaumau.org/why_burger_king_went_public_again Accessed 21 June 2012

administrators sold Traveland to an ill-equipped purchaser, and it was not long before the network of 270 franchised Traveland travel agencies was disbanded.[9]

## The Franchisor's Identity Within a Network

As already noted, the franchisor and its franchisees are but a part of the franchise network. This more complex structure leads to disconnects between the expectations the law addresses and the reality of the franchise business model. In addition to related entities, a franchisor negotiates arrangements with related and non-related entities that the franchisee must deal with. In some cases, franchisees are required to contract directly with these third parties; in others their franchisor is an intermediary in the contracting chain.

It is common for the franchisor-performed functions to be spread across several legal entities. Some of the entities may be truly independent of the franchisor; others may meet the tests of related entities under corporations' legislation. Functions to be performed through the franchisor may include recruiting franchisees, conducting franchisee training, exploring future directions for the network, owning and managing the intellectual property assets that the franchisees are licensed to use, negotiating and entering into leases, designing and fitting out the franchisees' premises, providing franchisee finance[10] or negotiating relationships with financiers to fund franchisee applicants. They also include sourcing and negotiating contracts for the supply of items of plant such as pizza ovens, delivery vehicles or cash registers, stationery and uniforms; sourcing and supplying via import, manufacture or distribution, the stock that the franchisees will sell to customers; and delivering stock to franchisees. Having a franchisor coordinating supply does not always result in the franchisees securing acceptable service from suppliers. For example, a Bakers Delight franchisee noted:

> In a traditional supplier/customer relationship there is likely to be immediate response to problems raised by the customer to a supplier. However where franchisees are forced to use a nominated supplier, the supplier no longer views the franchisee as 'the customer' even though it is the franchisee paying the invoice. The franchisor is seen as the customer and specific issues relating to individual franchisee may become inconsequential.[11]

[9] See J Buchan and L Frazer, 'The Domino Effect – How Ansett's failure impacted on Traveland' (Paper presented at the Academy of World Business, Marketing & Management Development (AWBMAMD) Conference, Paris, France. July, 2006) 1901–1911

[10] Bakers Delight Media Release, Unique Business Opportunity for Young Guns (2009) <http://www.bakersdelight.com.au/Assets/Files/1994895a-dac3-4386-8a08-cc0a4a5671ee.pdf> Accessed 16 June 2010. 'Bakers Delight will then help them [new franchisees] purchase a bakery through a combination of financial assistance – possibly including working capital, vendor finance and bonus schemes, as well as ongoing advice, training and operational support'. Frazer, Weaven and Wright, Franchising Australia 2006, above n 11, 54–55, report that 22.2% of franchisors provide [start-up] finance to franchisees, and for 17.7% of franchisees, the franchisor is the major source of finance

[11] 2 May 2007 Letter identity of sender withheld to ACCC re Third line forcing notification N92536 lodged by Bakers Delight Holdings Ltd. http://www.accc.gov.au/content/index.phtml/itemId/750777/fromItemId/729985/display/submission

Each franchise network is uniquely configured. For example, there are 98 Pets Paradise retail pet and pet supplies franchisees throughout Australia. Pets Paradise franchisees must enter contracts with several of the entities related or unrelated to the franchisor. For instance, they are required to engage the services of Budget Shopfitters Pty Ltd to fit out their premises. The franchisees are required to pay an ongoing royalty for use of the shop fitters' pet pens. The basic structure of the Pets Paradise network is typical of twenty-first century franchisors. It is outlined in *Pampered Paws Connection Pty Ltd (ACN 116 460 621) v. Pets Paradise Franchising (Qld) Pty Ltd (ACN 054 406 272) (No 3)*[12] ('Pets Paradise'). All eight different legal entities that made up the franchisor and its related entities were related for the purposed of section 50 of Australia's *Corporations Act 2001* (Cth).[13] In deconstructing the Pets Paradise model, Justice Mansfield stated:

> [e]ach of the [seven corporate] respondents is … implementing part of a system through the instruction of its director, the eighth respondent, and as part of the overall system of which they are a member through their proprietorship by the seventh respondent and the control over all of the eighth respondent.[14]

No part of the network is under the control of the franchisees, any of the entities can change hands subsequent to the franchisee joining the franchise system, and to maintain relationship with each of them, the franchisees depend on the franchisor.

Before moving our attention to franchisees, we will explore two specific aspects of the franchisors network: trademarks and retail premises leases.

## Franchisor's Trademarks

> The nature of franchising is that the franchisee is 'buying something that the franchisee can never sell, specifically, the trademarked "name on the door" and such support as the franchisor chooses to provide.[15]

Franchise agreements can be seen as sophisticated intellectual property licence agreements. In franchise agreements, franchisors generally claim to own the intellectual property and all improvements to it. A clause from the Australian Autobarn franchise agreement is typical:

> All rights in and to the Marks and the Industrial [ie intellectual] Property and any part thereof and any addition thereto shall be and remain the property of the franchisor and the

[12] [2009] FCA 138

[13] Under Australia's *Corporations Act*, s 50, where a body corporate is a holding company of another body corporate, a subsidiary or another body corporate or a subsidiary of a holding company of another body corporate, all the companies are related to each other and special rules, for example, re-disclosure, apply. See Philip Lipton, Abe Herzberg and Michele Welsh, *Understanding Company Law*, (16th edition Thomson Lawbook Co, 2012) 94

[14] [2009] FCA 138 para 21 (Mansfield J)

[15] Steinberg, P. and Lescatre, G. 'Beguiling Heresy: Regulating the Franchise Relationship' 2004 109, (1) *Penn State Law Review* 105, 116

Franchise Holder shall not acquire any right, title or interest therein except as provided in this agreement.[16]

Registered trademarks are personal property under Australia's *Trade Marks Act 1995* (Cth)('TMA').[17] Once registered, the trademark, as an item of intellectual property, may be assigned (e.g. to the purchaser of the franchisor), licensed (to franchisees) or sold by the owner (or a liquidator). Bruce Schaeffer and Susan Robbins[18] identify that intellectual property is 80% of the value of the business in franchise companies. Hadfield suggests that '[t]he more valuable the trade mark, the greater the price at which franchises can be sold and the greater the royalties collected'.[19] The registered owner(s) has extensive exclusive statutory rights in sections 20[20] and 22[21] TMA. Because key identifying elements of a franchise are its trademarks, franchisees could assume[22] that the franchisor has the right to control the trademarks, even if it does not own them.

---

[16] Copy of franchise agreement in author's possession

[17] Relying on provisions in Parts 10 and 11 *Trade Marks Act 1995* (Cth)

[18] Bruce S. Schaeffer and Susan J. Robbins 'Valuation of Intangible Assets in Franchise Companies and Multinational Groups' *Franchise Law Journal*, 2008 (27:3)

[19] Hadfield, G.K., Problematic Relations: Franchising and the law of Incomplete Contracts 1990, *Stanford Law Review* 42:927 at 949. This and related questions were tested and the results reported in Francine Lafontaine and Kathryn L. Shaw 'The Dynamics of Franchise Contracting: Evidence from Panel Data' *The Journal of Political Economy*, Vol. 107, No. 5 (Oct., 1999), 1041–1080.

[20] Section 20 *Trade Marks Act 1995* (Cth). Rights given by registration of trademark:

(1) If a trademark is registered, the registered owner of the trademark has, subject to this part, the exclusive rights:

   (a) To use the trademark

   (b) To authorise other persons to use the trademark, in relation to the goods and/or services in respect of which the trademark is registered

(2) The registered owner of a trademark has also the right to obtain relief under this act if the trademark has been infringed

(3) Omitted.

(4) If the trademark is registered subject to conditions or limitations, the rights of the registered owner are restricted by those conditions or limitations

(5) If the trademark is registered in the name of 2 or more persons as joint owners of the trademark, the rights granted to those persons under this section are to be exercised by them as if they were the rights of a single person

[21] Section 22 *Trade Marks Act 1995* (Cth) Power of registered owner to deal with trademark:

(1) The registered owner of a trademark may, subject only to any rights appearing in the register to be vested in another person, deal with the trademark as its absolute owner and give in good faith discharges for any consideration for that dealing

[22] *Trade Practices (Industry Codes – Franchising) Regulations 1998*. Clause 4 of the Franchising Code of Conduct 1998 (the Code) defines a franchise agreement:

4(1) A franchise agreement is an agreement (text omitted):

(c) Under which the operation of the business will be substantially or materially associated with a trademark, advertising or a commercial symbol:

   (i) Owned, used or licensed by the franchisor or an associate of the franchisor

   (ii) Specified by the franchisor or an associate or the franchisor

Research conducted in 2006 on the registered trademarks used by franchisees reveals a diversity of ownership and registration strategies.[23] In a franchise network, the rights the franchisor may grant franchisees to use rely on the legal nexus between the franchisor and the owner of the trademark. Trademarks are categorised in their owner company accounts as 'intangible' assets. They can form security for a loan. Yet, one surprise the data revealed was that only three franchisors[24] in the sample had security interests registered against their trademarks. This low level of registration of security interests points to a large untapped repository of security for franchisors wishing to raise debt capital.[25] The research revealed other surprising results, which suggest that master franchisees and franchisees need to be very careful not to assume anything when paying for rights to use trademarks.

The data was drawn from a sample comprising franchisors with franchisees occupying premises regulated by the *Retail Leases Act 1994* (NSW) ('RLA'). The franchisees each made an average initial investment of $234,000.[26] With a sunk investment of this magnitude each franchisee has a strong interest in its investment being based on the soundest possible foundations, a part of which is guaranteed rights to use the franchise network's trademarks. Of the then 850 known franchisors[27] in Australia, 337 were identified as having franchisees that occupied premises regulated by the RLA. From this sample 1,308 registered trademarks were identified as being in use. Up to 87% of franchise networks sampled used registered trademarks. The franchisor was the sole owner of its registered trademarks in 26% of networks and one of the owners in 29% of networks. In 3% of cases, there was more than one owner of individual trademarks. In 8% there were several individual owners of several individual trademarks. In some instances, the first trademark registered was owned by individuals, but subsequent trademarks in the network were owned by the franchisor or a related corporate entity.

---

[23] See Jenny Buchan, 'Franchisor's registered trademarks – empirical surprises' (2009) 21(7) *Australian Intellectual Property Law Bulletin* 154–157

[24] The Athlete's Foot that is owned by US companies and Australian franchisors Mountain Designs and RAMS Home Loans. In Mountain Designs, the bank has registered its interest in six of the nine registered trademarks

[25] But see Darin Neumyer. 'Future of Using Intellectual Property and Intangible Assets as Collateral' *The Secured Lender* New York: Jan/Feb 2008 Vol. 64, Iss. 1; 42

[26] Lorelle Frazer, Scott Weaven and Owen Wright, *Franchising Australia 2006* Griffith University

[27] The addresses of franchisees' premises were found and checked in the telephone directory. It was assessed whether the franchisees' premises would be regulated by the Retail Leases Act (NSW). This process identified 350 franchisors in the sample group. For 13 of these, no further information could be found and they were omitted. It is not possible to state with certainty that all eligible franchisors were included in the sample as there is no public record of franchise disclosure documents in Australia. It is also impossible to identify from some franchisors' websites which of its outlets are franchisee owned and which are franchisor owned

When the research was conducted, 7% of the franchise networks were foreign based. A foreign-based franchisor typically grants a national master franchisee the right to license individual unit franchisees to use the network's trademarks. In the sample, 16% of the trademark owners were foreign companies based in diverse jurisdictions – the Bahamas, Bermuda, Canada, Cape Province, France, Germany, Hong Kong, Japan, Mauritius, the Netherlands, New Zealand, the Republic of Ireland, the UK and the USA. Of note, only one[28] of the 53 Australian master franchisees had registered its interest as an authorised user [29] in the foreign franchisor's trademarks. An authorised user may bring an action for infringement under section 26(1) (b) TMA and may grant others (franchisees) the right to use the mark under section 26(1) (f) TMA. The other 52 Australian master franchisees and in turn their individual unit franchisees relied solely on contractual rights. For a national master franchisee that is not an authorised user, the process of defending the trademarks is cumbersome. In the absence of contractual rights between individual franchisees and the foreign franchisor, individual franchisees would risk losing the right to use the franchisor's marks if the Australian master lost the right to be the Australian master franchisee.[30] No individual unit franchisees had registered their interest as an authorised user of the franchisor's trademarks, although under TMA, section 6, they are permitted to do so. Franchisees, could record their interests as licensees under the provisions of Part 11 TMA. There was no evidence that they had done this either. It is thus vitally important for franchisees to have and maintain a contractual nexus with the trademark owner.

Fourteen per cent of franchisors in the sample did not have a registered trademark. They may have been trading under an unregistrable name. They may have been unaware of the wide scope of trademark law. For a further 14%, it was not possible to determine the legal identity of the franchisor entity. Thus, at least 14% of franchisors (and possibly up to 28%) did not use the statutory registration avenues under the TMA. Franchisors may defend unregistered trademarks by way of a statutory[31] or common law passing off action, but these are less certain, slower and more costly than an action under the TMA.

Possible consequences of the fragmented trademark ownership for franchisees whose franchisor enters administration or becomes insolvent will be addressed in Chap. 8.

[28] An interest in nine of the ten trademarks owned by franchisor Coldwell Banker Corporation (USA) in Australia is registered by an entity that is presumably the Australian master licensee, Australian Real Estate Systems P/L, pursuant to an authorised user agreement

[29] Section 8 *Trade Marks Act 1995* (Cth) an 'authorised user' 8 (1) uses the trademark in relation to goods or services under the control of the owner of the trademark

[30] For example, the Australian master franchisee for Canadian franchisor Kernel's Popcorn lost the right to be master franchisee by becoming insolvent. This resulted in the liquidator disclaiming the leases of the shops the franchisees were trading from

[31] Arguing misleading and deceptive conduct under Australia's *Competition and Consumer Act 2010* (Cth)

## Franchisor's and the Owners of Franchisees' Premises

Many franchisees trade from leased premises. In 2006, 44.7% of franchisors operating in Australia had franchisees operating from a retail site.[32] This numbered nearly 2,900 individual retail premises.[33] Sunk fit-out costs payable by franchisees ranged from $0 to $450,000 for retail franchisees in 2010 and up to $1,000,000 for non-retail franchisees.[34] The latter include, for example, hotel and serviced-apartment franchisees who nonetheless may sign premises' leases. Property interests can take many different forms.[35]

In terms of who takes control of the lease and who bears the legal risk, 12 common franchisee premises leasing models are outlined in Figs. 3.1, 3.2, 3.3, 3.4, 3.5, 3.6, 3.7, 3.8, 3.9, 3.10, 3.11 and 3.12 below.

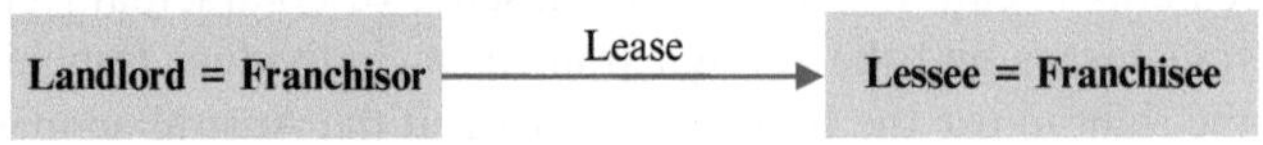


**Fig. 3.1** Franchisor owns the premises and leases to franchisee

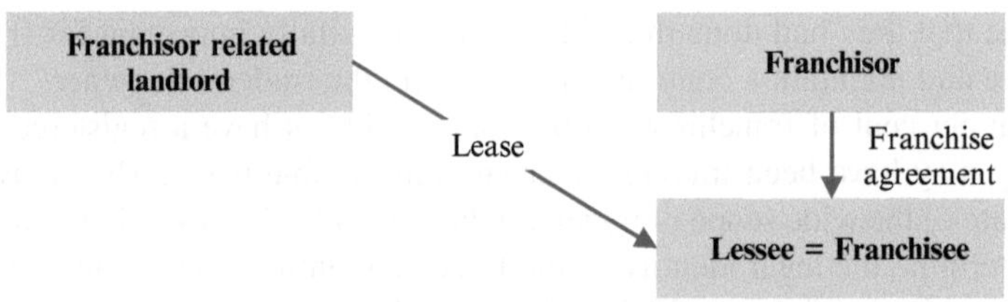


**Fig. 3.2** Legal entity related to franchisor owns the premises and leases to franchisee

[32] Lorelle Frazer, Scott Weaven, Owen Wright, *Franchising Australia 2006*, 28. The concept 'retail premises' was not defined in the survey so the figure does not equate perfectly with the definitions of 'retail premises' in the Australian legislative instruments. The data for the Franchising Australia 2008 survey was not analysed by reference to location of franchisees' business but by business type. In 2008, 28% of the 1,100 franchisors were identified as being in 'retail trade'. This figure excluded cafes and other food services, travel agencies, financial services and postal services. The figure for the separate categories of franchise cannot simply be added to the retail figure to provide a 2008 total as the café category includes accommodation, which is not retail and travel agencies, financial services and postal services may be conducted from retail or from non-retail premises. The mismatch between the 2008 survey data and the legal definitions of retail highlights the difficulty of using data that was collected for one purpose for another. In 2008, 47.1% of franchisees conducted their business from a retail site or kiosk; 29.3% from mobile unit, van or trailer; 26.8% were home based (office or garage); 21.8% of franchisees operate from specific commercial sites; and 4% operate from an industrial site, Frazer, Weaven and Wright *Franchising Australia 2008*, 27

[33] Jenny Buchan and Bill Butcher, 'Premises Occupancy Models for Franchised Retail Businesses in Australia: Factors for Consideration', (2009) 17(2) *Australian Property Law Journal* 143–4

[34] Frazer, Weaven and Bodey, *Franchising Australia 2010*, 48

[35] Some landlords insist on franchisors taking 'the head lease while others allow the franchisees to take the lease of the premises'. *Franchising Task Force, Final Report* to the Minister for Small Business and Customs (1991) 87

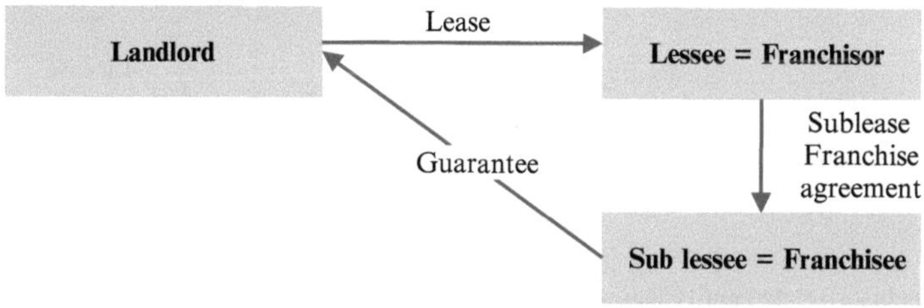


**Fig. 3.3** Franchisor leases premises from owner and subleases to franchisee

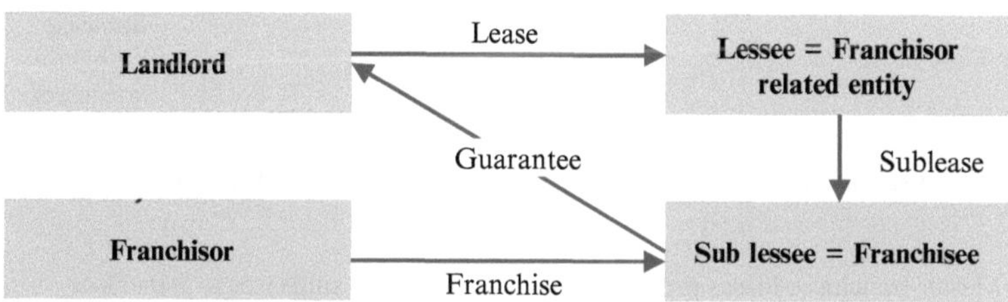


**Fig. 3.4** Franchisor-related entity leases premises from owner and subleases to franchisee

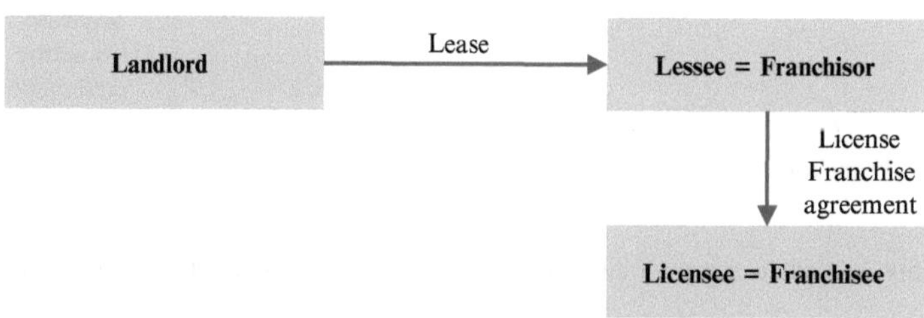


**Fig. 3.5** Franchisor leases premises from owner and grants licence to occupy to franchisee

Typically the premises leasing model is dictated by the franchisor's preference and the amount of control the landlord wishes to assert.[36] It is operationally convenient for a landlord owning numerous shopping centres/malls to deal with one tenant, the franchisor, instead of tens of individual franchisees spread throughout its centres. This enables the franchisor to maintain control of the outlets and may enable franchisors to negotiate better deals with large retail centre managers than would be

[36] See Rupert M Barkoff and Andrew C Selden, *Fundamentals of Franchising* (American Bar Association, 3rd ed, 2008), 67

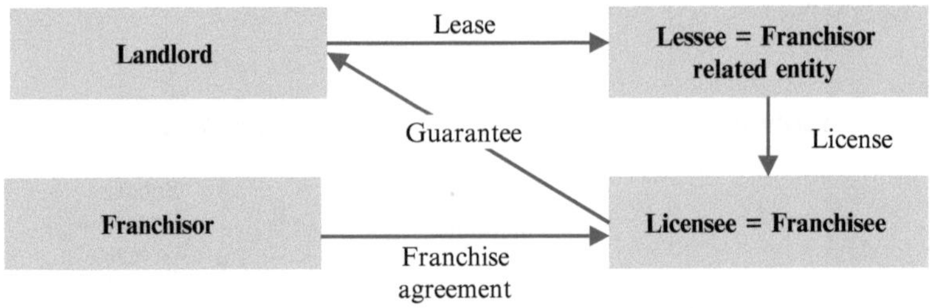


**Fig. 3.6** Franchisor-related entity leases premises and grants licence to occupy to franchisee

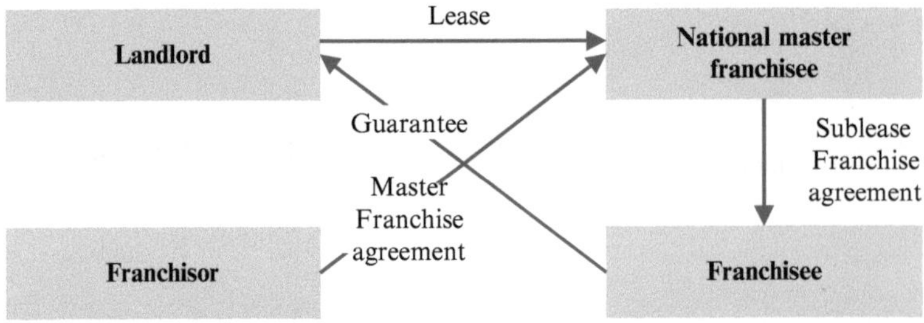


**Fig. 3.7** Master franchisee leases premises from a landlord and subleases to franchisee

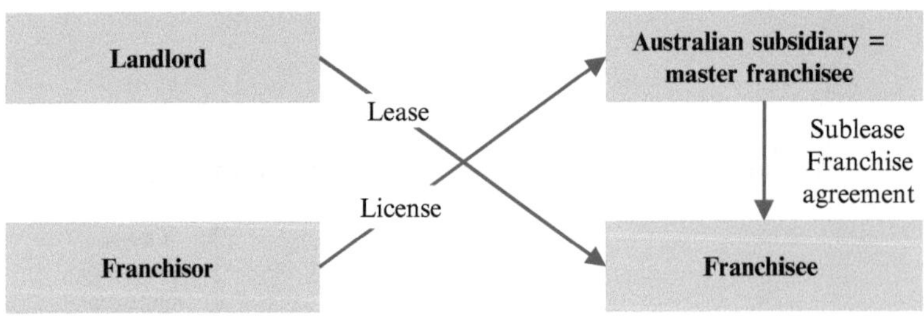


**Fig. 3.8** Entity related to master franchisee leases premises from landlord and subleases to franchisee

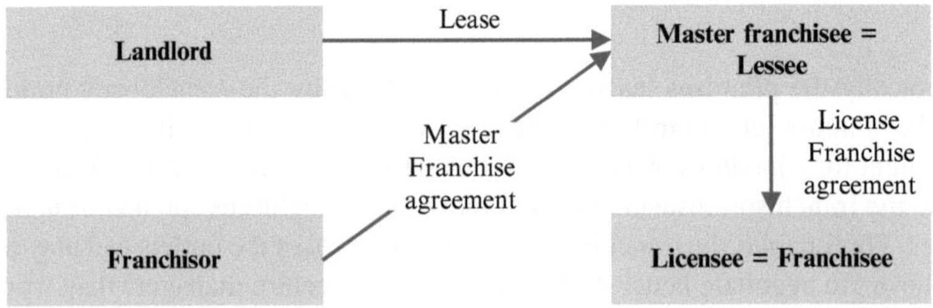


**Fig. 3.9** Master franchisee leases premises from landlord and grants licence to occupy to franchisee

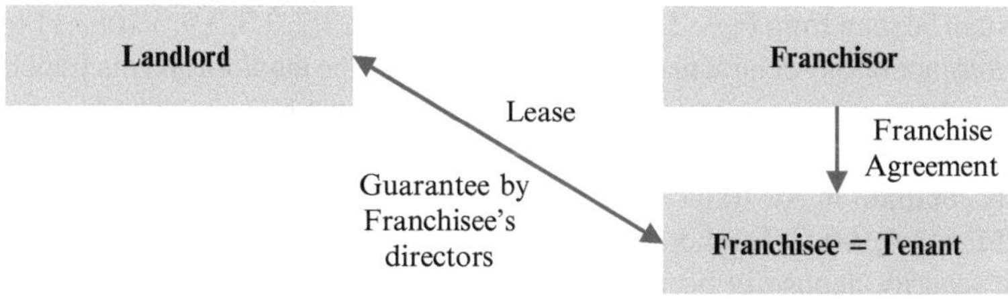


**Fig. 3.10** Franchisee or an entity related to franchisee leases premises direct from a landlord

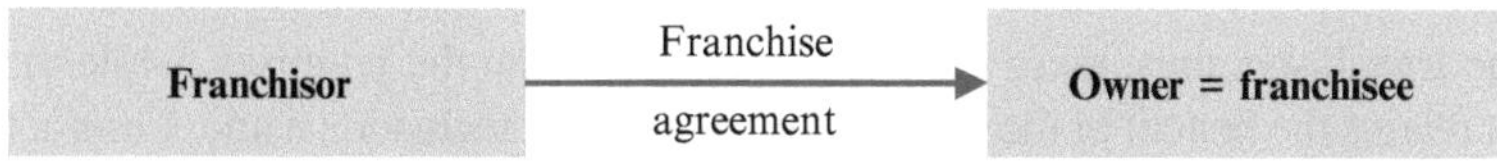


**Fig. 3.11** Franchisee or franchisee-related entity owns the premises

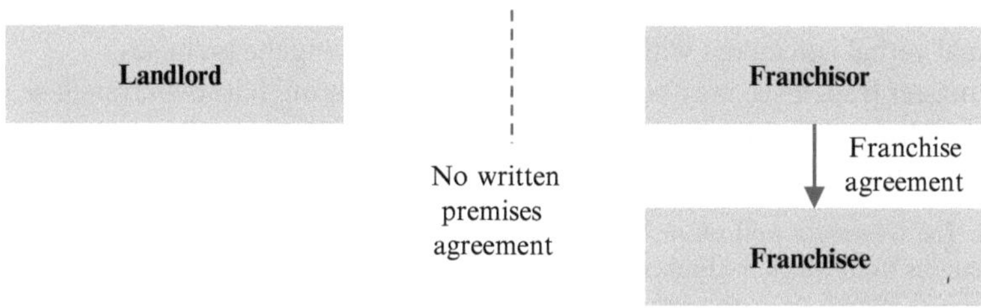


**Fig. 3.12** No formal occupancy arrangements

available to single tenants. However, this approach can backfire. At the time it became insolvent, RedGroup (owner of a franchised bookstore brand) was 'Westfield's second largest specialty tenant'[37] in Australia so the landlord Westfield suddenly found itself with a large number of highly visible vacancies. We will investigate REDgroup, its failure and the effect on its franchisees in detail in Chap. 8.

Figures 3.1, 3.2, 3.3, 3.4, 3.5, 3.6, 3.7, 3.8, 3.9, 3.10, 3.11 and 3.12 demonstrate the wide range of contractual relationships underpinning a franchisee's occupancy of retail premises. In some franchise systems, more than one model is chosen. In Australia where the franchise unit operates from a specific site, the head lease is held by the franchisee in 64% of cases. Twenty-six per cent of franchisors hold the head lease. Franchisors are more likely to hold the head lease in retail (both food and nonfood) systems.[38]

[37] James Thomson, 18 Feb 2011, smartcompany

[38] Lorelle Frazer, Scott Weaven, Owen Wright, *Franchising Australia 2006* (2006), Question A15, 30. Thus, Models 1–6. In an unpublished NSW Government Retail Tenancy Survey (2008), 33% of landlords required the franchisor to be the head tenant. The discrepancy between the 26% found by Frazer et al. and the 33% in NSW could be attributed to the configuration of the sample. Frazer surveyed franchisors across most industry sectors whereas the NSW Government survey focused solely on franchisors whose franchisees occupied premises that fell under the *Retail Leases Act 1974* NSW

As can be seen from Figs. 3.1, 3.2, 3.3, 3.4, 3.5, 3.6, 3.7, 3.8, 3.9, 3.10, 3.11 to 3.12, there may not be any contractual relationship between the landlord and the franchisee.[39] The franchisee may have protection as a lessee under the relevant retail leasing legislation, but in Australia this is not uniform as real property law is made at state level.[40]

It is common in Australia when the franchisor takes a head lease of retail premises (Figs. 3.4, 3.6, 3.7 and 3.10) for the franchisee to provide a personal guarantee or the security deposit to back the franchisor's performance under the head lease. The relevant clause in the franchise agreement might read:

> The franchisor shall hold the head lease to the store site. The franchisee shall make available the security deposit upon signing the sub-lease.[41]

The franchisee, thus, takes ultimate financial risk on the premises, while the franchisor retains the benefit of the site lease being in the franchisor's name. Contracts may be made between franchisee and landlord, as in Figs. 3.1, 3.10 and 3.11. Alternatively, the franchisee's contractual relationship may not be with the landlord; rather, the landlord is in a direct contractual relationship with the franchisor or its related entity, as in Figs. 3.3, 3.4, 3.5 and 3.6. The franchisee then enters a sublease, licence or has an informal verbal agreement with the franchisor concerning the premises.

A master franchisee may be contractually bound through its own franchise agreements with the franchisor to ensure the head leases in their territory are under their control. A franchise agreement, which used a Fig. 3.5 structure, stated that

> 8.1 The franchisor will on or before the Commencement Date enter into a lease of the Premises from which the Franchised Business is to be carried on.
>
> 8.2 The franchisee must, on the date this agreement is executed, enter into a licence agreement to occupy the premises on those terms and conditions contained in the Franchisor's Standard Occupation Licence.[42]

In Fig. 3.6, the franchisee's tenure is secured only by a licence. The following passage describes Fig. 3.6 from a franchisee's perspective:

> When a franchisee signs their franchisor's licence agreement, they are binding themselves to the lease, without having any of the protections offered by the lease. Neither the landlord nor the franchisor is required to provide the franchisee/licensee with any information about their negotiation process, nor does the franchisee see the landlord's disclosure document – if they even know it exists. As a Bakers Delight franchisee, I did not even see a copy of the leases for two of my stores until after I had signed the licence agreement. The third one I never saw.[43]

---

[39] In the case of a shopping centre, the franchisor commonly negotiates the lease agreement – or heads of agreement – with the owner's leasing manager. The franchisee then fits out the shop under the scrutiny of the centre manager. The centre manager is an employee of the shopping centre management company, which is normally a subsidiary of the shopping centre owner

[40] See Jenny Buchan and Bill Butcher, 'Premises Occupancy Models for Franchised Retail Businesses in Australia: Factors for Consideration' (2009) 17(2) *Australian Property Law Journal* 143–78 for discussion of the situation state by state

[41] Danoz Directions Franchise Agreement (2004) cl 3 original on author's file

[42] 2004 version of the Danoz Directions Franchise Agreement

[43] Evidence to Retail Tenancies Inquiry, Retail Tenancy Unit, New South Wales Government (Sydney) (2008) 3. Report embargoed. (Deanne de Leeuw former Bakers Delight franchisee) quoted with permission of the author

A clause such as the following provides clues as to the franchisor's preference, in this case for a Fig. 3.10 arrangement:

> Lease. The Franchisee must provide the Franchisor with details of its existing lease or licence of the Premises and of any proposed new lease or licence of the Premises.[44]

The problem for the franchisee in the situations depicted by Figs. 3.3, 3.4, 3.5, 3.6, 3.7, 3.8, 3.9 and possibly 3.12 is that there is privity of contract between the franchisor and landlord and franchisor and franchisee, but not between franchisee and landlord. The franchisee becomes vulnerable if the franchisor breaches the head lease in a way that permits the landlord to terminate it. If the franchisor does not pay the rent, the franchisee does not necessarily learn of the default under the head lease until the rent is in arrears.

As demonstrated by both Figs. 3.1 and 3.2, the franchisee is able to verify the premises' ownership and determine the extent of other registered interests by conducting a search of the title. For greater security, the franchisee could register its lease on the title. Property law recognises that several legal entities may have concurrent rights in the same premises. The most obvious example would be under a lease where an owner grants to a lessee/tenant the right to occupy the premises to the exclusion of all others, including the owner, for a specified period or a mortgage where the mortgagee has rights to conduct a mortgagee sale to recover moneys secured against the land if the mortgagor defaults. In addition to contract terms, real property in Australia is regulated by state and territory laws. Ownership, the strongest real property right, enables the owner (known as the registered proprietor) to do anything it wishes with the land[45] subject to any restrictions specifically imposed by statute. These restrictions can include planning requirements and laws that permit the government to compulsorily acquire land.[46]

All Australian states have adopted the Torrens system of land registration, issuing a title to each identified parcel of land. Part 6 of the *Real Property Act* 1900 (NSW)[47] provides for interests in land to be registered on the title. The effect of registration is to identify the registered proprietor of the property and alert third parties as to who, in addition to the owner, has a legal claim to an interest in the property. A mortgagee may register its interest. Lessees may also register their interests. Registered interests take priority over unregistered interests if an issue arises such as the financial distress of the registered proprietor. If a party has a registrable interest

[44] Draft Individual Unit Traveland Pty Ltd Franchise Agreement (undated) 14

[45] For example, *Real Property Act 1900* (NSW) s 42 states that the estate of the registered proprietor is paramount

[46] Land may also be subject to restrictions at common law, for example, nuisance, right of support and rights reserved to the Crown such as mining rights

[47] Similarly, in other states and territories, *Land Titles Act 1925* (ACT), *Land Title Act* (NT) part 3, *Real Property Act 1861* (Qld), *Real Property Act 1886* (SA), Land Titles Act 1980 (TAS), *Transfer of Land Act 1958* (Vic) and *Transfer of Land Act 1874* (WA)

but decides not to register, it may lodge a caveat on the title. If the owner (the 'mortgagor') defaults on its payments, the land can be sold by the lender (the 'mortgagee') to fund repayment of the loan. If there is a lease over premises on the land, the mortgagee, and subsequently the buyer, has to allow the tenant to remain in the premises for the term of its lease, or to pay it out, provided the *Real Property Act 1900* (NSW) s53 or its equivalent[48] has been complied with. Section 53 provides:

> 53 (1) When any land under the provisions of this Act is intended to be leased or demised for a life or lives or for any term of years exceeding three years, the proprietor shall execute a lease in the approved form.
>
> 53 (4) A lease of land which is subject to a mortgage, charge or covenant charge is not valid or binding on the mortgagee, chargee or covenant chargee unless the mortgagee, chargee or covenant chargee has consented to the lease before it is registered.

It is possible to register a sublease on title [49] but this is not common. Retail tenancy legislation enables the lessor to refuse to allow a tenant to grant a sublease.[50] Even if the lease is unregistered, the lessee's rights are preserved as long as any mortgagee of the premises has consented to the lease or any buyer of the premises has notice of it.[51] In that case the tenant will receive a notice instructing it to redirect the rent to the mortgagee. A problem arises for the franchisee when the mortgagee has not been formally notified of the lease.[52]

In the absence of a lease, the landlord or lessee may grant a licence to occupy to a franchisee. Property laws do not provide for a licensee to register its interest on the title to the premises. Nor can the licensee protect its interest by registering a caveat as a licence is a personal property interest, not an interest in real property. The fewest rights accrue to a mere occupier with no contract to define its rights. This is the situation depicted by Fig. 3.12.

A prerequisite for protection under retail leasing legislation is that the franchisor's occupancy situation falls under the legislation. A review of the definitions of 'landlord'/'lessor', 'tenant'/'lessee' and 'lease' as defined in the retail leasing legislation in Australia reveals that none of the legislation covers all of the configurations

---

[48] For example, *Land Title Act* (NT) s 67

[49] Real Property Act 1900 (NSW) s 53(1); Land Title Act 1994 (QLD) s 64; Real Property Act 1886 (SA) ss 116–17; Land Titles Act 1925 (ACT) s 82; Land Titles Act 1980 (Tas) s 64(1); Transfer of Land Act 1958 (Vic) s 661(1); Transfer of Land Act 1893 (WA) s 91; See B J Edgeworth, C J Rossiter, M A Stone and P A O'Connor, Sackville and Neave, *Australian Property Law* (8th ed, 2008), 870–871

[50] For example, *Retail Leases Act 1994* (NSW) s 42

[51] *Figgins Holdings Pty Ltd v. SEAA Enterprises Pty Ltd* [1999] HCA 20 and see Joycey Tooher, 'Let Mortgagees and their Buyers Beware: Figgins Holdings Pty Ltd v SEAA Enterprises Pty Ltd' (2000) 26(1) Monash Law Review 216; Peter Butt, 'Variation of Lease Binding Purchaser from Mortgagee' (1999) 73(12) *Australian Law Journal* 861

[52] We will return to this situation in Chap. 8

of franchisee occupancy outlined in Figs. 3.1, 3.2, 3.3, 3.4, 3.5, 3.6, 3.7, 3.8, 3.9, 3.10, 3.11 and 3.12. For example, in some cases, the protection is only available if the tenancy exceeds 12, 6 or 1 month's duration.[53] Franchisees occupying premises as licensees are not protected by most jurisdictions' legislation.[54]

## Conclusion

The increasing complexity of franchise networks calls for a rethink about how franchisees' investments should be protected. Both the trademark and retail-leasing patterns within franchise networks demonstrate that contractual relationships whose integrity is fundamental to the franchise system are vulnerable to 'the existence of divisible residual claims … which can generally be sold without permission of the other contracting individuals'.[55] Not only can they be sold. The most damaging claims for franchisees are triggered by the franchisor becoming insolvent. Before exploring the changes a franchise organisation can experience through the franchisor's insolvency, we need to examine the franchisee's role in the franchise system.

[53] *Retail Leases Act 2003* (Vic) s 12 (1) exempts some leases of shorter than 1-year duration. *Business Tenancies (Fair Dealings) Act 2003* (NT) s 7(1); s 13(8) exempts short-term leases from the provisions of the *Retail Shop Leases Act 1994* (Qld) and s 13(9) defines 'short term'; licences of 6 months or less for parts of common area in shopping centres are excluded from the *Fair Trading (Code of Practice for Retail Tenancies) Regulations 1998* (Tas) under Reg 1(b) and from the *Retail Leases Act 1994* (NSW) by s 6A. *Retail and Commercial Leases Act 1995* (SA) s 4(2)(ab)

[54] Licensees and franchisees are, however, specifically included under the definition of 'lease' in the *Duties Act 1997* (NSW)

[55] Michael C Jensen and William H Meckling, 'Theory of the Firm: Managerial Behavior, Agency Costs and Ownership Structure' (1976) 3(4) *Journal of Financial Economics* 305, 311

# Chapter 4
# The Franchisee

**Abstract** Franchisees outnumber franchisors many times. They perform distinct roles within the franchise network and have many responsibilities and few rights. In this chapter, franchisees are explored as parties to a contract and as consumers in a competitive market. In addition to being a source of funding to the franchisor's brand, they are an alternative workforce to employees and independent contractors. Thus, they are compared to these workers by reference to the 'Eleven Factors' test in the United States and tests applied in Australian law to determine a worker's status. The relevance of the categorisations in the contexts of consumer protection, goodwill, occupational health and safety and insolvency is introduced.

Franchisees are the tens of thousands of 'faces' of the brands they buy into. As we have seen, they outnumber franchisors significantly. They are on the front line, embedding their franchisor's brand into markets.

As I write from deep in the French countryside, I reflect on franchisees. Yesterday, I had lunch at a McDonald's franchise – not much else was open on a winter Monday – the day after New Year's Day. Alternatively, I may have found a Subway or Paul's – open while the usual purveyors of sandwiches were resting after welcoming the New Year in. What is it that drives franchisees to be open for business on public holidays, nights and odd hours when fully independent business owners and franchisors are spending their time how they wish? The franchisees were open and trading because that is what they had signed up for.

Franchisors sell franchisees the right to operate a business using the franchisor's blueprint. In exchange, franchisees agree to adhere to the franchisors operations manual and to make ongoing payments to the franchisor. The ongoing payments may include royalties, contributions to marketing funds and others. Franchisors may also receive commission from suppliers of stock purchased by their franchisees. In some systems, the payments are made by the franchisor to franchisee in the form of a commission.

J. Buchan, *Franchisees as Consumers: Benchmarks, Perspectives and Consequences*, DOI 10.1007/978-1-4614-5614-8_4, © Springer Science+Business Media New York 2013

At the beginning, being a franchisee can be like being a learner driver behind the wheel of a high-performance car: a steep learning curve, a bit terrifying. Unlike the learner driver, the franchisee has a franchisor to lean on. A person interested in franchising may be attracted by an advertisement such as that for cartridge company Inkspot which advertises that

> To become an Inkspot franchisee you need between $90 - $150 k for a turnkey Inkspot franchise; this includes everything from a fully designed, built and fitted out retail premise, all necessary machinery, fully stocked at openin [sic], right through to comprehensive training for you as franchisee and your staff.[1]

So, who becomes a franchisee? Having bought this notional high-performance car, what options do franchisees have? Can they choose when to stop for a rest, who to share the journey with, how fast to travel, whether to wear a seat belt, what type of fuel to use and which destination they will head for? How does the law see them? What is their role in the franchise network? How do they differ from employees and independent contractor suppliers? Can they return a flawed model to the manufacturer? How do they differ from the mortgagee who secured a loan from a bank and then had to endure numerous changes in the terms?

In terms of prior experience, data from Australia, France and the United Kingdom shows that immediately prior to entering the franchise, 52.6% of new franchisees in Australia had been in salaried work.[2] In France, a higher 66% came to franchising direct from salaried employment in 2010.[3] In the United Kingdom in 2006, 64% of franchisees were employees immediately before taking out their franchise.[4] In the United States, franchising has proved to be an attractive path for veterans to rejoin the civilian world. The International Franchise Association (IFA) reports that its 'VetFran program, founded in 1991, has enabled over 2,100 veterans to become franchise owners'.[5] The Franchise Council of Australia is experimenting with a program for attracting former elite football players to become franchisees. These former employee franchisees bring with them passion, drive and funds, but their immediate past work environment was one where employees were accorded numerous safeguards by the law. Neither their contracts nor the law offer franchisees many safeguards.

Franchising has been pitched to immigrants as a way of attaining immediate gainful work. Through becoming franchisees, they gain standing in the community and earn an income which they may not have been able to do using the qualifications gained in their country of origin. Australia's National Australia Bank ('NAB') specifically identifies franchising as 'a good way [for migrants] to minimise the risks that might otherwise be there for a new business'.[6] Other new franchisees may

---

[1] Sent to author via email from Franchise Business [eshots@e.franchisebusiness.com.au] 26 May 2012

[2] Frazer, Weaven and Wright, *Franchising Australia 2008*, Griffith University, Question B6 on page 35. And, 4% had 'other experience' (e.g. unemployed, parental duties). Forty three per cent had independent business experience immediately prior to becoming a franchisee.

[3] Enquette Annuelle sur la Franchise, Résultats 2010

[4] NatWest bfa United Kingdom, *Franchise Survey* (2006) 29

[5] IFA 2011 Annual Report, 5

[6] National Australia Bank 'NAB' Migrant News #8, 5

have been attracted to franchising as an opportunity to run their own businesses, which they lacked the confidence to do independently. Yet others select franchising because they do not have their own concept in mind on which to base a start-up business.

Neither youth nor seniority is a barrier.[7] Access to funding is, however, essential. As Gherke observes, in 2012,

> the overwhelming majority of franchisees are aged between 35 and 55. This means that people who are approaching the age of 35 and are now looking for franchises will increasingly be drawn from Generation Y (those born in between 1980 and 2000), compared to Generation X (1965-1980) and Baby Boomers (1945-1965). Unlike Baby Boomers and, to a certain extent, Generation X, which have both been conditioned to save for the future, Generation Y is often characterised as the 'spend it now' generation.[8]

Generation Y might be followed soon by a more prudent and frugal Generation Z as the GFC continues, and youth unemployment soars. This is yet to be seen.

New franchisees may be using a retrenchment payout to fund the purchase or may access funding through family members (referred to as the BOMAD or bank of mum and dad), savings or by accessing borrowing arrangements established by the franchisor. Some franchisors assist franchisees with access to funding by having the franchise offering pre-vetted by financiers who will lend to approved franchisees. In some cases, franchisors provide funding to assist new franchisees.

Through association with a franchisor, franchisees gain access to premium locations and favourable supplier terms. But, like the inexperienced driver at the wheel of the high-performance car, franchisees can quickly find themselves in a situation beyond their experience if anything threatens their relationship with the franchisor or the franchisor's relationship with its suppliers. Only then does the franchisee discover the extent of the risk it has assumed. The full force of the carefully crafted, franchisor-centric franchise agreement becomes apparent.

## A Contracting Party

The franchisor's mantra is that both parties are business people and that thus franchisees can negotiate contractual terms to protect themselves. The franchise agreement, examined in Chap. 5 and asymmetry in Chap. 6, exposes the flaws in this thinking. As we have seen, through contract-based relationships, franchisors convey risks, but few absolute rights, to franchisees.

---

[7] Banque Populaire, Deloitte, Frazer, Weaven and Bodey *Franchising Australia 2010*, 55 found that 9% of franchisees are under 30 years old, 67% are aged 30–50 years and 24% are over 50 years old

[8] Jason Gherke, Why BOMAD funding is critical to franchisee and franchisor growth, 27 March 2012, smartcompany.com.au

The franchisee supplies equity (the initial franchise fee paid to the franchisor and the investment in sunk costs of establishing or buying the franchise) and loan finance. For example, the franchisor of Boost Juice

> was able to roll out [a juice bar concept] around Australia at an extraordinary pace and with limited capital by developing a franchise system … We have been able to grow using other people's capital.[9]

Franchisees surrender control over aspects of their business. For example, a Californian court observed that the franchisor, through contracting, is able to give itself 'total control over'[10] the restaurant design and layout, advertising, preparation of food, the franchisees' price structure, what the franchisee and its employees wear and even closely supervises its franchisees' finances. This helps ensure standardisation but can have unintended consequences for franchisors as will be seen in Sect. 4.5.

Can franchisees protect themselves against the consequences of a rogue franchisor's exploitative, negligent, fraudulent or criminal behaviour by simply negotiating contracts better? The short answer is no. Even if the franchise agreement was more evenly weighted, it is only one of a suite of contractual relationships franchisees enter into. These consequential contract-based commitments occupy three categories: those entered into with the franchisor, including such agreements as licences to use intellectual property, software and premises and various finance arrangements.[11] Secondly, contracts entered into with third parties related to the franchisor, such as supplier agreements concerning stock, licence to use intellectual property, lease of premises and finance arrangements.[12] Third are contracts entered into with third parties unrelated to the franchisor, such as supplier contracts, vehicle leases, lease or licence of premises,[13] equipment leases, loan agreements – secured over real property or shares owned by the franchisee before it becomes a franchisee, local advertising and employment contracts with the franchisee's employees.

These consequential contracts seldom contemplate the franchisor breaching the common law or statute or becoming insolvent. They are drafted on the assumption that a franchisor is well motivated, successful, honest and solvent.

---

[9] Virginia Marsh, Entrepreneur enjoys fruits of fast-expanding juice chain – Janine Allis squeezed her way to success from humble beginnings. Financial Times, 24 June 2005, p. 5 quoting Boost's then chief operating officer, Simon McNamara

[10] *Shelley Lynn v. Keith Handley, Ivernia, Inc., McDonald's USA, LLC*, Does 1–10 Complaint and Demand for Jury Trial, CV12-02140 Filed Central District of California, March 14, 2012, para 104

[11] Frazer and Weaven, *Franchising Australia 2004*, Griffith University, found that 29% of franchisors provide finance to franchisees, with the most popular being direct finance supplied by the franchisor (59%)

[12] Frazer and Weaven, *Franchising Australia 2004*, found that of the franchisors providing finance in Australia, 4.9% did so through a company related to the franchisor

[13] In Australia, 47.1% of franchisees conduct their business from a retail site or kiosk; 29.3% from mobile unit, van or trailer; 26.8% home based (office or garage); 21.8% of franchisees operate from specific commercial sites; and 4% operate from an industrial site, Frazer, Weaven and Wright *Franchising Australia 2008*, Griffith University, 27

## A Consumer in a Competitive Market

> [I]ndividuals … have varying attitudes to risk depending on how risks are framed and what reference points are available, [they] violate rationality by overestimating their skills, over-project the current state, use rules of thumb or heuristics to solve problems and make decisions affected by transient emotion.[14]

Consumer law and consumer protection have been justified on the following bases: as a necessary response to market failure, or because of the extent of information asymmetry and the 'take it or leave it' character of the bargaining process and the resulting standard form consumer contract that cannot meet the needs of both supplier and consumer. Protecting consumers through statute can also be justified because, even if equipped with information, consumers do not behave rationally.[15]

The 1976 Swanson Review of Trade Practices in Australia identified that the definition of 'consumer'[16] is central in legislation that regulates anti-competitive conduct and protects consumers from its consequences. Although the dictionary definition of 'consumer' is 'a person who consumes, especially one who uses a product',[17] the Swanson Review urged that

> 'the definition of consumer should be sufficiently broad to provide protection to a range of business transactions, …to redress between supplier and consumer, inequalities in the technical expertise required to recognise, and the bargaining power to negotiate, a fair bargain'.[18]

To bring the sale of a franchise within the supplier/consumer framework, we need to move out of the business world of 1974 when Australia's *Trade Practices Act* was enacted and the internet was still more than a decade off being accessible to all[19] and there were still only a handful of franchisors operating. Now, in the twenty-first century, franchisee recruitment process and the type of contracts that result mimic consumer transactions. The Internet enables people to access phenomenal amounts of information, but in the absence of accessible, relevant hard data, it does not equip franchisees to evaluate and compare opportunities.

Australia's consumer protection regulator, the ACCC,

> 'believes that one of the key objectives of consumer policy is to empower consumers to participate in markets to access goods and services that meet their needs. Consumer policy

---

[14] Steven Kennedy, 'The Future of Consumer Policy: Should we Regulate to Protect Homo Economicus?' (Accord Industry Leaders Briefing, Old Parliament House, Canberra 13 August 2009) 10 citing Stefano Della Vigna, 'Psychology and Economics: Evidence from the Field' (2009) 47(2) *Journal of Economic Literature* 315, 316

[15] Distilled from Geraint Howells, Iain Ramsay and Thomas Wilhelmsson with David Kraft (eds) *Handbook of Research on International Consumer Law* (Edward Elgar, 2010) 10–11

[16] Trade Practices Act Review Committee Report to the Minister for Business and Consumer Affairs, August 1976, Australian Government Publishing Service, Canberra, 63. (Swanson Report)

[17] Bruce Moore (ed), *The Australian Oxford Dictionary*, (2nd ed, Oxford, 2004) 272

[18] Trade Practices Act Review Committee Report to the Minister for Business and Consumer Affairs, August 1976, Australian Government Publishing Service, Canberra, 64. (Swanson Report)

[19] Internet service providers did not open the internet to the general public until 1995. History of the internet, http://en.wikipedia.org/wiki/History_of_the_Internet

also plays a vital role in protecting vulnerable and disadvantaged consumers who have substantial difficulties in participating in markets'.[20]

For would-be franchisees, the market offers franchising as an opportunity to procure responsible work at a level they may not have been eligible to attain within an employment context. As consumers, franchisees have no difficulty participating in markets; franchisors compete for their investment dollars.

When responding to a franchisor's highly polished sales techniques and buying a pre-packaged business/product, the franchisee is not afforded the contractual or statutory protection of a traditional consumer who is able to return a product that is faulty or not fit for the purpose. Franchisees may not know until long after the expiry of any statutory 'cooling-off' period that the business or the franchisor is faulty. The franchisee's characterisation as consumer arises out of the nature of the franchise agreement, a high level of asymmetry and in market failure in the form of externalities.[21]

The traditional view in the late twentieth century was that markets worked things out over time, but '[i]n the case of a competitive market [such as franchise sales], there are a number of characteristics that may lead to a hypothesis that a market-based solution is unlikely to emerge'.[22] Michael J. Trebilcock identifies five situations where a market-led solution to the failure of consumer protection is unlikely to emerge. First, '[r]epeat transactions are rare, and consequently the performance incentives created by the possibility of repeat business from satisfied customers are blunted.'[23] Franchisees as consumers of the franchisor's business opportunity would often only purchase one franchise. Second, '[e]ntry and exit costs in the industry are low, leading to the possibility of a large number of fly by night operators with few sunk costs and only modest investments in reputational capital'.[24] Sometimes, entry costs in franchising are relatively low. However, even where entry and exit costs are very high for the franchisee business consumer, fly-by-night operators at franchisor and national master franchisee level still exist. Reputational capital may be only a modest investment for some franchisors; many trade through companies with forgettable names, in large markets, and can easily disassociate their own name and reputation from that of the failed entry.[25] Alternately, franchisors are able to hide

---

[20] ACCC submission to the Productivity Commission inquiry into Australia's Consumer policy Framework, June 2007, 146

[21] Externalities are defined as third-party (or spill-over) effects arising from the production and/or consumption of goods and services for which no appropriate compensation is paid. Externalities can cause market failure if the price mechanism does not take into account the full social costs and social benefits of production and consumption. http://www.tutor2u.net/economics/content/topics/externalities/what_are_externalities.htm

[22] Michael J Trebilcock, 'Rethinking Consumer Protection Policy' in Charles E F Rickett and Thomas G W Telfer (eds), *International Perspectives on Consumers' Access to Justice* (2003) 72

[23] Michael J Trebilcock, 'Rethinking Consumer Protection Policy' in Charles E F Rickett and Thomas G W Telfer (eds), *International Perspectives on Consumers' Access to Justice* (2003)

[24] Michael J Trebilcock, 'Rethinking Consumer Protection Policy' in Charles E F Rickett and Thomas G W Telfer (eds), *International Perspectives on Consumers' Access to Justice* (2003) 72

[25] One director of a now failed Australian franchisor went so far as to change his name by deed poll to distance his identity from his past as a solicitor who had been jailed for fraud following misuse of his firm's trust account

their true identify by using trusts, as occurred in *Australian Competition and Consumer Commission v. Chaste Corporation Pty Ltd (in liquidation)*.[26]

Third, '[m]any sellers or producers are extra jurisdictional, making redress through private law more difficult for customers. Sellers characteristically have few assets against which a judgment may be enforced'.[27] In addition, jurisdictional issues,[28] the language in the franchisor's jurisdiction, distance to travel to court,[29] the size of the dispute and the amount of time away from the business that litigation would necessitate contribute to the difficulty of securing redress for franchisees. In franchising, up to 25% of franchisors trading in Australia in 2010 were foreign based, with many more based in a different state or territory from the franchisee. This extra jurisdictional dimension to franchise relationships can hamper franchisees' ability to conduct due diligence. The franchisees' ability to conduct pre-contractual 'soft' due diligence beyond what can be found on the public record is much easier if the franchise network is locally based. Soft due diligence consists, for example, of speaking with suppliers to the network and existing and former franchisees to discover what the franchisor really is like to deal with? Further, akin to the seller with few assets, the franchisor entity is likely to have few assets. The franchisor's directors have ex ante the opportunity to shelter personal assets from its creditors.

Fourth, '[t]he costs to consumers of a "bad" transaction are delayed or potentially catastrophic, making *ex post* relief an inadequate or unsatisfactory solution'.[30] For example, except for rare instances of timing, a franchisor's administrator or liquidator is not appointed until after the franchisee has made the whole of its sunk investment. This investment must be made before the franchisee can start trading. The externalities of a failed franchisor often impact franchisees catastrophically. This is examined in detail in Chap. 8.

Finally, '[t]he small size of a typical transaction creates significant disincentive to seeking *ex post* relief through the courts'.[31] Although the size of the typical purchase of a franchise could often not be called 'small', a franchisor can find ways of making access to justice very expensive for franchisees.[32]

Today's franchisee is a consumer functioning in an environment where Iain Ramsay observes:

> [t]he 'responsibilisation' of the consumer is being pursued … governments are investing heavily in projects to ensure that individuals become responsible consumers through the

---

[26] [2005] FCA 1212

[27] Michael J Trebilcock, 'Rethinking Consumer Protection Policy' in Charles E F Rickett and Thomas G W Telfer (eds), *International Perspectives on Consumers' Access to Justice* (2003) 72

[28] For example, disputes must ultimately be resolved in Connecticut under all 'Subway' franchise agreements

[29] Even within Australia, litigation may be between one party based in NSW and the other in Western Australia, three time zones and several hours by air from each other

[30] Michael J Trebilcock, 'Rethinking Consumer Protection Policy' in Charles E F Rickett and Thomas G W Telfer (eds), *International Perspectives on Consumers' Access to Justice* (2003) 72

[31] Michael J Trebilcock, 'Rethinking Consumer Protection Policy' in Charles E F Rickett and Thomas G W Telfer (eds), *International Perspectives on Consumers' Access to Justice* (2003) 72, XX

[32] For example, Subway requires franchisees globally to pursue ultimate remedies in the courts of Connecticut regardless of home jurisdiction

use of information … These programs often make heroic assumptions about the ability of consumers to use and process information on market choices.[33]

The exploration of asymmetry between franchisor and franchisee in Sect. 6.3 demonstrates how the information supplied to educate franchisees to become more responsible may serve to mislead them about the risks they should consider before signing the franchise agreement. It also helps underscore Ramsay's concerns that the 'heroic assumptions' made by governments about franchisees are flawed.

Before moving on to contract law, it is useful to understand what differentiates employees from independent contractors/suppliers and both from franchisees.

## Categorisation of Work Arrangements

Franchisees undeniably experience a relationship of dependence and control with their franchisors. Dependence and control are the major features of the employer-employee relationship, but franchisors do not think of franchisees as employees.

### *Employee or Independent Contractor?*

From a customers' perspective, and functionally, employees, independent contractors, franchisees and even franchisors are indistinguishable. The law sees things differently. The person labelled 'franchisee' in the twenty-first century workplace occupies a different space in the law to employees and independent contractors. The criteria for identifying a worker as an employee or independent contractor are relatively well understood, but correctly categorising the franchisee is sometimes problematic because of the massive diversity within arrangements that call themselves franchises.

Although franchisors state clearly that their franchisees are independent contractors, the underlying reality of the franchisor/franchisee relationship is not always drawn as cleanly as the franchisor would like. Correct categorisation becomes significant if a regulatory compliance breach occurs or if an incorrect categorisation deprives workers of entitlements they would otherwise be entitled to[34] or where the revenue authorities determine which taxes or superannuation contributions are payable, and by whom, or if one party becomes insolvent.

The approach in the remainder of this chapter is to note in Table 4.1 characteristics that agencies and courts of Australia and the United States have identified as relevant to distinguishing employees from independent contractors. I then turn to

[33] Iain Ramsay, 'Consumer Law, Regulatory Capitalism and the "New Learning" in Regulation' (2006) 28(1) *Sydney Law Review* 9, 13

[34] For example, in the Australian case *Ace Insurance Ltd v. Trifunovski* [2011] FCA 1204, five agents, some of whom had been working for Ace Insurance for almost 30 years as 'agents', brought a claim against Ace Insurance for unpaid long service and annual leave. The court found that workers were employees

**Table 4.1** Features of employee and supplier/independent contractor

| Features of relationship | Employee | Supplier/independent contractor |
|---|---|---|
| *Behavioural control*[a]/terms of engagement | | |
| Type of instructions given/lawful authority to command | *Under a contract of service, the payer usually has the right to direct the manner of performance. What is important is the lawful authority to command that rests with the payer* | The hallmark of a contract for services is said to be that the contract is one for a given result. The contractor works on his/her own account to achieve the result in terms of the contract |
| Where to purchase supplies and services | *Employer entitled to stipulate* | Contractor typically decides subject to specific job specifications |
| Hours of work | *An employer expects an employee to devote the agreed amount of time to their work. An employer adopts policies to ensure this occurs, including policies for managing conflicts of interest* | Generally sets own hours of work |
| Place of performance/what tools and equipment to use | Worker under a contract of service will generally perform the tasks on the payer's premises using the payer's assets and equipment | *Generally provides all own assets and equipment* |
| Degree of instruction/how the work is performed/what order or sequence to follow | *Tasks are performed at the request of the employer.* The worker is said to be working in the business of the payer | Enters into a contract for a specific task or series of tasks. Maintains a high level of discretion and flexibility as to how the work is to be performed. Contract may contain precise terms as to materials used and methods of performance and still be one for services |
| Delegation/what work must be performed by a specified individual | *Employee has no inherent right to delegate tasks to another.* There may be a power to delegate some duties to other employees | Contractor chooses who will perform work. May delegate all or some of the tasks to another person and may employ others[b] |
| Leave entitlements | The contract generally provides for annual leave, long service leave, sick leave and other benefits or allowance | *Generally, an independent contract does not contain leave provisions* |

(continued)

**Table 4.1** (continued)

| Features of relationship | Employee | Supplier/independent contractor |
|---|---|---|
| Evaluation systems/performance reviews | *An entrenched aspect of employment* | |
| Termination | Employer reserves the right to dismiss an employee at any time (subject to state or federal legislation) | *Contracted to complete a set task. The payer may only terminate the contract without penalty where contractor has not fulfilled the conditions of contract*. Insolvency of either party a specified event of default |
| Training provided by the business | *May be trained to perform tasks in a particular manner* | Ordinarily uses own methods |
| *Integration* | *Services are usually merged into the firm's overall operation; the firm's success depends on those employee services*[c] | Services are usually separate from the client's business and are not integrated or merged into it |
| Results test | | An unlimited power to delegate work is an important indication that the worker is an independent contractor and that delegation is generally implied in a contract for services where the emphasis is on the results to be achieved[d] |
| *Financial control*[e] | Generally no opportunity to make a profit or loss outside | Can make profit or loss |
| Significant investment<br>Worker's investment | In many occupations, such as construction, workers purchase the tools and equipment they use and are still considered to be employees | *An independent contractor often has a significant investment in the equipment he or she uses in working for someone else* |
| Unreimbursed expenses | Generally reimbursed for expenses incurred in the course of employment | *Generally incurs own expenses and claims on personal tax* |

| | | |
|---|---|---|
| Opportunity for profit or loss/risk/financial control | Profit or loss is made by employer | *Stands to make a profit or loss on the task. Bears the commercial risk and the responsibility and liability for any poor workmanship or injury sustained in performance of the task. Generally, would be expected to carry their own insurance* |
| | The employer is generally responsible for any loss occasioned by poor workmanship or negligence of the employee | |
| | Bears little or no risk. Employee is not exposed to any commercial risk. This is borne by the employer. Employees are paid for services rendered | |
| Making service available to the market | Only makes his or her services available to the public through the employer's company | May advertise, carry business cards, hang out a shingle, or hold a separate business license |
| Method of payment/remuneration | Typically paid by the employer in regular amounts at stated intervals, such as by the hour or week. An employee in a middle or senior management position in a public company may be rewarded in the form of a bonus package of options or shares. They would then be free to trade these on the stock exchange at future dates and make capital gains | *Payment is based upon performance of the contract* |
| *Type of relationship*[f] | | |
| The factors, for the type of relationship between two parties, generally fall into the categories of: | | |
| How written contract classes the relationship | Employer/ee | Independent contractor |
| Whether the business provides employee-type benefits | The power to grant benefits (such as insurance, a pension plan, vacation pay or sick pay) carries with it the power to take them away, which is a power generally exercised by employers over employees | *Will finance own benefits out of the overall profits of the enterprise* |

(continued)

**Table 4.1** (continued)

| Features of relationship | Employee | Supplier/independent contractor |
|---|---|---|
| The permanency of the relationship | If the company engages a worker with the expectation that the relationship will continue indefinitely rather than for a specific project or period, this is generally considered evidence that the intent was to create an employer-employee relationship | *Fixed term, often long term and at will* |
| The extent to which services performed by the worker are a key aspect of the regular business of the company | If a *worker provides services that are a key aspect of the company's regular business activity*, it is more likely that the company will have the right to direct and control his or her activities. This would indicate an employer-employee relationship | |

[a] 'Behavioral' is first of three common law rules used in the United States to determine worker's status as employee or independent contractor. http://www.irs.gov/businesses/small/article/0,,id=179111,00.html; see *United States v. Silk* 331 U.S. 704 (1947) 'degree of control'

[b] ATO TR 2000/14, Attachment B

[c] http://www.twc.state.tx.us/news/efte/appx_e_twc_ic_test.html

[d] *Brilliant v. Commissioner of Taxation* [2010] AATA 267

[e] 'Financial' is second of three common law rules used in the United States to determine worker's status as employee or independent contractor. See http://www.irs.gov/businesses/small/article/0,,id=179113,00.html.

[f] 'Relationship' is third of three common law rules used in the United States to determine worker's status as employee or independent contractor. See http://www.irs.gov/businesses/small/article/0,,id=179116,00.html.

franchisees and assess how franchisees rate on each of the characteristics identified in Table 4.1. Here, I add features that have not been seen as significant for the employee/independent contractor decision but are relevant to franchising. In Sect. 4.5, I describe some consequences of categorisation where legal liability must be attributed. The consequences of the franchisor becoming insolvent are addressed in Chap. 8. I conclude this chapter with a ready reference table of the major factors as they occur chronologically throughout the relationship.

As they enter the relationship, parties typically identify how they want it to be categorised. What really matters is the nature of the underlying work performed, not what the parties choose to call the relationship. Common law tests, together with statutory criteria, are also applied in Australia. In Australia, Taxation Ruling TR 2005/16 states that the term 'employee' must have its ordinary meaning and that determining whether a person is an employee or an independent contractor

> is a question of fact to be determined by examining the terms and circumstances of the contract between them having regard to the key indicators expressed in the relevant case law. Defining the contractual relationship is often a process of examining a number of factors and evaluating those factors within the context of the relationship between the parties.[35]

In *Stevens v. Brodribb Sawmilling Company Pty Ltd,*[36] the High Court of Australia held that a number of common law tests should be considered in determining if the worker is an employee or a contractor and that it is 'the totality of the relationship between the parties which must be considered'[37] and that no single test will provide the answer. To look beyond the label in the contract, the US Internal Revenue Service ('IRS') applies the 'Eleven Factor' test[38] (based on the common law) to work out whether a person is an employee or an independent contractor for determining the coverage of various federal employment tax laws. The Eleven Factor test identifies factors under the headings[39] behavioural control, [40] financial control[41] and

[35] Paras 49, 50

[36] (1986) 160 CLR 16

[37] *Brilliant v. Commmissioner of Taxation* [2010] AATA 267

[38] See Internal Revenue Service, Employer's Supplemental Tax Guide (Supplement to Publication 15 22 (Circular E), Employer's Tax Guide) Edition, page 6 for use in 2012. http://www.irs.gov/pub/irs-pdf/p15a.pdf; see also Texas Workforce Commission http://www.twc.state.tx.us/news/efte/independent_contractor_tests.html viewed 21 April 2012. IRS Publication 15-A, 2010. Another IRS resource to assist in understanding the independent contractor tests is at http://www.irs.gov/businesses/small/article/0,,id=99921,00.html

[39] Adapted from Schedule B in ATO TR 2000/14, ATO SR xxx and IRS Eleven Factors

[40] 'Behavioral' is first of three common law rules used in the United States to determine worker's status as employee or independent contractor. http://www.irs.gov/businesses/small/article/0,,id=179111,00.html; see *United States v. Silk* 331 U.S. 704 (1947) 'degree of control'

[41] 'Financial' is second of three common law rules used in the United States to determine worker's status as employee or independent contractor. See http://www.irs.gov/businesses/small/article/0,,id=179113,00.html

type of relationship[42] that exists between the parties. Each specific case is determined, as would be expected, by applying the relevant factors to the facts.

Whilst we can all think of exceptions that prove each of these 'rules', the following are guidelines that are accepted by authorities in the United States and Australia. The italicised text in Table 4.1 is the situation that nearest describes a franchisee's role.

Terms in bold (non-italic) in Table 4.1 are the US criteria.[43] Eleven factors derived from the common law tests in the United States serve as guidelines to a worker's categorisation. As is always the case in applying guidelines, the facts will influence the extent to which the guidelines are applied. For example, while the notion of 'payment for a result' is expected in a contract *for* services, it is not necessarily inconsistent with a contract *of* service. Stephen J in the Australian High Court in *Federal Commissioner of Taxation v. Barrett & Ors*[44] found that land salesmen who were engaged to find purchasers and who were remunerated by commission only were employees and not independent contractors. Likewise, Australia's High Court in *Hollis v. Vabu*[45] considered that paying bicycle couriers per delivery, rather than per time period engaged, was a natural means to remunerate employees whose sole purpose is to perform deliveries. The Full Court of the Supreme Court of South Australia in *The Commissioner of State Taxation v. The Roy Morgan Research Centre Pty Ltd*[46] Mullighan, Nyland and Anderson JJ found that interviewers who were only paid on the completion of each assignment, not on an hourly basis, were employees and not independent contractors.

A recent Australian example is *Ace Insurance Ltd v. Trifunovski*[47] ('Ace'), where a court had to decide whether insurance agents who had been hired as independent contractors to sell income protection policies, were employees or independent contractors. Significantly, despite strong indications of a contractor relationship including being described as 'independent contractors' in their contracts, payment being paid according to number of policies sold, using their own vehicles and even going against the traditional wisdom of who could be an employee by a few being

[42] 'Relationship' is third of three common law rules used in the United States to determine worker's status as employee or independent contractor. See http://www.irs.gov/businesses/small/article/0,,id=179116,00.html.

[43] Adapted from Schedule B in ATO TR 2000/14, ATO SR xxx. Application of the US guidelines can be seen in *United States v. Silk* 331 U.S. 704 (1947)

[44] [1973]

[45] (2001) 207 CLR 21, 39 (Gleeson CJ, Gaudron, Gummow, Kirby and Hayne JJ) (McHugh and Callinan JJ dissenting). The majority found that a bicycle courier was a common law employee of Vabu and stated that '[v]iewed as a practical matter, the bicycle couriers were not running their own business or enterprise, nor did they have independence in the conduct of their operations'. [FN 27 in TR 2005/16]; *Hollis v Vabu* (2001) 207 CLR 21, 41 and TR 2005/15 para 32, 33

[46] [2004] SASC 288

[47] [2011] FCA 1204

incorporated[48] and engaging other employees (their wives) as administrative assistants, the court found that the agents were employees of Ace Insurance. Deciding factors included that the agents did not generate goodwill for their own business but rather for Ace Insurance's business; the agents were not in practice able to work for other principals because they were required to work very long hours; Ace Insurance provided training, including scripts for use with customers, so exercised control over the agents; and the agents were encouraged to hold themselves out as representatives of Ace Insurance.

## Features of Relationship When Franchisee Is Involved

When foundation employee/independent contractor decisions were being handed down (*United States v. Silk*[49] in 1949 and *Marshall v. Whittaker's Building Supply Co* in Australia in 1963), franchising was still in its infancy. It was not until 1952 that Neil Fox became the first McDonald's licensee.[50] Angus and Robertson[51] began franchising in Australia in 1977; by 1991, there were only 52 franchisors in Australia. Franchising and the implications of the franchisor/franchisee relationship hovered below regulatory radars for many years. While many of the identified features of the business relationship in Table 4.1 place the franchisee nearer to having an employment relationship than an independent contractor relationship with its franchisor, a genuine franchisee is a separate but an inextricably linked part of the franchisor's business. When their relationship is operating healthily, it is symbiotic and both franchisor and franchisees are indispensable. In Vabu, the majority of the High Court quoted the following statement made by Windeyer J in *Marshall v. Whittaker's Building Supply Co*:

> [T]he distinction between an employee and independent contractor is 'rooted fundamentally in the difference between a person who serves his employer in his, the employer's business, and a person who carries on a trade or business of his own.[52]

---

[48] Ace raised the issue of the ability to incorporate being a determining characteristic of an independent contractor. The court was not persuaded. 'All of the contracts permitted the agents to operate, if they chose, through a corporation. In relation to the sales representatives I regard this contractual opportunity as elusive and there was no evidence that any of these five agents had done so. There was also no evidence that the agents had incorporated at the level of the territory representatives. As sub-regional representatives, Mr Peries and Mr Trifunovski did at certain times conduct their operations through two corporations, Renham Pty Ltd and Heraclea Pty Ltd. One of Combined's witnesses, Mr Bosnic, also contracted through a corporation as a sub-regional representative. But these arrangements did not suggest that the services which were to be provided were other than those of Mr Peries or Mr Trifunovski or Mr Bosnic. In substance, the corporate vehicle merely allowed the commissions to be received by the companies and for the incurring by them of expenses' [2011] FCA 1204, para 95

[49] 331 U.S. 704 (1947)

[50] John F Love, McDonald's: *Behind the Arches*, (Bantam Books, 1986) 20

[51] Bookseller franchisors whose story is told in Chap. 8

[52] (1963) 109 CLR 210

This distinction is also referred to as the integration or organisation test. A problem in applying *Marshall v. Whittaker's* to franchising is that a franchisee both serves the franchisor in the franchisor's business and carries on its own business as a franchisee.

This section re-examines the characteristics identified in Table 4.1 in the context of franchising, focussing on the key indicators of behavioural control, financial control and the nature of the relationship.

## *Behavioural Control of Franchisees/Terms of Engagement*

Clause 10.16 of the Jax Tyres franchise agreement is typically found in franchise agreements:

> The relationship between the franchisor and the franchisee is strictly that of franchisor and franchisee. This agreement does not constitute either party a joint venturer, partner, agent, employee or fiduciary of the other.[53]

Similarly, Clause 10.1 of the Lenard's chicken shop franchise agreement states:

> The National Franchisor, the Master Franchisee and the Franchisee are each independent contractors. They are not and shall not be considered as joint venturers, partners or agents of each other and no fiduciary relationship shall be deemed to exist between them.[54]

Tasks are performed following the method prescribed by franchisors. Franchisees typically have little discretion about how and whether they perform the work. The franchisee is working in its own business within parameters mandated by the franchisor. *McDonald's Australia Holdings Ltd & Anor v Industrial Relations Commission of NSW & 2 Ors* [55] sets out the expectations for McDonald's licensees (i.e: franchisees):

> The foundation and essence of the McDonald's System is the adherence by licensees to standards and policies of McDonald's and its related corporations providing for the uniform operation of all McDonald's restaurants within the McDonald's System including, but not limited to, serving designated food and beverage products; the use only of prescribed equipment and building layout and designs; and strict adherence to designated food and beverage specifications and to prescribed standards of quality, service and cleanliness in restaurant operation.[56]

[53] *Jax Franchising Systems Pty Limited v. State Rail Authority (New South Wales); Jax Tyres Pty Limited v. State Rail Authority (New South Wales)* [2003] NSWLEC 397

[54] *Poulet Frais Pty Ltd v. The Silver Fox Company Pty Ltd* [2005] FCAFC 131 (Branson, Nicholson and Jacobson JJ)

[55] [2005] NSWCA 286

[56] *McDonald's Australia Holdings Ltd & Anor v. Industrial Relations Commission of NSW & 2 Ors* [2005] NSWCA 286, para 19 (Spigelman CJ, Mason P, Handley JA)

Given the prescriptive nature of the business environment for the McDonald's franchisee, it would arguably be open for the High Court to find that a McDonald's franchisee is an employee if it applied *Vabu* without considering additional distinguishing traits.

## Type of Instructions Given

The method of conducting a franchise is always set out in detail in operating manual(s). The franchisor has the contractual right to require franchisees to adhere to specific rules in the conduct of its business and to terminate the franchise if the franchisee does not follow the system.[57] In this regard, employment and franchising are indistinguishable.

## Right to Delegate

The behavioural control may extend to requiring the franchisee to be an owner-manager. Typically, franchisees may not delegate their management role except with the franchisor's express consent. Most franchisees have employees. Franchise agreements contain provisions for familial succession on death/incapacity of franchisor. For example, franchisor Mail Boxes Etc. mandates that:

> During this agreement the franchisee must not … without the Franchisor's prior written consent in any capacity whatsoever be directly or indirectly engaged in any business or undertaking which in the sole opinion of the Franchisor is considered competitive to the Business.[58]

The equivalent clause in a McDonald's licence agreement is:

> Best Efforts: Licensee or, where Licensee is a company, Principal shall … personally devot[e]e… his full time and attention to and exercis[e] his best efforts in the operation of the Restaurant. Licensee… shall keep free from conflicting enterprises or any other activities which would be detrimental to or interfere with the business of the Restaurant.[59]

---

[57] *Zuijs v. Wirth Bros Pty Ltd* (1955) 93 CLR 561; *Australian Mutual Provident Society v. Chaplin* (1978) 18 ALR 385; *Glambed v. FCT* (1989) 20 ATR 428; *Sgobino v. South Australia* (1987) 46 SASR 292; *Re Clothing Trades Award 1982* (1987) 19 IR 416; *City Motors (1981) Pty Ltd v. Commissioner of State Taxation (WA)* (1993) 26 ATR 291; *Samrani v. Roads and Traffic Authority of New South Wales* (1994) Aust Torts Reports ¶81–314; *Climaze Holdings Pty Ltd v. Dyson* (1995) 13 WAR 487; *Australian Building Construction Employees and Building Labourers Federation (WA Branch) v. Pacesetter Homes Pty Ltd* (1994) 56 IR 51; *Humberstone v. Northern Timber Mills* (1949) 79 CLR 389; *Stevens v. Brodribb Sawmilling Co Pty Ltd* (1986) 160 CLR 16; *Ready Mixed Concrete (South East) Ltd v. Minister of Pensions and National Insurance* [1968] 2 QB 497 (list sourced from CCH)

[58] Copy of franchise agreement in author's possession

[59] *McDonald's Australia Holdings Ltd & Anor v. Industrial Relations Commission of NSW & 2 Ors* [2005] NSWCA 286, para 23 of Judgment of Spigelman CJ

Another example is 7-Eleven, which requires a franchisee to work in the store full time for the first 6 months and thereafter at least 20 hours a week. Where a single franchisee operates multiple units of the same or a diversified portfolio of franchise units with more than one franchisor, they do so with the consent of their franchisors. Hadfield found that 12% of franchisors require the franchisee to manage its business full time.[60] Thus, in-term restraints are not a reliable distinguishing characteristic of the relationship.

Neither employee nor franchisee may have a choice of location. This is exemplified in the judgment of Justice Ryan in *Kaytonruby Pty Ltd & Ors v. Glev Franchisees Pty Ltd & Ors*[61] who noted:

> [the prospective franchisee] was … given several maps…on which were delineated "territories" … It was further indicated … that no franchise had by then been allocated in Victoria but Mr Leong would have to be quick. … [the franchisor's agent's observed that]…'I think Noble Park is a better area any way you look at it'. Eventually, … the franchisor's agent suggested that Mr Leong should consider taking a franchise in Malvern which [until] then had not been offered to prospective franchisees but had been reserved as a company shop.[62]

The only option for the franchisee was the suburb of Malvern.

## Degree of Instruction

Part of the reason franchising works is that franchisors train franchisees. They then sometimes control which suppliers franchisees deal with. The choice of suppliers can be a source of considerable franchisee dissatisfaction. The potential for conflict of interest is significant when the franchisor or a related entity is the supplier. Three typical positions franchisors have in relation to suppliers are exemplified by excerpts from three Australian individual unit franchise agreements.

At the least controlling level, the franchise agreement in *Jax Franchising Systems Pty Limited v. State Rail Authority (New South Wales) and Jax Tyres Pty Limited v. State Rail Authority (New South Wales)*[63] leaves Jax Tyres franchisees free to secure supplies from any supplier. This avoids conflicts of interest between franchisor and franchisee. The Jax Tyres franchise agreement stipulates:

> The franchisor shall not limit the suppliers from which such items may be purchased.[64]

A middle position existed in the Mail Boxes Etc (MBE) franchise agreement that stipulated, Clause 9.1:

> During this agreement the franchisee must not: Purchase those products, materials, equipment or services required by the Operating Manual to be purchased from suppliers approved

[60] Hadfield, 'Problematic Relations: Franchising and the Law of Incomplete Contracts', (1990) 42 *Stanford Law Review* 927, 943

[61] (1998) VG 438 of 1993

[62] *Kaytonruby Pty Ltd & Ors v Glev Franchisees Pty Ltd & Ors* (1998) VG 438 of 1993, para 24

[63] [2003] NSWLEC 397

[64] Jax Franchise Agreement, cl 9.6

> by the Franchisor from any person other than those suppliers without the written consent of the Franchisor.[65]

In comparison with the franchise systems mentioned above, the case of *Australian Competition and Consumer Commission v. Simply No-Knead (Franchising) Pty Ltd*[66] ('SNK') provides a glimpse into supply chain abuse by a franchisor. There, the franchisor required the franchisee to purchase most supplies through the franchisor, then refused to deliver the products ordered to the franchisees. This provided the first test case of the business-to-business unconscionable conduct provisions of the *Trade Practices Act*, s 51AC, introduced in 1998. SNK is now insolvent. Clearly, issues around sourcing and dealing with suppliers are one significant area where employment and franchising differs.

## Evaluation Systems

Performance reviews conducted by the franchisor help ensure franchisees maintain the standards set by the franchisor. For both employees and franchisees, a performance review may be comprehensive. The difference between employees and franchisees here is that employees may have statutory protection from summary dismissal, and trade unions to turn to for support. A franchisee has to go it alone in the courts. For example, for franchisees in the McDonald's network, as described in *Far Horizons Pty Ltd v. McDonald's Australia Ltd*[67]:

> The Store Owner must have a positive, co-operative and contributive attitude towards the McDonald's System. He/she must have demonstrated a pro-active record of sales building and involvement in their local community; an attitude which is in tune with today's competitive market place for good solid business rationale and one that will enhance the future growth of their store and the development of the McDonald's System.[68]

This was explained by the McDonald's witnesses as having two components:

> first an appropriate attitude towards the McDonald's organisation including other licensees, and, second, an appropriate attitude to the conduct of the business, including a readiness to engage in local activities which would promote the image of the business and of McDonald's'.[69]

Being subject to ongoing performance reviews is not a meaningful way of distinguishing employees from franchisees.

[65] This agreement has possibly been superseded as MBE was taken over by UPS, but it is not possible to be sure because of the absence of a franchise agreement database in Australia.

[66] [2000] FCA 1365

[67] [2000] VSC 310

[68] *Far Horizons Pty Ltd v McDonald's Australia Ltd* [2000] VSC 310, para 5(f)

[69] *Far Horizons Pty Ltd v. McDonald's Australia Ltd* [2000] VSC 310, para 32

### Training

The expectation of receiving training is one of the features of franchising that attracts new franchisees. In developing economies, 'the lack of business experience on the part of franchisees requires a significant investment in training from the franchisor'.[70] In this way, franchising is similar to employment in that the employee either responds to an advertisement for a person with their skills or will be trained to do the job if prior skill or knowledge is not required.

## *Financial Control of Franchisees*

The financial control factors that help differentiate an employee from an independent contractor fall into the categories of significant investment, unreimbursed investment, opportunity for profit or loss and services available to the market and method of payment.

### Significant Investment

Franchisees meet their own expenses, from establishment or purchase of their business through, in some franchises, to the cost of attending the franchisor's annual conference. To quote the Lenard's poultry franchisor, '[u]nless you [as franchisor] pile up a lot of debt, franchising is the only way to expand retail operations. It means that other people supply the capital'.[71] The amount of sunk costs depends on the type of franchised business. Here, franchisees resemble independent contractors.

A supplier/independent contractor may have taken significant steps, such as retooling, or committing to grow a particular crop in reliance on its contract with the franchisor, but it would normally have done so in the context of an already-established business. For example, a farmer will negotiate a supply agreement to grow potatoes, or a printer will negotiate to print labels to specific standards for a franchisor. A supplier is viewed by the franchisor as a strategic partner that is, effectively, making an investment in the whole network. The supplier relationship may have begun by the supplier successfully tendering. The franchisor and supplier negotiate and agree the terms of their contract. Although it will contain typical provisions, the supply agreement is relational but is not a standard form contract.

---

[70] Ilan Alon, Matthew C Mitchell and J Mark Munoz, 'Microfranchising in less developed countries' in Ilan Alon (ed) *Franchising Globally. Innovation, Learning and Imitation*, (Palgrave Macmillan, 2010) 164

[71] Derek Parker, 'Counting on His Chickens', The Australian (Sydney), 24 June 2005

## Unreimbursed Expenses

Franchisees provide their own equipment, stock and premises. They may sublease premises from the franchisor and be required to place orders through a centralised ordering system owned and operated by franchisor. They meet their own expenses. Taxation Ruling 2005/16 compares the employee and the independent contractor and states:

> [t]he weight or emphasis given to this indicator ... depends on the particular circumstances and the context and nature of the contractual work.[72]

In this regard, franchisees are the same as suppliers/independent contractors.

## Opportunity for Profit or Loss

The franchisee can make its own profit or loss and bears all risk for its own performance. Franchisees also bear the risk of the franchisor selecting an unprofitable site for the franchisee's business, underperforming or failing. In a franchising 'sleight of hand', franchisors often quote their annual profit or turnover in press releases and in submitting their applications for small business awards inclusive of that of their franchisees.

## Services Available to the Market

The franchise agreement will address the extent to which the franchisee is free to engage in work external to the franchise during the term; the franchised business is likely to command all the franchisee's work energy. To this extent, a franchisee is like an employee. The franchisee also expects to be able to sell their business. Ideally, franchisees make capital gains if their business succeeds, and here they are like an independent contractor.

## Method of Payment

In the majority of franchise relationships the franchisee does not receive commission from the franchisor but pays the franchisor a periodical royalty, regardless of results. The analysis in *The Commissioner of State Taxation v. The Roy Morgan Research Centre Pty Ltd,*[73] however, poses challenges for those franchisors whose franchisees are effectively commission agents. Such franchisees may be found to be employees.

---

[72] Paras 49, 50

[73] [2004] SASC 288

## *Type of Relationship Between Franchisors and Franchisees*

The factors determining the type of relationship that exists between two parties generally fall into the categories of written contracts, employee benefits, permanency of relationship and services provided as a key activity of the business.

### Written Contracts

A franchise agreement does not need to be written but usually is. The franchise agreement states explicitly that the franchisee is an independent contractor and is not in a joint venture, in employment or in partnership with its franchisor. Nevertheless, the classification in the contract is not conclusive.

In *Awuah v. Coverall North America Inc*[74] ('Coverall'), the Supreme Judicial Court of Massachusetts determined that Coverall's Massachusetts commercial cleaner franchises are in fact Coverall's employees. Under Massachusetts law, the court had to decide:

1. May a franchisor lawfully use customer accounts-receivable financing to pay a franchisee who is characterised as an employee under [G.L. c. 149, § 148B]?
2. Do the 'damages incurred' for which a misclassified worker can seek recompense under [G.L. c. 149, § 150,] include costs that an employer statutorily must bear?
3. May an employer lawfully withhold wages to an employee if the employer and employee agree that such wages are not earned until a customer remits payment?
4. May an employee and his employer lawfully agree that the employee will pay some or all of the cost of workers' compensation or other insurance coverage procured to alleviate the liability of the employer?[75]

As a consequence, franchisors become liable for the statutory liabilities they had hitherto shed. As journalist Janet Sparks observed, '[n]ot only will the franchisor get smacked for back wages and other employment fees, it will also be hit with reimbursing its employees with the franchise related fees and expenses that they paid the company, including franchise fees and ongoing funds'.[76]

---

[74] 460 Mass. 484 (2011)

[75] *Pius Awuah & Others* v. *Coverall North America, Inc.* SJC-10829. May 3, 2011. – August 31, 2011

[76] Janet Sparks, Coverall Doomed in Disguising Workers as Owners, 24 February 2012, http://www.bluemaumau.org/11303/coverall_doomed_efforts_disguise_employees_owners

## Permanency of the Relationship

Franchise agreements are typically for a fixed term,[77] occasionally for up to an indefinite term, not uncommonly for 20 years. Both an employee and a franchisee expect to be in the particular work relationship for a number of years; for an employee, this will vary with the nature of the job. For a franchisee, there is an expectation that the franchisee will be in the relationship for the term of the franchise agreement or will sell at a profit before then.

Post-termination restraints are an aspect of the relationship. Post-contract restraints apply to franchisees in Australia. The validity of the restraint depends on how reasonable it is – in time, scope and distance. Franchise-related restraint cases in Australia include *The Cheesecake Shop v. A & A Shah Enterprises* [2004] NSWSC 625 which discussed the following clause in the franchise agreement:

> 16. Post Termination Covenant Not To Compete. The Franchisee, Nominated Manager and the Guarantors shall not during the term or the period, after the expiration or earlier termination of this Agreement, as specified in the Schedule conduct on his own account or be concerned or interested in whether directly or indirectly as agent, representative, consultant, adviser, servant, employee, trustee, partner, shareholder, or director in any firm or corporation conducting a business similar to the Franchised Operation or in any cake manufacturing or cake retail or cake wholesale enterprise, within the distance [stipulated in the agreement] from the location specified in the Schedule.[78]

Justice Windeyer was not prepared to enforce a post-term non-compete covenant, writing:

> I cannot see how the restraint could be justified. It is really a prohibition against competition without any evidence to establish anything being competed against. ... In the absence of evidence the covenant would seem to operate to preserve an area for [The Cheesecake Shop] operations which do not presently exist and may never exist. ... such a restraint could not be upheld as it could not be shown to be necessary or reasonable to preserve the goodwill of [the franchisor].[79]

## Services Provided as Key Activity of the Business

A franchisee's business is part of the core activities of the franchise system, a core revenue source for franchisors. Evidence of this is the administrator's approach; even if the administrator closes many or most of the franchisor-owned outlets, he or she may require franchisees to remain open for business. The franchisee has no right to terminate contract if an administrator or liquidator is appointed to the franchisor.

[77] Frazer, Weaven and Wright, Franchising Australia 2008, above n 7, 23 report the initial terms of the current franchise agreement of the 264 franchisors that responded ranged from 1 to 50 years. Of these, 67% of franchisees have an initial term of 5 years

[78] *The Cheesecake Shop v. A & A Shah Enterprises* [2004] NSWSC 625

[79] *The Cheesecake Shop v. A & A Shah Enterprises* [2004] NSWSC 625, para 36

## Summary of Features

There are additional features of franchise agreements that have not been identified as indicia of whether a person is an employee or an independent contractor. They are useful in further clarifying whether a person is neither employee nor independent contractor but, instead, is a franchisee. They, together with the features from Table 4.1, are briefly summarised, ordered chronologically through the relationship, in Table 4.2.

**Table 4.2** Summary of features of employees, franchisees and independent contractors

| Feature of relationship | Employee | Franchisee | Independent contractor/ supplier |
|---|---|---|---|
| *Prior to commencement of relationship* | | | |
| Invest money directly in activity to get started | No | Yes | Yes |
| Invest in sunk costs in 'or's image /brand | No | Yes | Maybe |
| Decides where business will be located | No | No | Yes |
| Contract is the basis of the relationship | Yes | Yes | Yes |
| Consumer protection if advertisement is misleading or deceptive | Yes | Yes | No |
| *Once committed to relationship* | | | |
| Personal responsibility for premises costs | No | Yes | Yes |
| Right to choose suppliers | No | No | Yes |
| Owns improvements to intellectual property | No | No | Yes |
| Relationship recognised specifically by law | Yes | Yes | Yes |
| Duty of confidentiality | Yes | Yes | Yes |
| Restraints on other work that may be done during term of contract | Yes | Yes | Possibly |
| Vulnerable to capricious behaviour by other party | Yes | Yes | No |
| May join a trade union to enforce rights | Yes | No | Yes |
| Personally assumes financial risk on behalf of employer/franchisor/other party | No | Yes | No |
| May sell the role | No | Yes | Yes |
| *After relationship ends* | | | |
| Opportunity to make capital gain if enterprise succeeds | No | Yes | Yes |
| Owns the goodwill at the end | No | No | Yes |
| Post-relationship restraints | Sometimes | Sometimes | No |
| On termination of relationship, employee or franchisee usually has financial obligations re the employer/franchisors business | No | Yes | No |
| Clear statutory rights if other party becomes insolvent | Yes | No | Yes |
| Contract may be terminated on winding up of other party | Yes | Yes | Yes |

In many aspects, the franchisee and the employee are functionally indistinguishable. In *Majik Markets Pty Ltd v. Brake and Service Centre Drummoyne Pty Ltd and ors,*[80] the Supreme Court of New South Wales noted the vital role franchisees play when Handley JA observed:

> If the business was not operated by some franchisee, the franchisor would either have to employ staff of its own or sell or lease the site to an independent purchaser or lessee.[81]

Ideally, there will be no conflict of interest between franchisor and franchisee in relation to choice of suppliers or treatment of franchisees stemming from supplier issues. In theory, the franchisor's ability to negotiate on the basis of the combined buying power of the franchisees will secure better terms from suppliers than the franchisees could negotiate as sole operators.

Franchisees in Australia do not have a properly funded representative body that functions in the same way a trade union does. Franchisees sometimes feel vulnerable and disempowered on the occurrence of capricious or unreasonable behaviour by their franchisor and may have to go to court to attempt to assert legal rights. For example, in *Far Horizons,* Mr Hackett (director of a McDonald's franchise) makes his vulnerability as a franchisee obvious in his witness statement:

> Mr Xipolitos appeared to me to be determined and insistent on grading me as operationally unsatisfactory....
>
> I came to realise that my future security and prospects in the McDonald's System, being my $2 million plus investment in my restaurants and my desire to expand, were ultimately in the hands of a very subjective evaluation of my restaurants by one or two people and the personal relationship between myself as licensee and my Consultant.[82]

The increased vulnerability for a franchisee over an employee is that franchisees have sunk investments, their own employees, ongoing contractual obligations to the franchisor and third parties and consequential liabilities secured in contractual relationships. The franchisee does not have the option of finding another job without considerable financial loss.

## Relevance of Categorisation

### *Incorrect Classification in Contract of Appointment*

For franchisors, a re-categorisation as employees of the contractors they have called 'franchisees' is undesirable. This was the experience of the franchisors in *Coverall.* Similarly, in *ACE Insurance Ltd v. Trifunovski,* Flick J noted that the decision in the

---

[80] *Majik Markets Pty Ltd v Brake and Service Centre Drummoyne Pty Ltd and ors* (1991) 28 NSWLR 443 decision of Kirby P, Mahoney and Handley JJA

[81] *Majik Markets Pty Ltd v Brake and Service Centre Drummoyne Pty Ltd and ors* (1991) 28 NSWLR 443, 465

[82] *Far Horizons Pty Ltd v. McDonald's Australia Ltd* [2000] VSC 310, para 42

court of first instance that the insurance agents are employees not independent contractors 'will have an impact on Ace Insurance Ltd's payroll tax liability in Victoria …'.[83]

## *Consumer Protection*

The employment relationship is the subject of a comprehensive statutory regime that provides employees with 'cradle to grave' rights in relation to their employers. Depending on the jurisdiction, these can include statutory rights to accurate job advertisements, employer-funded superannuation, paid leave, recourse in the event of discrimination and recognised status and rights under the *Corporations Act 2001* (Cth) if the employer becomes insolvent.

Franchisees also have specific recourse in Australia to statutory actions if pre-contractual claims made to them and relied on turned out to be misleading or deceptive.[84]

## *Goodwill*

Goodwill is a complex issue and is a clear point of differentiation between an employee, independent contractor and a franchisee. Employers and contractors own the goodwill in their businesses. The franchisee situation opens the door for a debate about the type of goodwill that is being sold: is it goodwill that attaches to the person (the franchisee) or the brand (the franchisor) or the location (potentially either or both)? In ATO ruling 'PCD 8 Capital Gains: Goodwill'[85], possible viewpoints on the question of whether a franchisee can own goodwill are discussed.

Some franchise agreements state the matter clearly. For instance, Clause 17.2 of the MBE individual franchise agreement states:

> Consequences of Termination. The Franchisee shall have no claim against the Franchisor for … compensation for the loss of the business, loss of goodwill or any similar loss.

There is authority for the view that in the absence of a specific contractual provision to the contrary, on the termination of a franchise, the benefit of the goodwill remains in the franchisor. A franchisee would expect to receive some of the goodwill on the sale of a franchise *during* the term. The amount of time still to run under the franchise agreement will thus be relevant to the conclusion.

---

[83] [2012] FCA 235, para 15

[84] Australia's *Competition and Consumer Act 2010* (Cth) provides avenues for victims of misleading and deceptive or unconscionable conduct to seek redress

[85] Australian Taxation Office, PCD 8 Capital Gains: Goodwill (1995). Goodwill is also discussed by Ian Tregoning in 'Goodwill in the Context of Licensing, Leasing and Franchising: Some Considerations' (2009) 37 *Australian Business Law Review* 296

## *Occupational Health and Safety*

Whilst franchisees are widely assumed to be liable for the physical injury occurring on their premises, a franchisor has, on occasion, been found liable for the death of a franchisee's employee. For example, in two Australian cases,[86] the franchisor was held liable for the deaths of franchisees' employees. The franchisees and their employees followed the franchisor's methods and instructions to the letter, for example, by employing the franchisor's approved tradespeople to conduct work on the franchisee's site. The franchisor's prescribed methods or instructions were found by the courts to be flawed, resulting in the court attributing liability to the franchisor.

A different scenario arose in the Australian case *Samaan bht Samaan v. Kentucky Fried Chicken Pty Ltd.*[87] An incident in a franchisor-operated KFC outlet was found to be responsible for the plaintiff being sold contaminated chicken and becoming profoundly disabled as a result of eating it. Rotham J observed that

> [i]f this store were a franchise store, KFC would most likely not be liable, having taken all practical steps to ensure compliance with the procedures. However, this was not a franchise store.[88]

The Australian master licensee for Kentucky Fried Chicken in Australia was found to be liable for the poor food handling practices of its employees. Had a franchisee-operated store been conducted in the same way, the failure to adhere to the operating manual would have been a ground for terminating the franchise.

## *Insolvency*

Insolvency of the employer or franchisor generates very different outcomes for employees, independent contractors and franchisees. The employee loses his or her job if the employer's business fails. Some anticipate the employer's impending demise and leave before the administrator is appointed. Being paid wages fortnightly or monthly, employees would quickly know if they did not receive wages. An independent contractor is free to look for new work at any time, but franchisees may not become aware of their franchisor's insolvency until a supplier changes the terms of trade or news of the franchisor's demise appears in the media. The resulting problems for franchisees are addressed in Chap. 8.

[86] *WorkCover Authority of New South Wales (Insector Petar Ankucic) v McDonald's Australia Limited and anor* [2000] NSWIRComm 277 and *Workcover Authority of NSW (Inspector Ankucic) v McDonald's Australia Limited and anor*[2000] NSWIRComm 1123

[87] [2012] NSWSC 381, Rotham J. KFC has announced its intention to appeal. In the meantime, the franchisor is careful not to draw attention to the fact that the tragedy befell a customer who had bought chicken at a franchisor-owned outlet. http://www.kfc.com.au/about-us/news-kfc-statement-in-defence-vs-samaan.asp

[88] [2012] NSWSC 381, para 250

## Conclusion

Ultimately, it can be seen that within twenty-first-century franchise networks, the franchisees' relationship status on Facebook would most accurately not be 'single' or 'in a relationship' but 'it's complicated', very complicated! A key difference is the amount of risk the franchisee has assumed which is far more than an employee would normally have. But unlike independent contractors, franchisees have numerous restrictions imposed on them by franchisors. Franchisees have 'skin in the game',[89] without access to all of the 'up side' benefits available to the franchisor. Further, the amount of protection the franchisee receives is far less clear than the protection afforded an employee by the law.

If so much risk is shifted to franchisees why then do they still sign up? They subscribe to the franchisor mantra of 'be in business for yourself but not by yourself'. As Elizabeth Spencer says, '[d]espite being overburdened with risk, because of the standard form the franchisee is faced with the choice of accepting the contract terms [and all of the attendant risks and liabilities the various contracts expose it to] or giving up on the deal entirely'.[90]

Robert L Purvin Jr. writes, 'Perhaps the biggest myth of franchising is that a franchisee is an independent businessperson. [In reality,] most franchisees have fewer rights than common-law employees'[91] To Purvin, the franchise agreement consigns franchisees to 'indentured servitude'.[92] In this chapter, it has been demonstrated that franchisees also have fewer rights than regular consumers or contractors/suppliers.

Employment, independent contractor and franchise relationships are all created by contracts. If we accept that the lot of the franchisee might be to be like an indentured servant, could a franchisee avoid this predicament by signing a more balanced contract? To answer this question, an understanding of the principles of contract law and how they play out in the franchise context is essential. Thus, the next chapter is about contract law in the context of the franchisor/franchisee relationship.

---

[89] A term coined by investor Warren Buffett referring to a situation in which high-ranking insiders use their own money to buy stock in the company they are running. Read more: http://www.investopedia.com/terms/s/skininthegame.asp#ixzz1yghGKREE

[90] Elizabeth Spencer, 'Standard Form and Relational Aspects of Franchise Contracts' (Paper presented at the 20th International Society of Franchising Conference, Palm Springs, California, 24–26 February 2006) 21, quoting Silvana Sciarra, 'Franchising and Contract of Employment: Notes on a Still Impossible Assimilation' in Christian Joerges (ed), Franchising and the Law: Theoretical and Comparative Approaches in Europe and the United States (1996) in *Journal of Institutional & Theoretical Economics*, 152, 297–324

[91] Robert L Purvin Jr, The franchise Fraud, How to protect yourself before and after you invest. 1994, 76

[92] Robert L Purvin Jr, The franchise Fraud, How to protect yourself before and after you invest. 1994, 76

# Chapter 5
# Contract Law

**Abstract** Contract laws are the glue that holds the commercial world together. Franchise relationships are, however, difficult to document adequately. To date, contract law has been unable to accommodate the franchisor/franchisee relationship appropriately. In this chapter, the dated notions of certainty and freedom of contract are challenged for their inability to deliver a balanced franchise agreement. The specific demands placed on contract law by the franchise relationship are discussed through the lenses of relational contracts, incomplete contracts and exploitative contracts. Consequent on signing up to join a franchise system, franchisees enter numerous contracts with third parties. These are introduced in this chapter.

'Contractual relations are the essence of the firm, not only with employees but with suppliers, customers, creditors,'[1] master franchisees and franchisees. A franchise network is held together by contracts. The franchise agreement is the starting point for the courts and third parties such as landlords and administrators to determine the parties' rights.

Contract law rests on some long-accepted principles: sanctity of the contract, freedom of contract and an economic interest in certainty of contract. After conducting an inquiry into franchising in 2008, the Economics and Finance Committee of the South Australian Parliament concluded that

> [t]he basic premise on which the principles of freedom of contract and sanctity of contract rest is that contracts are negotiated at arm's length by equally positioned participants in the bargaining process … [This] is not fulfilled in the typical franchise arrangement.[2]

---

[1] Michael C Jensen and William H Meckling, 'Theory of the Firm: Managerial Behavior, Agency Costs and Ownership Structure,' (1976) 3(4) *Journal of Financial Economics*, 305, 311

[2] Economics and Finance Committee, Parliament of South Australia, *Franchises* (2008) 17

J. Buchan, *Franchisees as Consumers: Benchmarks, Perspectives and Consequences*,
DOI 10.1007/978-1-4614-5614-8_5, © Springer Science+Business Media New York 2013

For franchisors, however, casting the franchise agreement as a contract that documents a commercial relationship justifies their stressing the importance of these principles. In making the observation that 'the law of contract… has the greatest impact on interactions where freedom of choice and action and freedom from interference are most coveted',[3] Sir Edmund Thomas has identified the very reasons why franchisors the world over resist legislative intervention in the franchise contract so strenuously. Instances of this resistance are the Franchise Council of Australia's forceful but unsuccessful lobbying against franchise-specific federal legislation in 1997 and the International Franchise Association's reaction to the proposed *Californian Fair Franchise Bill* of 2012.[4]

Franchise agreements document the baseline obligations and rights of the parties. They document the consequences of the franchisee not adhering to its contractual obligations. Where the franchisee is a corporation, they also secure the obligations of third-party guarantors to underpin the franchisee's obligations. The contract provides a course of action to be followed where the franchisee is in breach. The contract law fills in the gaps through, for example, rules of interpretation and rules about remedies for breach of contract and how damages for breach are assessed.

Despite all the franchisor's words about support and nurturing that have resulted in the franchisee purchasing its business, the franchisor's position is clear. The 'inherent dynamic in franchisor/franchisee relationship … involves maintaining the franchisee in a subordinate position. This increases the franchisee's motivation to provide assurances of performance, among them taking on risk'.[5] The dynamic is reflected in the franchise agreement.

While franchisors and franchisees are both independent legal entities, they have different interests at different points in their relationship. Before the contract is signed, the franchisor wants to woo the franchisee to select their franchise rather than any other. The franchisor portrays the system as established and having the ability to deliver the franchisee a secure and profitable future. During the relationship, the franchisor wants control over dedicated and honest business owners and also wants to retain freedom to take the system in any direction it wishes. This might include taking significant risks and deciding to appoint an administrator. Decisions taken by franchisors once franchisees have signed on do not have to be made with the franchisees' best interests to the fore.

Whilst '[s]uperficially franchising is a very straightforward business operation; … it's probably the world's most complicated and intricate method of doing business'.[6] Because of the complexity of the franchise relationship and the intricacy

---

[3] E W Thomas, *The Judicial Process: Realism, Pragmatism, Practical Reasoning and Principles* (Cambridge University Press: 2005) 382

[4] See IFA's reaction to Californian Fair Franchise Bill quote from IFA annual report (2011, p 17)

[5] Elizabeth Spencer, 'Standard Form and Relational Aspects of Franchise Contracts' (Paper presented at the 20th International Society of Franchising Conference, Palm Springs, California, 24–26 February 2006) 21, quoting Silvana Sciarra, 'Franchising and Contract of Employment: Notes on a Still Impossible Assimilation' in Christian Joerges (ed), Franchising and the Law: Theoretical and Comparative Approaches in Europe and the United States (1996) *Journal of Institutional & Theoretical Economics*, 152, 297–324

[6] Knowledge @UNSW 29 March 2012 Franchising: Commercial Marriages from Heaven or Hell?

of the model, it would be naïve to think that the contract should be the last word on how the franchisor/franchisee relationship is regulated. This is even more so when an occurrence arises that is not contemplated in the agreement or where the franchisor has clearly used its superiority in the contracting process to the franchisees' detriment. Contract theory, explored here, together with asymmetry considerations that are explored in Chap. 6, helps explain how imbalances arise in relation to the franchise agreement and why they cannot be redressed by the common law.

## The Desirability of Certainty in Contracts

The myths of freedom and certainty of contract suit franchisors. Certainty in all dimensions is widely accepted as being desirable in commercial relationships. It is claimed that 'uncertainty is death for business'.[7] However, whereas one would assume that certainty is an outcome of the contracting process, 'as Sir Anthony Mason has observed: "It later emerged, as is the case with many legal concepts rooted in formalism, that the element of certainty was illusory"'.[8]

There is an assumption underlying a relational contract that the major foreseeable events, which could fundamentally change the relationship, are addressed in the contract. Other events are foreseeable but seem so unlikely to one or both parties that they are not included. The parties acknowledge, by implication, that some events are not foreseeable and will be the subject of negotiation if and when they occur. Where certainty is not possible, a balanced contract is not the outcome in a franchise agreement.

## Freedom of Contract

Parties to contracts act in their own interest. 'What rational person given the opportunity is going to create a contract that is not in their best interests?'[9] Yet as Sharma writes:

> [T]he liberal fiction that all the effects of a contract should be attributed to the will of those who made it still persists though contract law today even though the overwhelming majority of contracts are the product of the will of only one of the contracting parties.[10]

---

[7] Sky News, 'Australian Industry Group, Heather Ridout, with Kieran Gilbert', Agenda (5 May 2009)

[8] In *Bobux Marketing Limited v. Raynor Marketing Limited* [2001] NZCA 348, para 34 (Thomas J dissenting), citing AF Mason, 'Contract, Good Faith and Equitable Standards in Fair Dealing' (2000) 116 *Law Quarterly Review* 66, 70

[9] Courtenay Atwell, 'The Franchise See-Saw: Finding the elusive balance of power and control in the context of Australian Retail Franchising'. Unpublished paper UNSW, 2012

[10] K M Sharma 'From Sanctity to Fairness' (1999) 18 *New York Law School Journal of International and Comparative Law* 95, 115

Franchisors draft the agreement. It reflects the franchisor's will. The franchisor's interests are protected by the agreement. This makes sense to the extent that franchisors can thereby ensure that the major risks for the future integrity of the system are addressed and can achieve administrative efficiency through standardisation. For franchisors, standardisation of outcome is a more important result than letting a new franchisee enter the relationship in the mistaken belief that he or she has any bargaining power. There is little if any opportunity for franchisees to negotiate amendments to the single unit franchise agreement. Michael Webster's suggestions on negotiating franchise agreements should be read by all interested in becoming a franchisee.[11] The franchisee accepts the franchisor's unwillingness to negotiate because standardisation reinforces the franchisor's mantra – we know how to do it, trust us and sign on with us and you will be in control of your future before you know it.

This helps explain why franchisors make no mention of franchisor failure in franchise agreements. In not drawing attention to their own potential demise, they are acting in their own interest. Australian franchisors' equivocal response to compliance with the voluntary Franchising Code of Practice (1993–1998) is likely to be an indication of how franchisors would respond to the suggestion that all franchise agreements voluntarily include provisions addressing franchisees' rights if the franchisor failed.

Thus, the assumption that franchisors will act in their own interests is correct. The assumption that the weaker party to the contract, the franchisee, will act in their own interests, is incorrect. Not having, usually, bought a franchise before, a franchisee does not know what its own interests are. Of course, no one is forcing a franchisee to buy. Having decided to commit, a franchisee has no ability to put their own interests ahead of anything written in the franchise agreement or any pre-entry requirements mandated by the franchisor. To be accepted as a franchisee, they hand the franchisor all of their financial information, a gesture the franchisor does not have to reciprocate.

## A Standard Form Business Consumer Contract

The franchise agreement documents a relationship that has both supplier/consumer and commercial aspects to it. Prior to execution of the contract, the parties are the franchisor as a business supplier and a franchisee as a business consumer. The subject of the contract is a long-term business-to-business relationship. Documenting this hybrid consumer/business contract is the task of the franchisor. Even though it

[11] Michael Webster, 'Negotiating Your Franchisee Rights' on Don Sniegowski's Bluemaumau, (4 January, 2012) <http://www.bluemaumau.org/negotiating_your_franchisee_rights>

documents a commercial relationship, a franchise agreement is a standard form contract. Franchisors use standard form franchise agreements to optimise their position. For example, in 2001, an Australian court was told by Subway that a virtually identical dispute resolution

> clause appear[s] in [Subway] franchise agreements for over 14,000 Subway franchises throughout the world. The reason Subway Systems and Doctor's Associates[12] require disputes with franchisees to be resolved in accordance with clause 10 is that they want to develop an internationally consistent approach to dispute resolution with franchisees.[13]

From a management perspective, the Subway franchisor's stance is impossible to fault. The franchisor maximises its position by requiring disputes that cannot be resolved by negotiation or mediation at a national level to be resolved by arbitration or litigation in the location nominated by the franchisor, Connecticut, USA. This strategy benefits the franchisor but is a disincentive to robust dispute resolution for Subway franchisees outside the north east of the United States.

As Rick Bigwood points out, 'standardized [or standard form] contracts are mostly to be endured as beneficial in complex free market economies. This is largely because they reduce transaction costs'.[14] Bigwood acknowledges that 'consumer protection through market forces alone is weak'.[15] The inability of market forces to remodel franchise agreements to curb franchisor opportunism is evidenced by numerous submissions to Australian government inquiries and by court cases. For example, why does a standard form contract not anticipate the franchisor's death or insolvency? Franchise agreements always provide for the death or insolvency of the franchisee. Numerous franchisors, however, become insolvent. This will be addressed in Chap. 8.

In its submission to the Australian Consumer Law Consultation on Draft Provisions on Unfair Contract Terms, the Law Society of NSW provides examples of standard form contracts frequently used in conveyancing transactions and states that

> the Committee believes that the use of these forms has significant consumer benefits: [being] familiarity, comprehensiveness, compliance with legislative provisions, frequent updates, flexibility, efficiency, risk management, balance between the parties to the transactions.[16]

---

[12] Doctor's Associates Inc, an American corporation, is the owner of proprietary and other rights and interests in various service marks, trademarks, trade names and goodwill used in its business including the trade name and trademark 'Subway'. Subway Systems is the Australian licensee of Doctor's Associates. Subway Systems operates, and franchises others to operate, sandwich shops under the name 'Subway', using recipes and methods licensed by Doctor's Associates. *Timic v. Hammock* [2001] FCA 74, para 6

[13] *Timic v. Hammock* [2001] FCA 74, para 6

[14] Rick Bigwood, *Exploitative Contracts* (Oxford, 2003) 274

[15] Rick Bigwood, *Exploitative Contracts* (Oxford, 2003) 274

[16] Law Society of New South Wales, Australian Consumer Law – Consultation on Draft Provisions on Unfair Contract Terms (2009) Australian Government, The Treasury <http://www.treasury.gov.au/contentitem.asp?NavId=037&ContentID=1537> Accessed 4 June 2010

Whilst all of these points are valid in respect of standard form contracts drafted by an impartial party, they are invalid in franchising. Standard form agreements such as franchise agreements are drafted by the more powerful party in a consumer sales environment where the final result will be that the purchaser signs a contract documenting a commercial relationship. Franchisees are encouraged to read the franchise agreement, ask questions and obtain legal and financial advice, but any requests for changes are typically rejected by the franchisor. This prompts the rhetorical question: 'If the franchisor is going to require the franchisee to have legal counsel review the franchise agreement, will the franchisor agree to negotiate any and every term in good faith? Otherwise is the goal simply to add ballast to the usual disclaimers of no representations and no reliance?'[17] The franchisee accepts the franchisor's unwillingness to negotiate because standardisation reinforces the franchisor's mantra – we know how to do it, trust us and sign on with us and you will be successful before you know it.

Nevertheless, franchise agreements are

> long-term contracts [that] involve continuing financial commitment in the course of which the consumer, being imperfectly informed and not fully aware about his needs – is largely reliant on the advice, guidance and skills of his counterparty.[18]

Another way of expressing the problems caused by the standard form is that

> [c]onflicts of interest may, and do, create counter-incentives for [creating and] complying with contractual obligations. Especially in long term contracts and in conditions of asymmetric information, the possibility of opportunistic behaviour appears considerably increased not least because the value of the contract and the investment depends on the firm's performance after the point of purchase.[19]

It is easy to suggest that, having observed that other franchisees have already made the investment in the franchise business, franchisee consumers free ride and do not conduct extensive due diligence. This failure to conduct due diligence may be true in some cases, but maybe the effectiveness of due diligence for franchisees is overstated. Even if adequate due diligence were possible, the contract is not negotiable and the franchisor can change.

Willmott et al. write that '[s]tandard form contracts are typically used by parties who are in such a strong bargaining position … that they are able to prescribe the terms on which they are prepared to contract on a 'take it or leave it' basis'.[20]

---

[17] Email posted to ABA Forum on Franchising by Peter Lagarias, Thursday, 22 March 2012

[18] Andromachi Georgosouli, 'Investor Protection Regulation: Economically Rational?' (2006) Working Paper Series, University of London, Centre for Commercial Law Studies 10 <http://ssrn.com/abstract=893451> Accessed 4 June 2010

[19] Andromachi Georgosouli, 'Investor Protection Regulation: Economically Rational?' (2006) Working Paper Series, University of London, Centre for Commercial Law Studies 10 <http://ssrn.com/abstract=893451> at 4 June 2010, 10–11, fn 40 citing I D C Ramsey, 'Rationales for Intervention in the Consumer Marketplace' (1984) Occasional Paper for the Office of Fair Trading 28

[20] Lindy Willmott, Sharon Christensen, Des Butler, Bill Dixon, *Contract Law* (Oxford University Press 3rd ed, 2009) 583

The franchise agreement is an example of such a contract negotiation process. The franchisor supplier drafts the franchise agreement. The franchisee takes it or leaves it, seldom having the opportunity to vary the standard form. Anecdotally, the only franchisees in the position to negotiate non-standard terms into their franchise agreement may be the first franchisees of a new network or the first master franchisee entering a new state or country where a franchisor is very keen to establish a presence.

It is important to recognise that the franchise relationship is not purely commercial. Thus, to place the contract and the contracting process in perspective, we will now turn to aspects of contract that cast doubt on the wisdom or validity of slavishly applying the long-accepted contract law principles to the franchise agreement and associated contracts.

## Relational Contract

In addition to being commercial, consumer, standard form contracts, franchise agreements are relational contracts. They document ongoing relationships. Framing the franchise agreement as a relational contract is also to acknowledge that certainty need not be an objective, far less an outcome of the contracting process. Gillian Hadfield observes:

> [I]ncomplete contracts (such as franchise agreements) often exist deeply embedded in an ongoing relationship. The parties are not strangers; much of their interaction takes place "off the contract" mediated not by visible terms enforceable by a court, but by a particular balance of cooperation and coercion, communication and strategy.[21]

In one sense, Hadfield is right about the parties to a franchise agreement not being strangers, but in another sense, this assumption needs to be tested in new contexts. Anecdote suggests that many franchisors play 'good cop; bad cop'. The good cop is the salesperson who is the public face of the brand, who enthuses prospective franchisees about the brand, and the bad cop is the other member of the franchisor's family who is in charge of the day-to-day operation of the system. Additionally, as we saw earlier and will see again when we look at insolvency, the franchisor might sell the business, be bought out, or an administrator or liquidator might step into the shoes of the franchisor. The dynamic changes immediately on the occurrence of one of the above events – the parties are now strangers.

Franchise agreements are relational contracts and are necessarily incomplete. In a relational contract it is assumed that the major foreseeable events that could fundamentally change the relationship will be addressed in the contract and that other matters will be addressed if they arise. The franchise agreement has to remain

[21] Gillian K Hadfield 'Problematic Relations: Franchising and the Law of Incomplete Contracts', (1990) 42 *Stanford Law Review* 927, footnote 28 at 928

incomplete because of its long-term nature[22] and the unpredictability of both human relationships and commercial environments.

In theory, the incompleteness can be justified in a relational contract as being necessary to accommodate future changes in the commercial environment and in the specific franchise system. In practice, however, the incompleteness is one sided. Franchisees' obligations occupy many clauses and franchisors' few. Franchisees' obligations and the consequences of breach are spelled out in detail; franchisors obligations are almost entirely discretionary. Franchisors would argue that the level of discretion and the lack of balance in the contract are necessary to protect the brand. However, the absence of 'reciprocity of contractual obligation'[23] makes it difficult for franchisees to successfully prosecute a franchisor's breach of the spirit of the contract as it is easy for a franchisor not to breach the letter of a contract that requires little concrete of it. As Roger Blair and Francine Lafontaine observe:

> It would be unrealistic to expect a relational contract to cover all contingencies. From a franchisee's perspective, then, perhaps the biggest problem with franchising lies not so much in what it is, but rather what it is not and yet sometimes appears to be.[24]

'To a lawyer, a contract may be incomplete in failing to describe the obligations of the parties in each possible state of the world'.[25] It is thus difficult to explain why franchisors would knowingly leave gaps around the possibility of franchisor failure when 'the cost of making contracts complete in this sense is trivial'.[26] A flaw in applying the theory of trading off 'front-end and back-end costs'[27] to justify not providing for franchisor failure up front is that franchisors fail sufficiently often for the risk to be eligible for inclusion in the franchise agreement from the outset. It would be relatively inexpensive to insert provisions about franchisor failure into the franchise agreement, and the traditional justification that issues left for the back end will be resolved by the courts is not justifiable where the trigger event is the insolvency of one party.

---

[22] Shelby D Hunt, 'The Trend Towards Company-Operated Units in Franchise Chains' (1973) 49(2) Journal of Retailing 3, 10, reported that typically fast-food franchisors in the USA granted terms with a median length of 15 years and that frequently, the franchisee had an option to renew. Frazer, Weaven and Wright, *Franchising Australia 2008*, found the initial term of a franchise agreement in Australia across all sectors except motor vehicles varied from one to 50 years, with a median term of 5 years

[23] Bill Dixon, 'What is the content of the common law obligation of good faith in commercial franchises' (2005) 33 *Australian Business Law Review* 210

[24] Roger D Blair and Francine Lafontaine, *The Economics of Franchising* (Cambridge University Press, 2005), 221

[25] Robert E Scott and George G Triantis, 'Incomplete Contracts and the Theory of Contract Design' (2005) 56(1) *Case Western Reserve Law Review*, 187, 190

[26] Roger D Blair and Francine Lafontaine, *The Economics of Franchising* (Cambridge University Press, 2005), 221

[27] Robert E Scott and George G Triantis, 'Incomplete Contracts and the Theory of Contract Design' (2005) 56(1) *Case Western Reserve Law Review*, 187, 196

Justice Hammond in *Dymocks Franchise Systems v. Bilgola Enterprises Ltd* recognised that the

> underlying recognition is that a relational contract is of an ongoing, and often relatively open-ended, character; and that it is in society's interest to accord to each party to a contract of this kind, reasonable security for the protection of his or her justified expectations.[28]

Justified expectations are placed in jeopardy if the franchisor enters administration or fails completely.

## Incomplete Contract

Incompleteness is not an indication of poor drafting or poor planning. 'In contract theory, incompleteness is [also] due to the cost and sometimes unavailability of information'.[29] During the initial contract negotiations, 'parties incur ex ante transaction costs, including the costs of anticipating future contingencies and writing a contract that specifies an outcome for each one'.[30] 'Both *ex ante* and *ex post* contracting costs prevent parties from writing complete contracts and give rise to what economists refer to as the problem of incomplete contracts'.[31]

*Ex ante*, the parties might not foresee all possible contingencies, or they would have to incur prohibitively high negotiation and drafting costs to partition all contingencies sufficiently to provide for efficient obligations in each case. The contingency that the franchisor's business might fail is the least likely from a franchisees' perspective, as most believe they are buying a proven concept. 'A challenge for parties designing contracts is to preordain or at least constrain the course of future renegotiation so as to yield both *ex ante* and *ex post* efficiency'.[32]

Carter et al. identify that 'The absence of genuine [pre-contractual] negotiation can result in the weaker party signing an unfavourable contract. Partly in response to this, the law of contract implies terms into certain commonly occurring contractual relationships to complete the parties' bargain'.[33] Under the common law, some situations merit implying terms into contracts'.[34] These may be implied to give effect to

[28] *Dymocks Franchise Systems v. Bilgola Enterprises Ltd* 8 TCLR 612, 630

[29] Robert E Scott and George G Triantis, 'Incomplete Contracts and the Theory of Contract Design' (2005) 56(1) *Case Western Reserve Law Review*, 187, 191

[30] Robert E Scott and George G Triantis, 'Incomplete Contracts and the Theory of Contract Design' (2005) 56(1) *Case Western Reserve Law Review*, 187, 190

[31] Robert E Scott and George G Triantis, 'Incomplete Contracts and the Theory of Contract Design' (2005) 56(1) *Case Western Reserve Law Review*, 187, 190

[32] Robert E Scott and George G Triantis, 'Incomplete Contracts and the Theory of Contract Design' (2005) 56(1) *Case Western Reserve Law Review*, 187, 194

[33] J W Carter, Elisabeth Peden and G J Tolhurst, *Contract Law in Australia*, (LexisNexis Butterworths 5th ed, 2007), 8

[34] Des Butler, Sharon Christensen, Bill Dixon and Lindy Willmott, *Contract Law Casebook* (Oxford University Press, 2009) 73

the 'presumed intentions of the parties'.[35] The presumed intentions of the parties could rarely be proven, to the satisfaction of a court, to have included the franchisor's failure. It is thus not open to the franchisee to argue that clauses providing the franchisee with contract-based rights on the franchisor's insolvency were omitted because the contract did not reflect the intentions of the parties.

Alternatively, terms are implied into contracts 'regardless of intention'[36] because the type of contract or a specific statute mandates inclusion of that term. Currently, no terms are implied into franchise agreements to fit the second category following the appointment of a receiver, administrator or liquidator. The possibility of implying terms into franchise agreements by statute is addressed in Chap. 9.

Thomas adds a judicial perspective to the conclusions drawn by Carter writing that

> [i]t would be quite wrong to think that a contract that omits a provision to deal with a particular contingency is due to an oversight or the finite capacity of business people and their legal advisers to predict future events with accuracy. ... there are sound commercial and economic reasons why the parties may deliberately choose to enter into agreements in which no provision is made for known contingencies.[37]

Contracts may not be complete because they were never intended to be complete. In the franchising arena, for example, franchisors may negotiate directly with a landlord to reach heads of agreement in relation to the franchisees' premises; then, both franchisor and landlord may hand the negotiations over to the landlord's shopping centre manager or lawyer to complete the lease details with the franchisee. The heads of agreement may constitute a binding contract, but it is incomplete. Numerous practical constraints also impact on the amount of detail that will be committed to the written contract. Thomas also observes that in a typical commercial negotiation,

> [t]he decision as to what is the most efficient will be made having regard to ... the time available for further negotiations, the cost of more comprehensive drafting, the risk that the core bargain will be lost, the chances of the contingency actually occurring, and the consequences or alternatives available if the contingency does not occur. Further, with long-term or relational contracts ... the parties can anticipate that some terms of the contract will be renegotiated and developed in the light of experience or necessity.[38]

By taking each of the factors identified by Thomas and placing them in the context of the franchise sale and purchase process, it can be argued that franchise contracts are not the result of typical commercial negotiations. There is, in theory, ample time. The franchisee in many jurisdictions has a cooling-off period in which

[35] Des Butler et al., *Contract Law Casebook* (2009) 73–74

[36] Des Butler et al., *Contract Law Casebook* (2009) 78

[37] E W Thomas, *The Judicial Process: Realism, Pragmatism, Practical Reasoning and Principles* (2005), 296

[38] E W Thomas, *The Judicial Process: Realism, Pragmatism, Practical Reasoning and Principles* (2005), 296–297

to consider the deal. By this time, the franchise agreement has already been settled through a process of franchisor-centric drafting, and it is likely that no amendments will be agreed to. Cost is not the issue. The additional cost of drafting to provide a termination right for franchisees would be negligible, especially once that provision had been incorporated as standard into the franchisor's usual franchise agreement. However, the franchisee is required to sign the standard franchise agreement for the network. There is a perceived risk that the core bargain – the sale of the franchise to the franchisee – will be lost if the franchisee insists on additional terms. Once a franchisee has decided which franchise to buy it is very difficult to dissuade them. The damage resulting from franchisor failure is more widespread than that caused by the failure of an individual franchisee. When a franchisor fails, all of its franchisees are affected, most adversely. If an individual franchisee fails, the franchisor will not fail and nor will any other franchisees. Damage resulting from franchisor failure is identified in Chap. 8.

## Exploitative Contract

A franchisor has no incentive to include terms to protect the franchisee from the consequences of the franchisors' damaging behaviour. The franchisor has every incentive to put itself into a contractual position where it can exploit its franchisees if the relationship does not evolve as the franchisor expected. The concept of exploitative contracts has been investigated by Bigwood, who describes the contracting environment that permits exploitation to flourish. He writes:

> [T]he vulnerability that gives rise to the asymmetric power relation between the parties is such that [franchisees] ought to be excused … from having to exercise th[e] level of responsibility … expected and required of … contracting parties. … the exploitable circumstances condition presupposes a weakness or vulnerability that, in the circumstances, removes [franchisees] from the normal assumptions made about the bargaining 'game'… the crux of the exploitable circumstances criterion lie in the nature and extent of the power relation existing between the parties. What matters is that [the franchisees'] interests have become peculiarly sensitive to – that is, they can be directly, strongly and adversely affected by [their franchisor's] choices and actions and this resultant vulnerability becomes the source of [the franchisor's] bargaining power.[39]

The nature of the franchise agreement as a standard form contract means a franchisee is typically unable to negotiate amendments to provide it with rights if the franchisor fails. Consequently, the supplier franchisor is entering a franchise agreement that potentially exploits the franchisee consumer. If the franchisee is a corporation, the directors are required to personally guarantee the performance of the franchisee, but franchisors' directors seldom guarantee the performance of the franchisor.[40]

[39] Rick Bigwood, *Exploitative Contracts* (Oxford University Press, 2003), 143

[40] The author did manage to secure directors' guarantees from one franchisor that was granting a master licence where the franchise was structured as a commission agency. This structure meant all of the master licensee's cash flow was dependent on timely payment of commission by franchisor and left the master franchisees vulnerable to the franchisor's commission payment practices

In *Meridian* Madam, Justice Dodds-Streeton acknowledged that

> [implying] a term [of good faith], whatever the basis of its implication and whatever its precise content, may validly operate to protect a vulnerable or disadvantaged party 'from exploitative conduct which subverts the original purpose for which the contract was made'.[41]

If protection of franchisees from the consequences of franchisor failure is not achievable through the franchise agreement, how has the legislature responded? The inadequacy of legislative response to date is demonstrated in Chaps. 8 and 9.

## Consequential Contracts

The execution of the franchise agreement also means that the franchisee must enter a number of consequential contractual commitments. This was demonstrated in Chap. 3 by examinations of the franchisor and franchisees' contractual or lack of contractual relationships with the owners of the trademarks that identify the franchise network and its products and the premises that franchisees trade from. The franchisor

> serves as a nexus for contracting relationships and … is also characterized by the existence of divisible residual claims on the assets and cash flows of the [franchisor] which can generally be sold without permission of the other contracting individuals.[42]

These legally binding contract-based commitments will be noted and identified, but not explored in detail until Chap. 8 where they will be examined through the lens of insolvency. The first are contracts entered into with the franchisor. These include such agreements as licences to use intellectual property, software and premises and various finance arrangements.[43] The second are contracts entered into with third parties, related to the franchisor such as supplier agreements concerning stock, licence to use intellectual property, lease of premises and alternative finance arrangements.[44] Finally, parties that are unrelated to the franchisor might enter contracts with franchisees.

---

[41] *Meridian Retail Pty Ltd v. Australian Unity Retail Network Pty Ltd* [2006] VSC 223, para 210 at [4] citing Warren CJ in *Esso Australia Resources Pty Ltd v. Southern Pacific Petroleum NL (receiver and manager appointed)* [2004] VSC 477, who contemplated that only protection of a 'particularly vulnerable' party or a party 'at a substantial disadvantage' may justify curial interference. In Meridian, the franchisor's conduct was not considered to be exploitative

[42] Michael C Jensen and William H Meckling, 'Theory of the Firm: Managerial Behavior, Agency Costs and Ownership Structure' (1976) 3(4) *Journal of Financial Economics* 305, 311

[43] Frazer and Weaven, *Franchising Australia 2004*, found that 29 % of franchisors provide finance to franchisees, with the most popular being direct finance supplied by the franchisor (59 %)

[44] Frazer and Weaven, Franchising Australia 2004, found that of the franchisors providing finance in Australia, 4.9 % did so through a company related to the franchisor

## Conclusion

We return to Hadfield who points out that once the contract moves beyond negotiation or performance to litigation,

> [t]o the extent that courts cannot distinguish between the derogation of a commitment in an incomplete contract, and an exercise of the flexibility which is part of that commitment, incomplete contracts cannot fully function in their role as anchor for many complex transactions.[45]

The franchisee has limited options in the face of a detrimental decision by one of the other players in the network.[46] It remains bound to perform its obligations under the contract. A poor business decision by the franchisor, a member of the group of companies or one of its other stakeholders can damage franchisees. We will look at breach of contract by the franchisor under franchisor failure in Chap. 8.

Franchise agreements fall into many conflicting categories in the field of contract law. The relationship between the contracting parties starts as one between supplier and consumer. The consumer franchisee signs a non-negotiable, standard form and relational contract drafted by the franchisor party for the franchisor's benefit and in doing so becomes a party to a commercial, business-to-business relationship. If there is a purely contract-based dispute, the ACCC has no jurisdiction, and the parties need to go to court if they are unable to resolve it any other way. The (generally incorrect) nineteenth-century view that the franchise agreement is a negotiated contract and that the parties, having had the chance to conduct due diligence, must abide by the terms of the contract remains a strong deterrent to regulatory intervention.[47]

Even before franchisees enter the franchise system, asymmetry is exacerbated by structural, legal, financial and human barriers to the conduct of effective due diligence and by the non-negotiable nature of franchise agreements. Through these agreements, franchisors' shift risks that would normally be borne by an employer to the franchisee. In negotiated contracts, risks are normally measured and costed, then borne or rejected knowingly by contracting parties. This level of evaluation is impossible or prohibitively expensive in franchising. In addition, no amount of due diligence would make the terms in most franchise agreements negotiable.

When the franchisor/franchisee relationship is placed in jeopardy through the appointment of an administrator or liquidator to the franchisor, the franchise agreement is the first place an administrator or liquidator looks to determine what responsibilities the franchisor has and what rights its franchisees have. At that point, it is

---

[45] Hadfield, 'Problematic Relations: Franchising and the Law of Incomplete Contracts', (1990) 42 *Stanford Law Review* 927, 928

[46] Croonen EPM, and Brand MJ, 'Dutch Druggists in Distress: Franchisees Facing the Complex Decision of How to React to their Franchisor's Strategic Plans' (2010) *Entrepreneurship Theory and Practice*, 34(5), 1021–1038

[47] J Buchan, Chapter 16 in Robert Blackburn and Michael Schaper (eds) *Government, SMEs and Entrepreneurship Development: Policy, Practice and Challenges* (Gower, 2012)

too late for the franchisor and franchisee to negotiate a change in the terms of the franchise agreement. It is thus important to understand whether franchise agreements, as a genre, can realistically be expected to contain provisions relating to franchisor failure.

Private law matters to those who can use it effectively, for example, businesses that incorporate judicial rulings in standard terms or that seek judicial (or regulator[48]) rulings as a framework for structuring their business methods. Consumers have rarely been able to harness private law to have such systemic effects.[49]

To UNCITRAL, the 'franchise situation is a classic example of an unresolved treatment of contracts. Executory contracts, of which franchise agreements are an example, are not specifically considered in the UNCITRAL Legislative Guide on Insolvency Law'.[50] Vern Countryman defines an executory contract as 'one under which the obligation of both the bankrupt and the other party ... are so far underperformed that the failure of either to complete performance would constitute a material breach excusing the performance of the other'.[51] Rohrbacher explains that 'the troublesome issue in executory contracts is not that property and contracts are treated so differently but that debtors and creditors are treated so differently'.[52]

The franchise agreement purports to be a complete package of rights, distilling the franchisors and franchisees rights and obligations for the duration of the term. Nevertheless, almost without exception, franchise contracts make no reference to franchisees' rights on franchisor failure. This omission cannot be justified on the basis that it is so unlikely to occur that no provision needs to be made. The insolvency of the nexus triggers a move to a new equilibrium in which the administrator, and then the liquidator, controls the destiny of franchisees through the twin mechanisms of the franchise agreement and the *Corporations Act*.

The law of contract is incapable of satisfactorily 'regulating modern franchise relationships and practices'.[53] This is exemplified clearly when the franchisor fails. The report 'Opportunity not opportunism'[54] acknowledged that the current contractual arrangements between franchisor and franchisee are not satisfactory and

---

48 For example, Bakers Delight's successful application under *Trade Practices Act 1974* (Cth) s 47

49 Iain Ramsay, 'Consumer Law, Regulatory Capitalism and the 'New Learning' in Regulation' (2006) 28(1) *Sydney Law Review* 9, 33

50 United Nations Commission on International Trade Law, UNCITRAL Legislative Guide on Insolvency Law (2004) <http://www.uncitral.org/uncitral/en/uncitral_texts/insolvency/2004Guide.html> Accessed 5 June 2010

51 Vern Countryman, 'Executory Contracts in Bankruptcy' (1973) 57(1) *Minnesota Law Review* 439, 460 cited in B Rohrbacher, 'More Equal than Others: Defending Property-Contract Parity in Bankruptcy' (2005) 114(5) *Yale Law Journal* 1099, 1127

52 B Rohrbacher, 'More Equal Than Others: Defending Property-Contract Parity in Bankruptcy' (2005) 114(5) *Yale Law Journal* 1099, 1101, 1128

53 Tanya Woker, 'Franchising – The Need for Legislation' (2005) 17 *South African Mercantile Law Journal* 49

54 Joint Committee on Corporations and Financial Services, Australian Senate, *Opportunity Not Opportunism: Improving Conduct in Australian Franchising*, (2008) Recommendation 4 [6.40] xv

recommended 'that the [Australian] government explore avenues to better balance the rights and liabilities of franchisees and franchisors in the event of franchisor failure'.[55] The franchise agreement, in its current form, is unable to address franchisor failure satisfactorily nor will it evolve, unaided, to provide an adequate solution.

An action for breach of contract presupposes that there has been a breach. Franchise agreements always permit the franchisor to terminate the franchise agreement if the franchisee commits an act of bankruptcy but seldom makes provision for franchisees' rights following the administration or insolvency of the franchisor. Franchise agreements also require franchisees to obey all relevant laws, with failure to do so constituting a breach of the franchise agreement and entitling the franchisor to terminate. Franchise agreements only require the franchisor, as a term of the contract, to comply with the Franchising Code of Conduct ('the Code'),[56] not with the *Corporations Act*. Thus, a breach of the *Corporations Act* or of any other financial regulation by the franchisor does not pave the way for the franchisee to argue that the franchisor has breached the franchise agreement.

The justifications for a contract not to be comprehensive in its terms – that it is relational, or too expensive to include all possible future contingencies, or that the franchise agreement needs to be standardised for ease of administration – do not support the omission of terms about franchisor failure, an event whose possibility is real and whose consequences can be devastating for the franchisee consumer. It can be concluded that incomplete, relational contracts are ill equipped to deal with franchisor failure *ex post*, as the very event that triggers a need to renegotiate; failure of the contract drafter, also signals the impending end of the relationship between the drafter (franchisor) and the counter party (franchisees).

Ultimately, there is no equitable, logical or cost-based justification for the franchise agreement making extensive provision for some known possible events that would have a relatively minor effect on the network, such as the possibility of a franchisee dying, while failing to provide for known and potentially network-debilitating events, such as franchisor failure.

The franchise agreement is, in theory, negotiable. It may be possible for the franchisee to insert a provision in the contract that gives the franchisee the right to 'walk away' from the franchise system and to retain the right to use the premises, if the franchisor fails. In reality, the possibility of the franchisor failing is generally the furthest thing from the new franchisee's mind, and the franchise agreement is seldom negotiable.

Summarising the franchise agreement, it documents a business-to-business commercial relationship that begins as an exchange between the supplier (franchisor)

---

[55] Joint Committee on Corporations and Financial Services, Australian Senate, *Opportunity Not Opportunism: Improving Conduct in Australian Franchising* (2008) Recommendation 4 (para 6.40) xv

[56] *Trade Practices (Industry Codes – Franchising) Regulations 1998*, Statutory Rules 1998 No. 162 as amended made under the *Trade Practices Act 1974*

and a consumer (franchisee). The franchisee never relinquishes the role of consumer; it assumes the additional role as business owner. Negotiation is minimal, and the contract signed is standard form and relational. The franchise agreement is drafted by the franchisor. It locates control in the franchisor and ownership and risk with the franchisee. Risk that would knowingly be borne by an employer and a lender in a traditionally modelled business is outsourced to franchisees in the franchise model. For the employee, the law provides back-up if the principal defaults. The lender is protected by private law and its status in the insolvency regime. No such legal safety nets are in place for franchisees.

Andrew Selden writes that 'franchise agreements used in the US continue [in 2008] for the most part, to be heavily one-sided, overbearing and structurally self-conflicted'.[57] Once executed, the franchise agreement sits gathering dust until one party needs to invoke legal rights. Then, as we know, it commands centre stage until the issue is resolved. The franchise agreement, in its current form, is unable to address franchisor failure satisfactorily. If protection of franchisees from the consequences of franchisor failure cannot be achieved through the standard franchise agreement, it is logical to ask how the legislature has responded. In Chaps. 6 and 7, the effectiveness of legislative initiatives in providing consumer protection for franchisees of failed franchisors is considered. However, before moving to the legislature, I will explore the asymmetry of the franchisees' world in Chap. 5.

---

[57] Andrew C Selden 'Beyond the Law and Contracts: Strategies for Effective Franchise Relationship Self-Management' in Elizabeth C Spencer (ed) *Relational Rights and Responsibilities: Perspectives on Contractual Arrangements in Franchising*, (Bond University Press, 2011) 159

# Chapter 6
# Asymmetry in the Franchisor/Franchisee Relationship

**Abstract** The seemingly intractable problem of asymmetry bedevils relationships where one party holds far more of almost everything than the other. This chapter explores the many faces of asymmetry within franchise relationships: information, adviser, education and regulator, risk and reward, resource, contract and regulatory asymmetry. It identifies how they conspire to perpetuate the imbalances between franchisors and franchisees. Within the context of asymmetry, impediments to franchisees' ability to conduct due diligence are discussed.

Thomas may have been referring to a franchise agreement when he wrote, '[t]he sheer commercial absurdity of this lopsided bargain prompts the question as to how it could have come about'.[1] In relation to commercial absurdity of the franchisees' position all the way from the lead-up to signing the franchise agreement, right through to a franchisor's possible failure, part of the explanation for the extremely lopsided bargain lies in asymmetry.[2] Asymmetry exists in every aspect of franchising: in the structure of the franchise network, the timing of events, the contents of contracts and the legislation designed to protect consumers. Franchisees make their investment based on fatally flawed information. This devalues the due diligence process, reduces the effectiveness of franchisee protection regulation and limits franchisees' ability to plan an effective exit strategy from an insolvent franchisor. It compromises the franchisees' awareness of the need to self-protect and their opportunity to do so. Asymmetries of risk, information, adviser, reward, regulation and rights that favour franchisors' over franchisees' interests are pronounced. Some examples of how asymmetry exists in franchising are now identified.

[1] *Bobux Marketing Limited v. Raynor Marketing Limited* [2001] NZCA 348, para 18 (Thomas J, dissenting) in relation to a distributorship agreement

[2] Asymmetry: a situation in which one party in a transaction has more information than another and this information has an important bearing on the price or terms of the transaction. *Australian Government Best Practice Regulation Handbook*, August 2007, x

J. Buchan, *Franchisees as Consumers: Benchmarks, Perspectives and Consequences*, DOI 10.1007/978-1-4614-5614-8_6, © Springer Science+Business Media New York 2013

## Information Asymmetry

Information asymmetry extends from information available on the public record to assist a franchisee in conducting its due diligence to information about the difference between what is written in the contracts and what is the 'culture' of a particular franchise. To return to my high-performance car analogy in Chap. 3, the beginner driver franchisee does what it can to check the car works beautifully and is duly impressed by its power, but because of the way the car sale process is conducted, does not think to lift his/her eyes from the road. A look around would have disclosed that the road ahead is closed or a different type of vehicle is required to traverse it.

The first introduction to a specific franchise network may be at a franchise business opportunity expo. These are held in major population centres annually and are a widely accepted franchise promotion method. Regardless of the source of information, there is a sameness about all franchise opportunity advertising. In the words of American franchise lawyer and commentator Richard Solomon:

> If you look at all the franchise adverts for franchise opportunities in any business category, they all say the same thing -- we know how to do it -- we can show you how to do it -- you save a lot of money and reduce risk of failure if you do it with us -- we have the 'secret' to success -- we will support you to achieve success -- we have the proven system -- we have the name recognition -- we get you up and running quickly. In actual fact, most of this is not even remotely true.[3]

Prospective franchisees reading franchise advertisements feel secure buying into a long-established franchise, believing it to be well proven. They trust the information supplied by the franchisor and have difficulty obtaining objective third-party perspectives. A prospective franchisee attempting to conduct due diligence to verify information disclosed by the franchisor, is confronted with numerous impediments. Unlike the United States where a franchisor's disclosure information is available on the public record, in many countries (including Australia), neither the franchisor's disclosure documents nor its pro forma franchise agreements can be obtained other than direct from a franchisor. This means that the franchisee's advisers cannot compare the offering before them with either the usual documentation for franchisees in the network or with the franchise agreements of other comparable franchisors. This limits the value of professional advice as it is unable to be contextualized. Despite frequent submissions to the contrary to the many government enquiries in Australia involving franchising since 2006, there is still no requirement in Australia for the disclosure document to be registered or for the franchisor to be identified as a franchisor in any public register. The *Opportunity not opportunism* report represents incremental progress in thinking that has not yet been adopted as policy. It proposed that

[3] Richard Solomon, 'License to Lie, Cheat and Steal: Impact of Acknowledgement & Integration Clauses' (2008) Blue Maumau <http://www.bluemaumau.org/license_lie_cheat_and_steal_impact_acknowledgement_integration_clauses> Accessed 15 May 2008

the government investigate the benefits of developing a simple online registration system for Australian franchisors, requiring them on an annual basis to lodge a statement confirming the nature and extent of their franchising network and providing a guarantee that they are meeting their obligations under the Franchising Code of Conduct and the Trade Practices Act. [4]

Even if Recommendation 2 were adopted, franchisees and their advisers would still not have a means of establishing a context for the specific franchise agreement being advised on and signed. Although required to do so by law in Australia, franchisees often do not register their business names.[5] It is thus impossible to verify from the public record, the identity of the owners and former owners of franchisees of franchised outlets.[6] To comply with the disclosure provisions of the Code, Australian franchisors are required to disclose the following information about litigation.

4 Litigation
- 4.1 Details of:
  - (a) current proceedings by a public agency, criminal or civil proceedings or arbitration, relevant to the franchise, against the franchisor or a franchisor director in Australia alleging:
    - (i) breach of a franchise agreement; or
    - (ii) contravention of trade practices law; or
    - (iii) contravention of the Corporations Act 2001; or
    - (iv) unconscionable conduct; or
    - (v) misconduct; or
    - (vi) an offence of dishonesty; and
  - (b) proceedings against the franchisor under:
    - (i) section 127A or 127B of the Workplace Relations Act 1996; or
    - (ii) section 106 of the Industrial Relations Act 1996 of New South Wales; or
    - (iii) section 276 of the Industrial Relations Act 1999 of Queensland.
- 4.2 Whether the franchisor or a director of the franchisor has been:
  - (a) in the last 10 years—convicted of a serious offence, or an equivalent offence outside Australia; or
  - (b) in the last 5 years—subject to final judgment in civil proceedings for a matter mentioned in paragraph 4.1 (a); or
  - (c) in the last 10 years—bankrupt, insolvent under administration or an externally administered body corporate in Australia or elsewhere.
- 4.3 For items 4.1 and 4.2—the following details (where relevant):
  - (a) the names of the parties to the proceedings;
  - (b) the name of the court, tribunal or arbitrator;
  - (c) the case number;
  - (d) the general nature of the proceedings;

---

[4] Joint Committee on Corporations and Financial Services, Australian Senate, Opportunity not opportunism: improving conduct in Australian franchising, Commonwealth of Australia 2008, Recommendation 2, para 4.81

[5] Australia: *Business Names Registration Act 2011* (Cth)

[6] The 2008 Amendments to the Disclosure Document under the Code partially rectified this problem by S 11.2 of Annexure 1 (the Disclosure) in that it requires disclosure of 'Details of whether the territory or site to be franchised has been subject to a franchised business operated by a previous franchise granted by the franchisor and, if so, details of the franchised business, including the circumstances in which the previous franchisee ceased to operate'

(e) the current status of the proceedings;
(f) the date and content of any undertaking or order under section 87B of the Act;
(g) the penalty or damages assessed or imposed;
(h) the names of the persons who are bankrupt, insolvent under administration or externally administered;
(i) the period of the bankruptcy, insolvency under administration or external administration.

The problem here for franchisees attempting to conduct due diligence is that the process mandated in the Code for resolving disputes is mediation. In Australia, hundreds of franchise disputes are mediated every year. Mediation is a confidential process. A franchisor thus may have been involved in mediations with numerous franchisees, and there is no way for potential franchisees to discover that fact or what the disputes were about.[7] Comments from South Australian Inquiry identify some of the consequences of confidentiality:

> It is not in the best interests of good business that people can put in place confidentiality clauses in contracts [for example contracts to resolve mediated disputes] and whatever and then proceed to do the wrong thing, potentially.[8]
>
> Mediation requires little or no government involvement for administration or enforcement. Because of the confidentiality of the process it is difficult to gauge the effectiveness of this strategy. … Mediation … is easy for franchisors to control and thus reinforces the imbalance of power …[9]
>
> What you have is a high settlement rate [via the Government-funded office of the Franchise Mediation Adviser] of 72 per cent for mediation. The problem is that there were 300 of those, but there were another 770 inquiries [that did not proceed to mediation] and no-one knows what happened to them. … Somebody had a big enough problem to call the Office of the Mediation Adviser and ask for help, and we have no idea what happened to them. … but franchisors know what happens in the case of the disposition of mediat[ed] disputes. They can go on and use that information with their other franchisees. But individual franchisees, because of the confidentiality of the process, do not share that information.[10]

Thus, the efficient and inexpensive mediation processes designed to redress the prohibitive costs and time lags associated with accessing justice through the courts for franchisee consumer's become instead a mechanism for disempowering these same consumers. In addition, as Dimity Kingsford Smith notes, in the context of consumer investor redress in the financial services arena, there is a

[7] Jenny Buchan, Jennifer Harris, Gehan Gunasekara, 'Franchise Mediation: Confidentiality or Disclosure: A Consumer Protection Conundrum'. (Paper presented at the 25th Annual International Society of Franchising Conference, Boston, USA June 2011)

[8] Economic and Finance Committee, Parliament of South Australia, Franchises (2008) Evidence to South Australian Inquiry (Oral submission, 14 November 2007, Max Baldock and John Brownsea, State Retailers Association of South Australia)

[9] Economic and Finance Committee, Parliament of South Australia, Franchises (2008) Evidence to South Australian Inquiry (Submission 13, Elizabeth Spencer)

[10] Parliamentary Joint Committee on Corporations and Financial Services, Commonwealth, Inquiry into the Franchising Code of Conduct (2008) Evidence to Commonwealth Inquiry, (Submission 12, Elizabeth Spencer)

'tension between the practical resolution of disputes and accountability for individual decisions'.[11]

All details of mediation conducted to satisfy the requirements of the Code remain confidential including the names of the parties. Thus, information about franchisors other than information they supply in disclosure or on their own websites is difficult and/or expensive to obtain, and breaches of the disclosure regime are usually impossible to detect unless they lead to litigation.

The problem of not being able to obtain accurate information about the culture within a franchise has been expressed as: 'Each contract says what it says, but the culture underlying the way parties choose to operate the levers that contract gives them may be producing quite a different effect than appears to a superficial or even a close reading'.[12] This problem is exacerbated by the mediation process. On settlement of a mediated dispute, the parties agree not to discuss any details of the mediation with third parties. This prevents franchisees from responding to mediation-related questions from researchers and also from giving candid responses to intending franchisees who make contact to seek information about 'what's it like being a franchisee in the system'? There is no incentive for anyone involved in the franchise sales process, nor for any current franchisee of the network, to mention any unsatisfactory aspects of the system.

## Adviser Asymmetry

Franchisors receive legal and accounting advice from, typically, highly specialised advisers at the big end of town. Franchisors frequently use professional advisers who have created numerous franchise agreements for a range of franchise models. For example, a partner of a global law firm says: '[m]y firm would represent over 300 franchisors (due to our size, we do not have a large franchisee constituency)'.[13] Large legal and accounting firms also have experience in advising franchisors on how to shelter personal assets from franchisees.

Franchisees choose a range of advisers. They may go to their lawyer and accountant who has served the family well through the many mundane transactions that require their services. The chances are that they know nothing more about franchising than their client does. The calibre and expertise of their advisers have a bearing on a franchisee's understanding of what they are signing. It also has a bearing on whether any meaningful pre-purchase or post-failure negotiation occurs. If a franchisee wants to engage advisers with franchise expertise, they may have difficulty identifying those

[11] Dimity Kingsford Smith, 'Financial services regulation and the investor as consumer' in Geraint Howells, Iain Ramsay and Thomas Wilhelmsson with David Kraft (eds) *Handbook of Research on International Consumer Law* (Edward Elgar, 2010) 434

[12] Evidence to Economic and Finance Committee, Parliament of South Australia, Official Hansard Report, 6 February 2008, 38 (JR Rau MP)

[13] Evidence to Economic and Finance Committee, Parliament of South Australia, Official Hansard Report, 6 February 2008, 33 (Stephen Giles)

people. The identity of professional advisers is found through advertisements in franchise magazines, their presence at trade shows or searching the internet. Lawyers with specific areas of expertise can be found through the state or territory law society. The business law expert is superficially the ideal lawyer to provide franchisee advice. But as Solomon observes a competent read of a contract 'isn't really the due diligence on the transaction itself.... a business lawyer who is not up to date on what is happening in the franchise industry most probably will not spot many of the contract language traps'.[14] Solomon continues, '[t]he franchise industry... uses that lack of available [legal and also accounting] expertise to enable rampant misrepresentation'.[15]

Franchisees will seek an accountant's advice in relation to the feasibility of the business opportunity described in the disclosure document. Australian accountants are either members of the Institute of Chartered Accountants of Australia ('CAs') or members of CPA Australia ('CPAs'). As a generalization, the CAs advise larger commercial clients (franchisors and master franchisors), work in the city, include liquidators in their number, and may be members of the FCA. The CPAs who would typically advise franchisees are often suburban or country-town accountants, less likely to join the FCA as their practices would not specialise in franchising and could not justify the expense. Accountants are not necessarily able to predict the future solvency of the franchisor, even with access to the disclosure document. In testing the return on investment, the accountant is not likely to model the return based on the franchisor itself failing 1 or 2 years into the relationship.

The 'acid test' of the value of advice is whether, having required its prospective franchisees to have legal counsel and financial advisers review the franchise agreement and disclosure, the franchisor will agree to negotiate terms. Usually not.

## Education and Regulator Asymmetry

Regulators lament the apparent lack of due diligence on the part of franchisees. The 2006 UK franchise survey, for example, reports that its initial source of information about the franchise industry was equally (20–21%) magazines, newspapers and friends/relatives.[16] In the United Kingdom, information about a specific franchisor came from magazines (18%) and exhibitions (20%).[17] None of these are objective information sources. To blame franchisees for their absence of extensive due diligence beyond trusting ones 'gut feeling' is an attractive 'out' for franchisors. In Australia, the Matthews Report identified that

[14] Richard Solomon, 'License to Lie, Cheat and Steal: Impact of Acknowledgement & Integration Clauses' (2008) Blue Maumau <http://www.bluemaumau.org/license_lie_cheat_and_steal_impact_acknowledgement_integration_clauses> Accessed 15 May 2008

[15] Richard Solomon, 'License to Lie, Cheat and Steal: Impact of Acknowledgement & Integration Clauses' (2008) Blue Maumau <http://www.bluemaumau.org/license_lie_cheat_and_steal_impact_acknowledgement_integration_clauses> Accessed 15 May 2008

[16] NatWest bfa United Kingdom, *Franchise Survey* (2006) 30

[17] NatWest bfa United Kingdom, *Franchise Survey* (2006) 20

> [t]he ACCC and peak industry associations undertake an important role in providing education and information resources for franchisees and franchisors. These resources should strengthen the message to prospective franchisees in particular that they should seek advice from suitable and independent franchise sector advisors.[18]

The government agreed with this recommendation.[19] Regulators can do more to raise franchisees' general awareness of possible pitfalls of the franchise model. However, their ability to warn franchisees of risks of specific networks will always be hampered by the differences among franchisors' legal structures and their varying approaches and attitudes to risk sharing.

Although 21.2% of franchisors ranked 'difficulty in finding franchisee finance'[20] as the third greatest hindrance to growth in 2006, all four major trading banks in Australia have specific policies to assist in the purchase of franchisee businesses. All four – ANZ, CBA, National Australia Bank (NAB) and Westpac (WBC) – are 'service provider' members of the FCA. None of the four mentions the risk of franchisor failure on their websites. This suggests one of two things. Either the area of the banks dealing with loans that have 'gone bad' and the business lending and the marketing areas of the banks do not communicate with each other about specific customers, or banks decide that because they have adequate collateral security from franchisees and are not worried that their policies of lending to the franchising sector will trigger awkward questions at shareholders' meetings. The situation of failed jewellery retail franchisor Kleins and the NAB (below) is a clear reason why banks need to monitor the ongoing viability of the franchisors they approve. Failure to do so places them at risk of misleading franchisees that the franchisor's business is still a sound investment.

Turning to each of the banks to see what their customers might be able to learn from them about the franchisors whose franchisees they will fund and about franchisor failure, we see the following. The ANZ does not publicise the names of those franchisors to which it has accorded preferred status. It states:

> We work from the basic belief that franchise businesses are different and usually inherit some strengths and capabilities from the franchisor. … ANZ offers ANZ Preferred status to selected franchisors to reflect the value of their franchise system.[21]

The CBA 'may be able to offer preferential lending terms and competitive pricing on a range of services and solutions to our preferred franchise systems'.[22]

We are told that

> NAB Franchise Bankers understand the franchisor-franchisee relationship, and the different financial needs on either side. For franchisees, 'Joining a NAB Accredited Franchise System

[18] Graeme Matthews, Review of the Disclosure Provisions of the Franchising Code of Conduct (2006), 37, Recommendation 9

[19] Australian Government Response to the Review of the Disclosure Provisions of the Franchising Code of Conduct (2007) 4

[20] Lorelle Frazer, Scott Weaven, Owen Wright, *Franchising Australia 2006*, Griffith University, 43

[21] ANZ, ANZ Franchising <http://www.anz.com/australia/business/IndustrySpecialisation/Franchising.asp> at 24 May 2012

[22] Commonwealth Bank, *Franchise Banking* <http://www.commbank.com.au/corporate/your-industry/franchising/default.aspx> Accessed 24 May 2012

> means that you may be able to borrow up to 70 per cent of the total set up cost of a new franchise, or purchase cost of an existing franchise, without necessarily providing your home as collateral for the loan.[23]

The message to prospective franchisees is that each of these Accredited Franchise Systems is a reputable, secure investment in the eyes of the NAB. The list of NAB Accredited Franchise Systems included Kleins on 23 May 2008.[24] As at May 2008, there was no public record that any of the three central companies that make up the Kleins group had filed any documents with ASIC since January 2003. On seeing Kleins on the NAB list, between KFC and McDonald's, prospective franchisees would have been entitled to conclude, as late as 23 May 2008 that NAB had confidence in Kleins as an investment. But, NAB was identified in May 2008 as the biggest secured creditor of the Kleins group (in administration), being owed approximately A$15million. This raises issues of the bank's duties to its Kleins franchisee customers and the extent to which it exposes itself to claims by Kleins' disenfranchised franchisees.

In WBC

> [f]ranchise lending is one of the four core business units in the TPD [Third Party Distribution] system. ... The business maximises Westpac's share of the franchising market by developing profitable relationships with franchisors, providing referrals and expert advice to Business Banking sales people; and also providing input into WBC's franchising policies and systems.[25]

This indicates that WBC manages its risk exposure by securing loans over the franchisees' home. This protects the bank from losing money if a franchisor fails but exposes the franchisee to the risk of significant loss. Westpac also recommends that prospective franchisees should consider the following questions:

> What's the franchisor's track record (financial and management)?
> How much control do you (and the franchisor) have?
> What are the renewal and termination terms and conditions?
> Do you see your investment in a franchise as a long-term commitment?[26]

These questions are generic and are not supported by examples or placed within a context. They will not make a franchisee ask questions about the franchise network or the consequences of franchisor failure.

Governments and banks direct prospective franchisees to additional sources of general franchise information. These include national franchise industry groups and Do-It-Yourself or primer books. None is sufficient to put the franchisee on notice that the franchisor might fail. The FCA in Australia, for example, provides information through its website, its publication The Franchise Review and its education

[23] NAB, NAB Accredited Franchise Systems <http://www.nab.com.au/wps/wcm/connect/nab/nab/home/business_solutions/8/6/4> Accessed 24 May 2012

[24] NAB Website <www.nab.com.au> Accessed 23 May 2008

[25] Westpac Bank Website <www.westpac.com.au> Accessed 1 May 2008

[26] Westpac Bank Website <www.westpac.com.au> Accessed 1 May 2008

programs. None of these provide any information about franchisor insolvency. There is no incentive for them to do so. The FCA website also states:

> … the nature of the franchise relationship was open to exploitation prior to 1998 in Australia, when franchising operated in a de-regulated environment. As a consequence the public perception of franchising was tarnished by several high profile franchise failures … Behaviour in the sector was not universally appropriate, and franchisees had far less investment security. Since 1998 the sector has not only grown, but matured and developed into one of the primary engines for economic growth in Australia.[27]

An inference to be drawn from this statement is that prior to 1998, when pre-contract disclosure was voluntary for franchisors, there were some unprofitable franchisors and some of them failed but this does not happen any more.

## Risk and Reward Asymmetry

The franchise agreement is effectively a contract uberrimae fidei[28] for the franchisee, but not for the franchisor as the franchisor entity has only specific disclosure requirements. The shifting of risk that is achieved by appointing franchisees is a significant benefit to the franchisor. A fundamental aspect of franchising is the separation of ownership, by the franchisees, from control, which remains with the franchisor. This can also be expressed as a separation of risk bearing, again by the franchisees, and decision functions, which rest with the franchisor.[29] For example, as was seen in Chap. 3 when the franchisor takes a head lease of retail premises in its own name, it is common for the franchisee to become the guarantor of the franchisor's performance under the head lease. The franchisee, thus, takes almost all the risk on the premises, while the franchisor retains the full benefit of the site lease being in the franchisor's name. The franchisor executes the franchise agreement and requires the franchisee, and if the franchisee is a corporation, its guarantors, to sign, whereas the franchisor's directors rarely provide personal guarantees to franchisees.

Another example of risk shifting is the practice of structuring a franchise relationship to function like a commission agency. Here, the franchisee attracts the customers, but payment by the customers for the products or services they purchase is made directly to the franchisor. The franchisor then pays a commission to the franchisee. The two risks that the franchisee assumes in this scenario are that the franchisor will

---

[27] Franchise Council of Australia, Franchise Insolvency Leads to a 'Rebirth' for Franchisees <http://www.franchise.org.au/scripts/cgiip.exe/WService=FCAWWW/ccms.r?PageID=10184> Accessed 7 October 2009, 7

[28] Trischa Mann (general ed) and Audrey Blunden (consulting ed), *Australian Law Dictionary* (2010), 585, Utmost Good Faith

[29] See Eugene F Fama and Michael C Jensen, 'Separation of Ownership and Control' (1983) XXVI(2) *Journal of Law and Economics* 301, 304 who do not include franchise networks in the spectrum of organizations discussed

be prepared to chase customers for payment and that the franchisor will remit the commission to the franchisee, both in a timely manner.

Research on approaches to risk in franchising has been carried out by Paul Rubin, and Lafontaine and Bhattacharyya. Neither study factored the failure of the franchisor into their risk research. Looking at the franchise investment as a proportion of an individual's entire portfolio of assets Rubin's view is that 'since franchisees commonly invest a large share of their assets in acquiring the franchise, it is unlikely that'[30] franchisors are more risk averse than franchisees. Lafontaine and Bhattacharyya consider the role of risk in franchising[31] from the perspective of the investment in the single franchise unit rather than as a component of an individual's entire investment portfolio. After examining a number of factors in the franchisor/franchisee relationship, they conclude that franchising is not necessarily selected for its risk-shedding potential. One of the factors evaluated by Lafontaine and Bhattacharyya was failure rates. They confined their inquiry to the failure of franchisees and of franchisor-owned outlets and did not extend their inquiry to entire networks. They note that

> failure rates will still be sensitive to franchisor moral hazard; if a franchisor shirks, or behaves opportunistically, this will increase the probability of failure for all units in the chain and is likely to show up in the discontinuation statistics.[32]

Lafontaine and Bhattacharyya conclude that

> there are patterns in the data that seem to imply that franchisees bear more risk than franchisors. Under models based on efficient risk allocation, this leads to the conclusion that franchisors are more risk averse than franchisees, a conclusion we find unappealing given their respective sizes and differential access to capital markets.[33]

In reply to the question are there risks the intending franchisee's business plan cannot address? the ACCC wrote in 2009: '[e]very business faces risk. One risk to franchisees is the franchisor becoming insolvent, which can sometimes happen unexpectedly'.[34]

---

[30] Paul H Rubin, 'The Theory of the Firm and the Structure of the Franchise Contract' (1978) XXI(1) *The Journal of Law and Economics* 223, 225 in Francine Lafontaine (ed), Franchise Contracting and Organization (2005) 18, 20

[31] Francine Lafontaine and Sugato Bhattacharyya, 'The Role of Risk in Franchising' (1995) 2 Journal of Corporate Finance 39, 55 in Francine Lafontaine (ed), *Franchise Contracting and Organization* (2005) 164, 180

[32] Francine Lafontaine and Sugato Bhattacharyya, 'The Role of Risk in Franchising' (1995) 2 Journal of Corporate Finance 39, 55 in Francine Lafontaine (ed), *Franchise Contracting and Organization* (2005) 164, 180

[33] Francine Lafontaine and Sugato Bhattacharyya, 'The Role of Risk in Franchising' (1995) 2 Journal of Corporate Finance 39, 55 in Francine Lafontaine (ed), *Franchise Contracting and Organization* (2005) 164, 180

[34] Australian Competition and Consumer Commission, 'Understanding the Issues in Franchising' (2009) Franchise Review 65. This risk is explored further in Chap. 8

When it comes to reward asymmetry, the sale of the franchisors' business is relevant. The franchisees have no say in who buys the franchisor's business from the franchisor or the franchisor's administrator or receiver. Nor are they paid a share of the profits in the way an employee or shareholder would be paid.

## Resource Asymmetry

It is assumed that parties to a long-term contract will perform comprehensive due diligence on each other as prospective business associates and on the business offering. In Australia, the franchisor provides the franchisee with the information that it wants the franchisee to know and complies with the disclosure requirements of the *Competition and Consumer Act 2010* (Cth) ('CCA'). Beyond this, franchisees are advised to conduct their own due diligence. Despite the requirement of pre-contractual disclosure, franchisees as consumers seldom anticipate the possibility of the franchisor's business failing or the effect that event may have on their rights and obligations as a franchisee. Accordingly, due diligence does not extend beyond the franchisor and the specific business opportunity being evaluated. Such information is often not capable of being objectively verified.

The FCA acknowledges that there are disadvantages to the franchise model including

> 3. The prospective franchisee may find it difficult to assess the quality of the franchisor. This factor must be weighed very carefully by the potential franchisee for it can affect the franchisee in two ways.
>    A. Firstly, the franchisor's offer of a business-format package may not amount to what it appears to be on the surface.
>    B. Secondly, the franchisor may be unable to maintain the continuing services which the franchisee is likely to need in order to sustain their business.
> 6. The franchisor's policies may affect the franchisee's profitability. For example, the franchisor may wish to see his franchisee build up to a higher turnover from which he gets his continuing franchise fee, while the franchisee may be more concerned with increasing his profitability, which does not always necessarily follow from increased turnover.
> 7. The franchisor may make mistakes in their policies. They may arrive at decisions, relating to innovations in the business which turn out to be unsuccessful and detrimental to the franchisee.
> 8. The good name of the franchised business and its brand image may become less reputable for reasons beyond their own control.[35]

Prospective franchisees would have difficulty assessing whether a specific franchisor has any of the possible flaws listed above. Disadvantages 6, 7 and 8,

---

[35]Franchise Council of Australia http://www.franchise.org.au/scripts/cgiip.exe/WService=FCAWWW/ccms.r?PageId=10111 Accessed 22 June 2010

like insolvency, refer to future matters. Even with unlimited resources, it is impossible for a franchisee to make an informed assessment about these issues. Franchisees are blamed by courts, commentators and franchisors for failure to conduct adequate pre-purchase due diligence. For example, a delegate of the FCA, when asked to comment on a report about franchisor failure, dismissed the seriousness of the issue by replying that '[f]ranchising is risky and some people might not be adhering to the correct process'.[36] Such a response by an industry representative tends to make prospective franchisees think that as long as they follow the processes established by any regulation, and their franchisor, they will not be part of a franchisor failure. The facts do not support this. In fact, the market for franchises is a little like 'the market for cigarettes: manufacturers compete among themselves for market share but have a common incentive not to disclose information about the risks from smoking so long as these risks apply to all cigarettes'.[37] Any franchisor may fail. All franchisors have an interest in holding the line that they will succeed. Trebilcock notes that the high costs of investigating the safety of an unfamiliar product prior to purchasing leads to the consumers entering the market with the expectation that products 'are acceptably safe [and this] is a crucial assumption of most consumer behaviour, influencing the value that consumers place on information'.[38] Exactly the same thinking is encouraged by franchisors who allow prospective franchisees to draw conclusions that simply because a franchisor calls itself a franchisor and is a member of its national franchisor industry body, then it is proven and successful, fit for its purpose like other safety-tested products.

Due diligence cannot anticipate the events that precede some franchisor administrations or insolvencies, and no franchisee or franchisee's professional adviser could predict when a franchisor might to embark on a course of strategic insolvency.[39] Any disclosure document is a snapshot of the franchisor's business at the date it is made. It is always going to be of limited value for that reason.

[36] Jacqui Walker, 'Help for Squeezed Business', Business Review Weekly (Melbourne), 30 March 2006, 24

[37] Michael J Trebilcock, 'Rethinking Consumer Protection Policy' in Charles E F Rickett and Thomas G W Telfer (eds), *International Perspectives on Consumers' Access to Justice* (2003), 70

[38] Michael J Trebilcock, 'Rethinking Consumer Protection Policy' in Charles E F Rickett and Thomas G W Telfer (eds), *International Perspectives on Consumers' Access to Justice* (2003), 70

[39] Noakes D, 'Measuring the Impact of Strategic Insolvency on Employees' (2003) 11(12) *Insolvency Law Journal* 91, n 5, quoting Peta Spender 'strategic insolvency arises when the bankruptcy is invoked due to strategic decision-making rather than being a passive response to market forces'. Mokal RJ, 'The Search for Someone to Save: A Defensive Case for the Priority of Secured Credit' (2002) 22(4) *Oxford Journal of Legal Studies* 687, suggests at 698 that 'because a significant part of the [small firm] shareholder-managers' wealth is likely to be invested in the [small] firm, as an undiversified investment, far from being ready to liquidate them strategically, shareholder-managers can be expected to fight … single-mindedly to keep them afloat'. Mokal's proposition may help explain the franchisees' response to impending failure but is inapplicable to franchisors that diversify business risks through their franchisees

## Contract Asymmetry

Rights and liabilities recorded in the franchise agreement are asymmetrical. In economic terms, the 'role of contract law is to minimize the cost of the parties writing contracts + the cost of the courts writing contracts + the cost of inefficient behaviour arising from poorly written or incomplete contracts'.[40]

'Standardised contract terms are … [a] regulatory instrument'[41] that places all of the power to regulate the difficult times the relationship will experience, in the hands of the drafter, the franchisor.

In the context of economics, contract terms play a dual role: 'creating the correct marginal incentives on a contractually specified measure of (or proxy for) performance, and … the creation of rents sufficient to make the relationship self-enforcing'.[42] In franchising, the marginal incentives created within the franchise agreement do not outweigh the disadvantages to the franchisees whose franchisor operates its business so poorly or recklessly that an administrator or liquidator is appointed. In theory, franchisees can negotiate some protection into the franchise agreement. In practice, most cannot.

Hadfield observes that '[e]ither because current regulation is piecemeal or more fundamentally, because franchise relationships are too complex to reduce to precise statutory terms, the heart of franchising's legal structure is still contract'.[43] At negligible cost through amending its standard franchise agreement, a franchisor can include a provision to give franchisees the right to terminate the franchise agreement if an administrator is appointed. Yet, anecdotal evidence suggests that only one franchisee in each of the 270-franchisee Traveland and the 60-franchisee Beach House Group ('BHG') networks had a clause in their agreements permitting a franchisee to terminate the agreement if the franchisor failed.[44] Franchisors have no incentive to write contracts that fully acknowledge both parties' risks.

The nature of the franchise agreement, the difficulty of conducting adequate affordable due diligence, the possibility of strategic insolvency, the fact that the Code may not bind administrators and the stay on proceedings during administration and insolvency mean that the most solid avenue forward for fair franchise contracts is for terms to be implied into all franchise agreements via legislation.

---

[40] D Wittman, *Economic Foundations of Law and Organization* (2006) 194

[41] Michael J Trebilcock, 'Rethinking Consumer Protection Policy' in Charles E F Rickett and Thomas G W Telfer (eds), *International Perspectives on Consumers' Access to Justice* (2003), 77

[42] Benjamin Klein, 'The Economics of Franchise Contracts' (1995) 2 Journal of Corporate Finance 9, 19 in Francine Lafontaine (ed), *Franchise Contracting and Organization* 2005, 323

[43] Gillian K Hadfield, 'Problematic Relations: Franchising and the Law of Incomplete Contracts' (1990) 42 *Stanford Law Review* 927, 939

[44] Liquidator appointed by the court 18 December 2008, ASIC, National Names Index <http://www.search.asic.gov.au/cgi-bin/gns030c?acn=098_577_667&juris=9&hdtext=ACN&srchsrc=1> Accessed 19 December 2008

## Regulatory Asymmetry

> [R]isk is a key concern for policymakers. All other things being equal and where possible, we aim to reduce the overall level of risk and complexity in society.[45]

Regulatory asymmetry exists, despite the best endeavours of policy makers to understand franchising. One widely adopted mechanism policy makers support to reduce the imbalance of contracting power between franchisor and franchisees and to mitigate some aspects of asymmetry is pre-contract disclosure. This is a regulatory tool that packages much of the information that a franchisee needs to be aware of before signing a franchise agreement into one document. Australia enacted its Franchising Code of Conduct ('the Code') in 1998.[46] The Code was enacted as a mandatory industry code of conduct pursuant to the then *Trade Practices Act* s 51AE (now the CCA). To comply with the Code, all franchisors must maintain a franchise disclosure document and supply it in prescribed situations. The franchisor is required to disclose over 250 discrete items of information about itself, its associates and the franchise opportunity. Franchisees are encouraged to seek legal and financial advice in relation to the material disclosed. Part 3 of the Code contains some limitations on the contents of franchise agreements and mandates a cooling-off opportunity for franchisees. Part 4 addresses dispute resolution by establishing a mediation regime and making it accessible to parties who are 'in a dispute arising under a franchise agreement or this code'.[47]

The express purposes of the disclosure, expressed in s 6A, are twofold:

(a) to give to a prospective franchisee, or a franchisee proposing to enter into, renew, extend or extend the scope of a franchise agreement, information from the franchisor to help the franchisee to make a reasonably informed decision about the franchise and

(b) to give a franchisee current information from the franchisor that is material to the running of the franchised business.

Its overall objective is 'to regulate the conduct of participants in franchising towards other participants in franchising'[48] by levelling the playing field between franchisors and franchisees. Regulation is achieved under the Code through three avenues: by requiring franchisors to provide disclosure (Part 2), by implying terms into franchise agreements (Part 3) and by mandating a dispute resolution process (Part 4).

---

[45] Steven Kennedy, 'The Future of Consumer Policy: Should we Regulate to Protect Homo Economicus?' (Accord Industry Leaders Briefing, Old Parliament House, Canberra 13 August 2009) 10, 15

[46] *Trade Practices (Industry Codes – Franchising) Regulations 1998* (Cth)

[47] *Trade Practices (Industry Codes – Franchising) Regulations* Part 4, s 24

[48] *Trade Practices (Industry Codes – Franchising) Regulations* 1998 (Cth) s 2

In an attempt to prevent dependence from becoming a form of predation or servitude,[49] Part 3 of the Code implies terms into the franchise agreement. These terms provide a cooling-off period for franchisees (13), require franchisors to provide a copy of the premises lease in some circumstances (14), forbid the franchisor from preventing franchisees or prospective franchisees to associate with each other (15), prohibit the franchisor from requiring franchisees to sign a general release from liability (16), mandate audit and reporting requirements in relation to franchise network marketing and other cooperative funds (17), require disclosure of materially relevant facts by the franchisor to the franchisees within 14 days of the franchisor becoming aware, including contravention of the *Corporations Act* by the franchisor and the franchisor becoming an externally administered body corporate (18), require the franchisor to provide a current disclosure document if the franchisee requests it (19) and forbid the franchisor from unreasonably withholding a franchisee's request to be permitted to transfer its franchise (20).

A risk that is currently addressed in both franchisor agreements and the Code is the risk of the franchisee's business failing – there is no reciprocal statutory attention if the franchisor fails. As we saw in Chap. 5, contracts remain incomplete to the disadvantage of franchisees. The legislation does not provide the level playing field it was enacted to provide in response. In defence of its decision not to amend the Code to extend the rights provided for franchisors in regulation 23 to franchisees, the government commented in 2009 that

> The inclusion of an automatic right of termination for franchisees (in the Franchising Code) in the event of franchisor failure would give one area of small business an advantage over others (preferential treatment). It would also provide franchisees with an automatic right under the Franchising Code that is not available to franchisors.[50]

Australia's Government fails to appreciate that franchisors already have the right to automatically terminate franchisees to which receivers or administrators are appointed. They give it to themselves in the standard franchise agreements. They do not need legislative protection.

Steven Kennedy identifies that 'government actions tend to reallocate risk between different groups'.[51] This reallocation is partly a result of lobbying. At least one researcher has suggested that 'the dearth of information on franchisor failure is largely a reflection on the strength of the franchise lobby constituted by franchisors and their representatives'.[52] Similar franchisor-biased representation is prevalent in

[49] Elizabeth C Spencer, 'Conditions for effective disclosure in the regulation of franchising' (2008) 22(4) *International Review of Applied Economics* 509

[50] Joint Committee on Corporations and Financial Services, Australian Senate, *Opportunity Not Opportunism: Improving Conduct in Australian Franchising* (2008), 22

[51] Steven Kennedy, 'The Future of Consumer Policy: Should we Regulate to Protect Homo Economicus?' (Accord Industry Leaders Briefing, Old Parliament House, Canberra 13 August 2009) 10, 15

[52] Benjamin Morris, Franchisor Insolvency (B Laws Honours Thesis, University of Technology Sydney, 2006)

the Australian, American, Canadian and British context. A Franchisees Association of Australia Incorporated was established in 1983 but lacked funding and did not function like a trade union; the Franchise Council of Australia claims to represent franchisors and franchisees, but 'current figures suggest that only 200 franchisors of 1100 in total are members, which represents less than 20% while the percentage of franchisees who are members is even lower'.[53]

## Conclusion

The franchisee investigates the franchise opportunity believing the business is sound and viable. It may be impossible to conduct due diligence beyond what the franchisor has disclosed. From every perspective, information, adviser, education, risk and reward, resource, contract and regulation, franchisees experience significant asymmetry, always to their detriment. Franchisees remain vulnerable to the vagaries of the environment their franchisor creates.

[53] Elizabeth Crawford Spencer, 'All for One and One for All: A Survey of Franchise Trade Associations' Roles in the Governance of the Franchise Relationship.' (Paper presented at the 23rd Annual International Society of Franchising Conference, San Diego, California, 12–14 February 2009) 15

# Chapter 7
# Corporate Governance

**Abstract** Although franchisees function like a division of a corporation, they do not receive the benefit of the checks and balances the law has built into corporations through corporate governance principles. In this chapter, the OECD Principles of Corporate Governance and the eight basic corporate governance principles for public listed corporations identified by the Australian Stock Exchange are explored for the contribution they could make to the governance of a franchise system. Conflict of interest, franchisor succession planning and the corporate governance of listed franchisors are pursued as specific lines of inquiry.

## Introduction

'Checks and balances are imposed on corporations and corporate groups through divisions of enterprise with different functions, clear levels of authority, and a management structure'[1] all underpinned by corporate governance principles and legislation and closely overseen by regulators. These checks and balances function to mitigate the exploitation of minority shareholders by the majority and prescribe directors' duties, shareholder remedies, public disclosure, audits, independent directors, securities laws and insolvency procedures.[2]

To Oliver Hart, '[c]orporate governance issues arise in an organisation whenever two conditions are present. First, there is conflict of interest (or an agency problem)

[1] Lessing, J. 2009. The Checks and Balances of Good Corporate Governance. Corporate Governance ejournal. [Online]. Available at: http://works.bepress.com/john_lessing Accessed 10 June 2011

[2] Lessing, J. 2009. The Checks and Balances of Good Corporate Governance. Corporate Governance ejournal. [Online]. Available at: http://works.bepress.com/john_lessing Accessed 10 June 2011

J. Buchan, *Franchisees as Consumers: Benchmarks, Perspectives and Consequences*, DOI 10.1007/978-1-4614-5614-8_7, 

…second, the conflict of interest or agency problem cannot be dealt with through contract'.[3] Although conflicts of interest abound between franchisor and franchisees, the franchising model has neatly circumvented the troublesome issues that good corporate governance would address because franchisees are not members of the franchisor's company. Franchisors and franchisees' businesses are legally separate, yet neither role exists independent of the other. Franchisees rely on their franchisor being wise and ethical. If the franchisor makes a bad decision, the franchisees have to live, or sink, with it. Good corporate governance recognises that '[b]oard members should act on a fully informed basis, in good faith with due diligence and care and in the best interests of the company and the shareholders',[4] but this level of responsibility does not extend to the best interests of the franchisees. Franchisors do not have to secure their franchisees' consent or sign off to any of their decisions, even though these decisions may have a positive or negative effect on the franchisees and their success. An emerging challenge posed by franchising is thus corporate governance.

A narrow interpretation says that 'corporate governance is concerned with "the ways in which suppliers of finance assure themselves of getting a return on their investment"'.[5] Broader definitions such as the following include a wider class of stakeholders by defining corporate governance as comprising

> a system of structuring, operating and controlling a company … to achieve …a culture based on a foundation of sound business ethics and fulfilling the long-term strategic goal of the owners while taking into account the expectations of all the key stakeholders, and in particular:
>
> - considering and caring for the interests of employees, past, present and future
> - maintaining excellent relations with both customers and suppliers
> - taking account of the needs of the environment and the local community
> - maintaining proper compliance with all the applicable legal and regulatory requirements under which the company is carrying out its activities.
>
> … a well-run organisation must be structured in such a way that all the above requirements are catered for and can be seen to be operating effectively by all the interest groups concerned.[6]

Neither approach above mentions franchisees. This omission highlights the fact that the law does not acknowledge the role of franchisees within the franchisor's

[3] RP Austin and IM Ramsay, *Ford's Principles of Corporations Law* (LexisNexis Butterworths 13th ed, 2007) 317 citing Oliver Hart 'Corporate Governance: Some Theory and Implications' 1995 105 *Economic Journal,* 678

[4] OECD Principles of Corporate Governance, 2004, 24

[5] RP Austin and IM Ramsay, *Ford's Principles of Corporations Law* (LexisNexis Butterworths 13th ed, 2007) 317 citing A Shleifer and RW Vishny, *A Survey of Corporate Governance* National Bureau of Economic Research Working Paper Number 5554, 1996

[6] Applied Corporate Governance; Definition of Corporate Governance at http://www.applied-corporate-governance.com/definition-of-corporate-governance.html Accessed 2 September, 2011

business model accurately. As a consequence, it fails to accommodate their interests as key stakeholders in the franchise network. Franchisors, as a class, are not held accountable for exploiting franchisees. This is despite the reality that the interests of the franchisor and the franchisee are not always aligned, franchisees supply finance, their existence relieves a company of the need to hire a larger number of employees and the franchisor exercises a high degree of potentially exploitative control over franchisees through the non-negotiable franchise agreement.

> Corporate governance is one key element in improving economic efficiency and growth as well as enhancing investor confidence….Good corporate governance should provide proper incentives for the board and management to pursue objectives that are in the interests of the company and its shareholders, and should facilitate effective monitoring.[7]

Should corporate governance then be relevant in a franchise system? What should franchisees expect of sound corporate governance in franchise networks? We will look at two sources of corporate governance principles and then at the public statements about governance in franchise networks. Specific aspects of governance will be highlighted, including stakeholders, conflicts of interest and succession planning. This chapter ends with a look to a future that could include a more inclusive approach to corporate governance in franchise networks.

## Principles

Corporate governance principles set out by the OECD and the Australian Stock Exchange provide guidance to directors in formulating appropriate responses.

### *OECD*

The OECD Principles of Corporate Governance ('the Principles') shed light on the issue of why franchisees, as parties who have only a contractual relationship with the franchisor, matter in corporate governance of the franchisor. The six principles state that the corporate governance framework should:

1. Promote transparent and efficient markets, be consistent with the rule of law and clearly articulate the division of responsibilities among different supervisory, regulatory and enforcement authorities.
2. Protect and facilitate the exercise of shareholders' rights.
3. Ensure the equitable treatment of all shareholders, including minority and foreign shareholders. All shareholders should have the opportunity to obtain effective redress for violation of their rights.

[7] OECD Principles of Corporate Governance, 2004, 11

4. Recognise the rights of stakeholders established by law or through mutual agreements and encourage active co-operation between corporations and stakeholders in creating wealth, jobs and the sustainability of financially sound enterprises.
5. Ensure that timely and accurate disclosure is made on all material matters regarding the corporation, including the financial situation, performance, ownership and governance of the company.
6. Ensure the strategic guidance of the company, the effective monitoring of management by the board and the board's accountability to the company and the shareholders.[8]

The OECD 'principles focus on governance problems that result from the separation of ownership and control.... this is not simply an issue of the relationship between shareholders and management.... In [some] countries, employees have important legal rights irrespective of their ownership rights. The Principles therefore have to be complementary to a broader approach to the operation of checks and balances.... Creditors play an important role in a number of governance systems and can serve as external monitors over corporate performance'.[9]

## *ASX*

The Australian Stock Exchange has identified eight basic corporate governance principles for public listed corporations. The principles are that 'corporations should (1) lay solid foundations for management and oversight, (2) structure the board to add value, (3) promote ethical and responsible decision-making, (4) safeguard integrity in financial reporting, (5) make timely and balanced disclosures, (6) respect the rights of shareholders, (7) recognise and manage risk and (8) remunerate fairly and responsibly'.[10] All eight principles are relevant to the operation of franchisors and franchisees within franchise networks. ASX Principle 3 is concerned with companies actively promoting 'ethical and responsible decision-making'.[11] This principle is referring to decisions that comply with the law but also 'take into account the reasonable expectations of their stakeholders including: shareholders, employees, customers, suppliers, creditors, consumers and the broader community in which they operate'.[12] No rational argument could locate franchisees outside this list of a franchisor's stakeholders.

---

[8] OECD Principles of Corporate Governance, 2004, http://www.oecd.org/dataoecd/32/18/31557724.pdf

[9] OECD Principles of Corporate Governance, 2004, 12

[10] Australian Stock Exchange 'Corporate Governance Principles and Recommendations with 2010 Amendments 2nd edition, 10–12

[11] Australian Stock Exchange 'Corporate Governance Principles and Recommendations with 2010 Amendments 2nd edition, 22

[12] Australian Stock Exchange 'Corporate Governance Principles and Recommendations with 2010 Amendments 2nd edition, 22

# Specific Areas

## *Conflicts of Interest*

Corporate governance plays, as Hart has pointed out, an important role in the management of conflicts of interest. Franchising is replete with such conflicts, and in the absence of an inclusive corporate governance framework, franchisees have limited options in the face of any detrimental decision by their franchisor.[13] Where conflicts of interest arise between corporations in a group or between directors, shareholders and employees, their respective rights are protected by entrenched statutory rules and by guidelines such as OECD principle VI that recommends 'Boards should consider assigning a sufficient number of non-executive board members capable of exercising independent judgment to tasks where there is a potential for conflict of interest'.[14]

Where conflicts arise between franchisor's interests and franchisees' interests, the franchisees, with only contract-based rights, inevitably lose out to the superior statute-protected claims of the franchisor's directors, shareholders, employees and creditors. The administrator of a franchisor may, for example, decide to sell the failed franchisor's business to a competitor without the need to satisfy franchisees that the competitor will retain them and the brand.

## *Succession Planning*

When a traditional business is sold, the shareholders benefit in the price received via dividends or shares in the acquiring company. Franchisor's businesses are frequently sold for huge sums, but the franchisees do not receive a dividend or any form of payment. The franchise agreements are assets that the franchisor sells; the purchaser is untroubled by any need to adjust the price for holiday pay, long service leave, payroll tax or superannuation payments that would normally need to be considered when buying an employee-hungry business. For example, Australia is home to a franchise brand called Boost Juice:

> A deal was signed in May [2010], giving [US venture capitalist] Riverside about 70 per cent of Boost for about $80 m. Using the modus operandi of most private equity houses -- working on the basis of acquiring a business, adding some value and then selling it for a profit -- it is expected that Feiglin will seek to bulk up the Retail Zoo and pretty it for sale in the next three to five years.[15]

[13] Croonen, E.P.M. and Brand, M.J. 2010. Dutch Druggists in Distress: Franchisees Facing the Complex Decision of How to React to their Franchisor's Strategic Plans. *Entrepreneurship Theory and Practice*, 34(5), 1021–1038

[14] OECD Principles of Corporate Governance, 2004, 25

[15] Tracy Lee, Smoothie chain is in for a boost , The Australian, 29 January 2011

The exit options available to franchisors differ from those available to franchisees as franchisees almost without exception have a licence for a finite period of time. For franchisors, the choices include family succession, management buyout, listing, merger and ceasing to trade. Referring to a business owner who is not a franchisor, John Hawkey suggests '[t]he best option is the option that will maximize the value of an owner's equity and be the most favourable from a personal satisfaction and financial point of view'.[16] He presents the options below (Table 7.1).[17]

All exit options excluding number six are also available to a franchisor but not all play out satisfactorily for the exiting franchisor's franchisees. Option six is employed sometimes by administrators of insolvent franchisors and will be addressed in Chap. 8. Whilst new owners undoubtedly provide a welcome exit strategy for founder-franchisors, investor-franchisors purchase a franchise network as an investment. The franchise agreements and franchisees are assets that are expected to provide an income stream; the investment must generate a competitive return, or it will be wound up. In this context, franchisees risk being viewed as commodities to non-founder owners, not partners in a joint business activity.

Senator Joyce of Massachusetts captures the position the franchisor's exit predicament poses for its franchisees in saying:

> The reality today … is a franchise[e] could invest their equity as well as their sweat equity and build something that they would like, not just for themselves, but perhaps also for their children and the next generation. But one day the parent company could be sold to a hedge fund or to a foreign investor or simply have a change in policy and decide, "we don't want any franchises any more, we want to have company-owned stores." That franchisee … would have scant protections.[18]

## Corporate Governance of Listed Franchisors

Listed franchisors publish their corporate governance policies and implementation strategies in their annual reports. For example, in McDonald's, the Finance and Governance Committee is a standing committee of the Board of Directors. 'This Board has long believed that good corporate governance is critical to our fulfilling our obligations to shareholders'.[19] From the way the responsibilities are drafted on the McDonald's website, there is no sense that a governance duty is owed to the franchisees.

---

[16] John Hawkey, *Exit Strategy Planning: Grooming Your Business for Sale or Succession*, (Gower Publishing Limited, England, 2002) 43

[17] John Hawkey, *Exit Strategy Planning: Grooming Your Business for Sale or Succession*, (Gower Publishing Limited, England, 2002) 44

[18] Bluemaumau, 2011. An example in Australia is the *Meridian Retail* case

[19] Corporate governance principles Adopted by the Board of Directors with effect as of February 28, 2011. http://aboutmcdonalds.com/mcd/investors/corporate_governance/guidelines_and_policies/corporatre_governance_principles.html

**Table 7.1** Exit options for franchisors

| Exit option | 1. Can I achieve maximum value? | 2. What is the risk factor in disposal? | 3. Can I retain control after sale? | 4. Will this be good for my personal financial planning? | 5. Will I be assured payment? | 6. Will I have deal flexibility? | 7. What will my personal satisfaction be? |
|---|---|---|---|---|---|---|---|
| 1. Family succession | Yes | Moderate | Probably | Yes | No | Yes | Very high |
| 2. Employees or managers (MBO/MBI) | Yes | Moderate | No (unless on terms) | Yes | Depends on terms | Yes | Moderate to high |
| 3. Sole trader merger | Yes | Moderate | Some | Yes | Yes | Yes | Moderate |
| 4. Third-party sale | Depends on timing | Low | No | Depends on timing | Depends on terms | Probably not | Moderate to low |
| 5. Public listing | Yes | High | Yes | Yes | Yes, for initial offering | No | High |
| 6. Franchising | Yes | Moderate | Yes; of franchisor business | Yes | No | No | High |
| 7. Managed close-down | No | Low | No | Probably not | Yes | No | Low |
| 8. Liquidation-fire sale | Definitely not | Low | No | No | Yes | No | Very low |

Burger King has separate sections of its website for 'franchising' and 'investor relations'. Corporate governance is included under the investor relations heading.[20] This implies that franchisees are not acknowledged to be investors. Within the corporate governance section are Codes of Ethics and Conduct which define the BURGER KING ®SYSTEM as 'Burger King Corporation, its subsidiaries and affiliates, its franchisees and/or their representatives, BURGER KING ® restaurants and BURGER KING ® purchasing agents and/or their representatives'.[21] The function of Burger King's Nominating and Corporate Governance Committee is to exercise 'general oversight with respect to the governance and performance of our board, as well as corporate governance matters applicable to us and our employees and directors'.[22]

In 2011, a listed Australian franchisor Harvey Norman had 195 franchised outlets that generated sales revenue of $A5.08billion and 96 company-owned stores that generated an income of $A1,556.38million.[23] Its Board of Directors' responsibilities are

(a) 'establishing strategic objectives for the Company and monitoring the execution and implementation by management of the measures, targets and initiatives necessary to execute those strategic objectives;
(b) monitoring compliance with regulatory requirements, ethical standards and external commitments; and
(c) appointing and reviewing the performance of the Chief Executive Officer'.[24]

No mention of franchisees is made in Harvey Norman's Board Charter which instructs the Board members to act

(a) in a manner designed to create and continue to build sustainable value for shareholders; and
(b) in accordance with the duties and obligations imposed upon the Board by the Constitution and by law.[25]

A perfunctory search of high-profile proprietary company-owned franchisors in Australia reveals nothing about their corporate governance policies or practices on their websites.

---

[20] http://www.bk.com/en/us/company-info/about-bk.html

[21] Burger King. The Code of Business Ethics and Conduct for vendors, May 2008. http://media.corporate-ir.net/media_files/irol/87/87140/VCC_May2008.pdf Accessed 2 June 2012

[22] Burger King investor relations, Nominating and Corporate Governance Committee Composition, http://investor.bk.com/phoenix.zhtml?c=87140&p=irol-govCommComp Accessed 2 June 2012

[23] Harvey Norman Holdings Limited 2011 Annual Report, http://www.harveynormanholdings.com.au/pdf_files/2011_Annual_Report.pdf Accessed 2 June 2012

[24] Harvey Norman Holdings Limited A.C.N. 003 237 545 Board Charter, http://www.harveynormanholdings.com.au/pdf_files/HNHL_Board_Charter_Sept_2009.pdf Accessed 2 June 2012

[25] http://www.harveynormanholdings.com.au/pdf_files/HNHL_Board_Charter_Sept_2009.pdf

# The Future

> A major set of problems with internal control systems are associated with the curbing of what [Jensen] call[s] active investors. Active investors are individuals or institutions that hold large debt and/or equity positions in a company and actively participate in its strategic direction. Active investors are important to a well-functioning governance system because they have the financial interest and independence to view firm management and policies in an unbiased way. They have the incentives to buck the system to correct problems early rather than later when the problems are obvious but difficult to correct. Financial institutions such as banks ... are natural active investors but they have been shut out of boardrooms and firm strategy by the legal structure, by custom and by their own practices.[26]

Franchisees are active investors, similarly shut out of board rooms. Stephen Spinelli writes that '[t]he real power of franchising comes to life when it leverages significantly different partner [franchisor and franchisees'] skill sets'.[27] This result is achieved in some systems through 'private solutions negotiated within individual franchise systems, [which], are proving to be quite effective to coordinate strategies, allocate costs and benefits, implement strategic adaptation and minimise dissatisfaction and conflict within franchise systems'.[28]

It is beyond the power of the franchisees to influence the franchisor's management choices. As Doug Frazey observes:

> While franchisees are typically required to meet a number of conditions in their franchise agreements (such as sales quotas), franchisors do not share the same responsibilities. ... a franchisee is usually powerless to correct a poorly managed franchisor, even though the effects may weigh more heavily on the franchisee.[29]

Not everyone in the franchise should be the key decision-maker; not all should be involved in high-level governance. A franchise network is not a collective management structure; each player has a role that they need to perform fully in order for the whole to thrive. High-level governance should thus remain a role for franchisors. They are the stakeholders responsible for driving the direction of the franchise network. They have the overarching vision.

However, with the high-level governance right comes the responsibility to ensure that decisions that are made by the franchisor and administrators are consistent with good governance and accordingly are not damaging to the franchisees' businesses.

---

[26] Michael C Jensen 'The Modern Industrial Revolution, Exit, and the Failure of Internal Control Systems' *The Journal of Finance*, Vol XLVIII, No 3, July 1993, 831 at 867. Referring to Roe (1990, 1991), Black (1990) and Pound (1991)

[27] Stephen Spinelli, 'Franchises Without Borders' 18 (1) *Business Strategy Review*, 50 at 51

[28] Andrew C Selden 'Beyond the Law and Contracts: Strategies for Effective Franchise Relationship Self-Management' in Elizabeth C Spencer (ed) *Relational Rights and Responsibilities: Perspectives on Contractual Arrangements in Franchising*, (Bond University Press, 2011) 160

[29] Doug Frazey, 'Case Note: When 'Good Cause' Goes Bad: Minnesota Restricts Protection for Dealers under HUMEDA – River Valley Truck Ctr., Inc V. Interstate Cos' (2006–2007) 33(2) William Mitchell Law Review 711, 728 quoting David Hess, 'The Iowa Franchise Act: Towards Protecting Reasonable Expectations of Franchisees and Franchisors' (1995) 80 *Iowa Law Review* 333, 338–9

# Chapter 8
# Franchisor Failure

**Abstract** Franchisor insolvency attracts increasing attention as the Global Financial Crisis rumbles on. It transpires that the law does not accommodate the franchisees' interests in a neat or predictable way if its franchisor's business fails. In this chapter, the concept of insolvency (administration followed by winding up) and the roles of the key players are explained. A case study of the failed REDgroup and its franchisor Angus & Robertson is presented, and some consequences of franchisor failure for franchisees are set out. This chapter also presents statistics on franchisor failure and identifies examples of strategic insolvency in the franchise context. International dimensions of franchisor insolvency and trademark issues are explored. The inability of ex ante measures, such as pre-contractual disclosure and the standard form franchise agreement to protect franchisees are addressed.

## Introduction

The franchisee's business is predicated on and inextricably linked to the solvency of the franchisor. Not all franchisors succeed in business. The demise of a well-known franchisor is often mentioned in the business pages of the press. One if its franchisees may rate a mention in the local newspaper. In the eyes of the law and their customers, franchisees quickly fade, just like the Cheshire cat, leaving behind only 'a vacant store, a painted-over sign, or a Google search that references an outdated website'.[1]

The interrelated nature of the franchisor's and franchisee's business together with the pattern of contractual relationships that bind the franchise network together are

[1] Jason Gherke, 10 April 2012, Why franchisors fail: Lessons from the Titanic. Smartcompany.com Accessed 12 April 2012

J. Buchan, *Franchisees as Consumers: Benchmarks, Perspectives and Consequences*, 
DOI 10.1007/978-1-4614-5614-8_8, 

strengths that become weaknesses for franchisees if a franchisor fails. The 'standard form of the franchise agreement [limits] the ability of the franchisee to self protect'.[2] Only a few franchisees and even national master licensees have had previous experience with the consequences of franchisor failure, and most do not realise that in this respect, their investment is largely unprotected by the law. Insolvency legislation, in existence long before franchising became popular, exposes the full extent of the franchisees' vulnerability. Nowhere are the differences between employees, suppliers/independent contractors and franchisees more exaggerated than if the franchisor fails. The currency liquidators trade in is 'debtors and creditors', 'assets and liabilities'. Franchisees find they inhabit a world where business failures are seen as

> a productive mechanism. ... part of a process in which inefficient and unprofitable businesses are replaced by efficient and profitable ones. ... [where economies get better through a process of experimentation and natural selection.[3]

Returning to the analogy of the high performance car, it is only when the car crashes that it becomes clear that it did not come equipped with air bags. The law did not require them to be fitted as a standard feature of the car by the manufacturer; the manufacturer did not offer them as an extra, the driver assumed they were there, but they were not. Similarly, the franchisee is ill suited to weather the crash of its franchisor. In this chapter, I outline the procedures surrounding administration and insolvency. I present franchisor failure statistics and map out the impact of franchisor failure on its franchisees through a case study. The chapter concludes with a look at the capacity of any disclosure document or contract to protect a franchisee's investment in the face of franchisor failure.

## What Is Insolvency?

> A drastic fall from corporate grace can occur if those in charge lost their way. [4]

Insolvency, known as bankruptcy in the USA, is a set of statutory procedures through which a company can move or be moved from a situation of financial stress to a resolution of that stress. In the first stage, called administration, an administrator is appointed to determine whether the company is able to be (1) returned intact

[2] Wayne Jenvey, 'Rocky Roads and Rollercoasters – Turnaround Strategies for Distressed Franchise Systems' (Paper presented at the Legal Symposium at the Franchise Australia Annual Conference, Gold Coast, 24 October 2006) 2

[3] Bickerdyke I, Lattimore R, and Madge A, 'Business Failure and Change: An Australian Perspective' (Productivity Commission Staff Research Paper, 2000) 3

[4] Justice Owen, The failure of HIH Insurance: The HIH Royal Commission Report (Commonwealth of Australia, 2003)

to the control of the directors or (2) restructured and returned to the control of the directors or (3) put into liquidation.[5] Strict time frames are accorded to each step in the insolvency process. In Australia, for example, from the time the administrator is appointed, the first meeting of creditors must be held within eight business days. Following the first meeting of creditors, the administrator has up to 30 business days in which to evaluate the potential for the company, formulate a recommendation to creditors and hold the second creditors meeting. At the second creditors meeting, the creditors vote to pursue outcome 1, 2 or 3 above. If option 2 is preferred, the restructure begins through the deed administration process. If option 3 is chosen, the administrator immediately becomes the liquidator and proceeds to wind the company up.

## *Role of Administrators*

Administrators are effectively handed the keys to our fast car, and control over its use. Administrators must adhere to the powers they are given by statute.[6] The franchise agreement is the first place an administrator looks to determine what responsibilities the franchisor has and what rights its franchisees have. At that point, it is too late for the franchisor and franchisee to negotiate a change in the terms of the franchise agreement. 'The voluntary or deed administrator appointed to a franchisor will have to act quickly to maintain the franchise contracts on foot, assuming some viability in the franchise, in order to sell the franchise business. The difficulty of maintaining the confidence and continued acceptance of contractual obligations of the franchisees and other third parties such as landlords throughout that process cannot be underestimated'.[7]

## *Role of Liquidators*

If the company is to be wound up, a liquidator is appointed. The liquidator's role is to dispose of the failed company's assets, pay creditors and report to the regulator about what caused the failure of the company.

[5] http://www.asic.gov.au/asic/ASIC.NSF/byHeadline/Resources#4

[6] In Australia, the *Corporations Act 2001* (Cth) sets out administrators' powers in ss 437A, 442A–442F, additional powers in s 442A and fiduciary obligations in s 437A. The administrators' powers in relation to the insolvent company's property are contained in ss 437D and 442D

[7] Jenny Buchan, 'Challenges that Franchisees of Insolvent Franchisors Pose for Liquidators' (2008) 16:1 *Insolvency Law Journal* 26, 38

Both administrator and liquidator have a statutory right to disclaim onerous property.[8] There are several aspects of the franchisor/franchisee situation that may give them cause to exercise this right. Franchise agreements themselves are contracts that may be disclaimed by the franchisor's liquidator as unprofitable.[9] The liquidator can thereby eliminate less successful franchise agreements while retaining the more productive ones that are generating higher royalty fees or other income streams for the franchise. Unless specific prior security arrangements have been agreed, claims by terminated franchisees are unsecured. For example, if the franchisor holds the disclaimable head lease, the right to disclaim has implications for the franchisee that may have, at best, a tenuous claim to remain in occupation of the premises. Following the disclaimer, the franchisee has a right to lodge a proof of debt in the liquidation as an unsecured creditor for its loss.[10] Loss does not include franchisee's sunk costs.

An underperforming franchisee that occupies premises where the franchisor holds the head lease can be a liability to a liquidator. There may be an exclusive territory provision in the franchise agreement, prohibiting the liquidator from locating a more profitable franchise in a nearby location. Additionally, the insolvent franchisor may be liable itself for any shortfall in rental payments made by underperforming franchisees where the franchisor is the tenant under the lease and had subleased premises to those franchisees.

Traditional suppliers of debt finance are known as creditors in insolvency. Traditional suppliers of equity finance, shareholders, have taken the risk of the entity becoming insolvent and invested in reliance on information supplied in a prospectus

[8] See *Corporations Act* Part 5.6, Division 7A – 'Disclaimer of Onerous Property' and Michael Murray, *Keay's Insolvency: Personal and Corporate Law and Practice* (5th ed, 2005) 340. 'In some cases liquidators do not wish to retain property because it is too onerous, worth little or is unsalable. In such circumstances, liquidators wish to get rid of the property in order to avoid responsibilities and costs in relation to it. In disclaiming, the liquidator gives notice to others that he or she wishes to be rid of any interest in the property. If a person suffers loss as a consequence, those persons to whom notice has been given are required to try to mitigate their loss. They may lodge a proof of debt in the liquidation in respect of the amount of that loss. The liquidator may disclaim property referred to in Section 568(1) *Corporations Act 2001* (Cth) (including) land burdened with onerous covenants (for example a lease of retail space in the franchisor's name that is licensed to a franchisee as occupier with no status on the title and no privity of contact with the landlord) and contracts (including franchise agreements).' This procedure is also explained in *Enviro Systems Renewable Resources v. Australian Securities & Investments Commission* (2001) 80 SASR 1; 36 ACSR 762; 2001 WL 115336; [2001] SASC 11 by Martin J. 'In essence, the documentation provides that Enviro (franchisor) offers participants (franchisees) the right to use identified (property). Participants do not have a registrable interest in any of the land. One parcel is leased by Enviro. The lease provides that if the lease is terminated as a consequence of default by Enviro, the lessors are entitled to take possession of the land and trees planted on the land become the absolute property of the lessors'. The same applies to a lease of a shop

[9] *Corporations Act 2001* (Cth) Part 5.6 Div 7A. For example, Sue Mitchell, 'Signature Out of Pulp But Not Out of Juice', The Australian Financial Review (Sydney), 1–2 April 2006, 10. 'After disclaiming 17 leases on the loss-making bars [i.e. the leases of premises occupied by Pulp franchisees], the only assets the liquidators had available to sell were 'fridges, blenders and mixers'

[10] *Corporations Act 2001* (Cth) s 568D(2)

that has met rigorous standards. When negotiating, they had the opportunity to become secured creditors and/or to price the unsecured risk accordingly. Franchisees seldom have these options.

Although franchisees may be creditors, that status does not fully recognise the extent of their investment in the franchise, or their losses when the franchisor fails. In fact, if a liquidator is appointed to a franchisor, the franchisee may experience outcomes it had not contemplated by way of the liquidation crystallising not only the claims of the franchisee but also the liabilities the franchisor required the franchisee to take on to third parties. A franchisee's ability to meet these liabilities is contingent in practical terms on, but not legally conditional on, the continued right to remain a franchisee.

## Data on Failed Franchisors

The existence of widespread franchisor failure is acknowledged by franchise lawyers.[11] Beyond attempts at establishing how many franchisors fail and when in the franchisor life cycle the failure occurs, franchisor failure has received little academic,[12] practitioner or government attention.

Academic studies of the number and timing of franchisor failures have been conducted in the United States, the United Kingdom and France.[13] Researchers have noted the difficulty of obtaining accurate data and the possible inaccuracy of non-government-sourced data.[14] For example, the USDOC stopped reporting on franchise failures in 1988.[15]

The number of franchisor failures identified from 1971 onwards includes '54 entire restaurant franchise systems [in the US] that turned "belly up" over a 2-year period'.[16] In another US study,

[11] For example, the Franchise Council of Australia's annual conference legal day scheduled a session on franchisor failure every year from 2006 to 2009 inclusive

[12] Benjamin Morris, Franchisor Insolvency (B Laws Honours Thesis, University of Technology Sydney, 2006) 3. An exploratory study was conducted by Jenny Buchan in 2004–2005 in Australia and reported in 'When the Franchisor Fails', CPA Australia. The report focussed on consequences of franchisor failure

[13] Australian, British, French and United States franchising and franchise research are referred to throughout this book. In all four countries, the franchise sector thrives, and statistics exist on franchisor failure

[14] In John Stanworth, David Purdy and Stuart Price, 'Franchise Growth and Failure in the USA and the UK: A Troubled Dreamworld Revisited' (1997) 2(2) *Franchising Research: An International Journal* 75, 78 citing Janes Cross, 'Franchising Failures: Definitional and Measurement Issues' (Paper presented at the International Society of Franchising Conference, Las Vegas, Nevada, 13–14 February 1994) 1

[15] Roger D Blair and Francine Lafontaine, *The Economics of Franchising* (Cambridge University Press, 2005) 272

[16] Harold Brown, Franchising: Realities and Remedies (1973) 40 cited in Shelby D Hunt, 'Franchising: Promises, Problems, Prospects' (1977) 53(3) *Journal of Retailing* 71, 75 citing a study in Urban B Ozanne and Shelby D Hunt, *The Economic Effects of Franchising* (1971) 93

> 104 franchisors operating 5,423 outlets failed during 1987 … The volume of 1986 sales represented by failed firms amounted to $[US] 1.7 billion, of which the franchisee-owned portion was $[US]1.5 billion.[17]

While this only amounted to fewer than 5 per cent of the total number of franchisors, the number of franchisees affected is high. The fact that the franchisors' failure has an impact on them has been noted[18] but has not been the subject of systematic research. In the UK, researchers have concluded that up to a quarter of franchisors fail over a 10-year period and that '[a]round half the sample was judged to have failed completely and utterly'.[19] This pattern is mimicked in France where researchers found that during the period 1992–2002, only 42.13% of franchise networks survived.[20] For franchisors granting franchisees the right to trade as a franchisee for terms of up to 20 years and accepting upfront franchise fees for the entire term[21], the failure within 10 years of the franchisor grantor begs the question of what rights the franchisee grantees have on the failure of their franchisor only half way through the term.

Research into the timing of the failures has also been conducted in the USA and Australia. Whereas 'Shane suggests heavy failure rates of new franchise systems in the first four years, followed then up to the ten year period by only modest further losses, …. Lafontaine and Shaw report … steady and sustained failure rates from franchise format adoption onwards'.[22]

In Australia, estimates of the size of the problem range from a ratio of six franchisor failures to one success over a period of 20 years,[23] to 72 per cent exiting franchising over the period 1999 to 2011.[24] The 72% included franchisors that had

---

[17] Roger D Blair and Francine Lafontaine, *The Economics of Franchising* (Cambridge University Press, 2005) 272

[18] Franchisor exits, whether it be a departure from franchising or a business failure, [have an impact] on the survival or growth of the franchised units that were tied to it. Roger D Blair and Francine Lafontaine, *The Economics of Franchising* (Cambridge University Press, 2005) 44

[19] Francine Lafontaine and K L Shaw, 'Franchising Growth and Franchisor Entry and Exit in the US Market: Myth and Reality' (1998) 13(2) *Journal of Business Venturing* 95–112, in Frank Hoy and John Stanworth (eds), *Franchising: An International Perspective* (Routledge, 2003) 164

[20] Rozenn Perrigot and Gérard Cliquet, 'Survival of Franchising Networks in France from 1992 to 2002' (Paper presented at the 18th Annual International Society of Franchising Conference, Las Vegas, Nevada, 6–7 March 2004)

[21] Rozenn Perrigot, 'Services vs Retail Chains: Are There Any Differences? Evidence from the French Franchising Industry' (2006) 34(12) *International Journal of Retail & Distribution Management* 925

[22] Francine Lafontaine and K L Shaw, 'Franchising Growth and Franchisor Entry and Exit in the US Market: Myth and Reality' (1998) 13(2) *Journal of Business Venturing* 95, in Frank Hoy and John Stanworth (eds), *Franchising: An International Perspective* (2003) 163

[23] Emma Connors, 'The Brave New World of Franchising', The Weekend Australian Financial Review (Sydney), 6–7 February 2010, 39 quoting franchise consultant Gary Williamson

[24] Buchan J, Qu C and Frazer L 'Protecting Franchisees from Their Franchisor's Impending Failure: A Way Forward for Consumer Protection Regulators Using Indicators?' (Paper presented at the First International Conference on Comparative Law and Global Common Law 'Exchange and Integration of the Contemporary Legal Systems' College of Comparative Law, China University of Political Science and Law, 24–25 September 2011, Beijing)

**Table 8.1** Examples of Australian failed franchisors

| Franchisor | Number of franchisees when franchisor failed | Number of years franchisor's company trading (total including franchising) |
|---|---|---|
| Angus & Robertson | 61 | 125 |
| Beach House Group | 60 | 17 |
| Kleenmaid[a] | 22 | 24 |
| Kleins Jewellery | 134 | 26 |
| Speeds Shoes | 75 | 94 |
| Traveland | 270 | 43 |

[a]The Kleenmaid franchisees paid initial fees of $60,000–$120,000 each plus set-up costs. They subleased premises from the franchisor's associate, Kleenmaid Property. Deloitte, The Kleenmaid Group (Administrators appointed) Administrators' Report to Creditors pursuant to Section 439A Corporations Act 2001 at 14

exited franchising but possibly remained in business and others like those in Table 8.1 that are no longer trading.

Research on the impact of franchisor failure on franchisees and the economy has been hampered by lack of data, the cost of buying data and the difficulty of locating and interviewing former franchisees who are often emotionally traumatised by their experience. They, like the Cheshire cat, often disappear from view with alarming speed when the franchisor fails. This inability to access data on which to found empirical research has hampered the evolution of policy to address any deficiencies in the law.

## Why Franchisors Fail

Common sense suggests that franchisors do everything in their power to make their business a success. This is not always the case. As well, despite the endeavours of the regulator, and the due diligence of the franchisor, there are franchises promoted and sold that are just not viable. The concept may be a fad, or the promoted returns were never possible.

The Franchising Task Force Report of December 1991 ('Task Force') in Australia [25] concluded that the

> most vulnerable franchise systems are those that have recently commenced franchising and have less than, say, 12-15 units.[26]
>
> Franchisees are clearly vulnerable to the collapse of the franchisor, however, even when the franchisor has collapsed, some franchisees are capable of surviving as independently owned and operated outlets …
>
> However newer franchisees or franchisees already suffering severe financial strain are unlikely to survive the complete collapse of a franchise system.[27]

[25] Robert W Fitzgerald, Franchising Task Force Final Report to the Minister for Small Business and Customs (1991) 2.7–2.10

[26] This conclusion can be questioned in the light of evidence since 1991

[27] I have listed only the reasons that are within the control of the franchisor, omitting those that are a function of the broader economy

Three years after the Task Force filed its report, Stanworth, Purdy and Price report that James Cross identified some causes of SME (small- and medium-sized enterprise) failure as being generic and concluded that failures of this type should actually be remedied or reduced by franchising.[28] These causes are undercapitalisation, absence of economies of scale, lack of business acumen and inability to survive intense competition in sectors where barriers to entry are low.

Failure as a result of franchising-related factors was seen by Cross as falling essentially into five key categories: business fraud, intrasystem competition involving franchise outlets being located too close to one another, insufficient support of franchisees, poor franchisee screening and persistent franchisor/franchisee conflict.[29] Failure of the parent company and strategic insolvency following the inability of investors to exit via a public listing can be added to this list.

## *Reasons Why Some Australian Franchisors Failed*

Blame for the failure of franchisors is attributed by franchisors, administrators and the media to a wide range of causes. Examples include the following:

An unsuccessful attempt at expanding to another country led to the demise of Mini-Tankers International. Although it already operated franchises in Australia, Canada and New Zealand, it 'collapsed in September [2003] owing $10.7million as a result of an unsuccessful attempt to launch an operation in the United States'.[30]

Litigation by franchisees sunk franchisors A1 Mobile Radiators[31] and Cut Price Deli[32] that were successfully prosecuted for misleading and deceiving their franchisees, and Simply No-Knead that was successfully prosecuted for behaving unconscionably towards its franchisees.[33]

---

[28] In John Stanworth, David Purdy and Stuart Price, 'Franchise Growth and Failure in the USA and the UK: A Troubled Dreamworld Revisited' (1997) 2(2) Franchising Research: An International Journal 75, 78 citing Janes Cross, 'Franchising Failures: Definitional and Measurement Issues' (paper presented at the International Society of Franchising Conference, Las Vegas, Nevada, 13–14 February 1994) 1

[29] In John Stanworth, David Purdy and Stuart Price, 'Franchise Growth and Failure in the USA and the UK: A Troubled Dreamworld Revisited' (1997) 2(2) *Franchising Research: An International Journal* 75, 78–79

[30] Kath Walters, 'Fuel for Shareholders Anger', Business Review Weekly (Sydney), 13 May 2004, 17

[31] *Australian Competition & Consumer Commission v. Trayling* [1999] FCA 1133

[32] *Cut Price Deli Pty Limited, Cut Price Deli Franchising Pty Limited and Enzo Sgambellone v. Christian Roger Jacques, Catherine May Jacques and Pourquoi Pas Pty Limited* [1994] FCA 1101; (1994) 49 FCR 397; *Airberg Pty Ltd & Ors v. Cut Price Deli Pty Ltd & Ors* [1998] FCA 893

[33] *Australian Competition & Consumer Commission v. Simply No-Knead (Franchising) Pty Ltd* [2000] FCA 1365; *Australian Competition and Consumer Commission v. Simply No-Knead (Franchising) Pty Ltd* (2000) 104 FCR 25

An illegal tax avoidance scheme dressed up as a franchise was how NoRegrets was ultimately portrayed. It was an online lingerie retail business. Franchisees were enticed to invest in a virtual franchise store 'launched in 1998 as a tax-effective scheme, with the help of prospectuses that set a new standard in steamy financial documents complete with pictures of scantily clad women'.[34] The franchise was based on an aggressive tax avoidance scheme where 'investors put in about [A] $12,500 cash for each so-called virtual franchise store they bought but claimed tax deductions of up to $51,000'.[35] It was described as a 'financial and operational flop'.[36] It is estimated that the 600 franchisees lost 'in excess of [A] $7million through a combination of their original franchise fee, then big bills sent by the tax office as part of a crackdown'.[37]

Fraudulent conduct by Mr Lloyd Scott led to franchisor Lloyd Scott Enterprises failing in June 2001. The media reported

> the fallout continues from the [A]$40 million fraud that brought down Newcastle photocopier franchise Lloyd Scott Enterprises. ... Lloyd Scott had been fraudulently writing multiple leases on photocopier equipment, a step that had flooded his company with cash, but which had required him to perpetrate more frauds to keep the various leases paid up.[38]

Badly run public companies can fail. CarLovers Carwash franchise, for example, became insolvent in 2003 through a combination of poor negotiation by franchisors in relation to premises leases and consequential franchisee revolt. The franchisor

> locked itself into expensive leases of up to 20 years, on sites where the carwashes didn't reach expectations and the company made big write downs. ... [I]n 1998 CarLovers' problems with its leases were compounded with what became an even greater problem: an increasing number of franchisees stopped paying franchise fees, claiming that CarLovers was not providing the services ... it had promised.[39]

Sadly for the franchisees, the administration was also a disaster with the administrator/liquidator abusing the opportunity to require the franchisees to continue trading for several years until he was ultimately prosecuted and finally banned for life from practising as a liquidator.[40]

---

34 Neale Prior, 'Lingerie Firm's Rescue Looks A Little Scanty', The Australian Financial Review (Sydney), 22 May 2004, 6

35 Neale Prior, 'Investors in Norwood's NoRegrets Left with Plenty of Them', The West Australian (Perth), 4 February 2005, 37

36 Neale Prior, 'Investors in Norwood's NoRegrets Left with Plenty of Them', The West Australian (Perth), 4 February 2005, 37

37 Neale Prior, 'Investors in Norwood's NoRegrets Left with Plenty of Them', The West Australian (Perth), 4 February 2005, 37

38 Greg Ray, 'Fraud Fallout Action Settled', The Newcastle Herald (Newcastle), 24 July 2004, 4

39 Neil Chenoweth, 'CarLovers is All Washed Up', The Australian Financial Review (Sydney), 19 July 2003

40 The Senate, Economics references Committee, *The regulation, registration and remuneration of insolvency practitioners in Australia: The case for a new framework*, September 2010, Commonwealth of Australia http://www.asic.gov.au/asic/asic.nsf/byheadline/09-150AD+Liquidator+%28Stuart+Ariff%29+banned+for+life?openDocument

Franchisor, Stockmans Australian Cafes identified what were believed to be critical mistakes that led to its failing. These were its

> Failure to provide sufficient field support to franchisees.
>
> Appointing master franchisees. ... [which] gave third parties the authority to grow and represent the franchisor [without their having] the requisite skills and passion.
>
> [Absence of] internal compliance standards and tolerance of non-complian[t] franchisees.
>
> Having a very wide geographical spread of franchisees, but small numbers. [The franchisor] had all the costs of servicing a national network without many of the economies.
>
> Failure to invigorate the network with new product and innovation.
>
> Poor communication and complaints management processes.
>
> Growth that was too fast and master franchisees that were too focussed on selling franchises rather than providing the necessary support to franchisees.
>
> Poor recruitment standards and policies.
>
> Lack of detailed monitoring and bench marking.[41]

Oversaturation of the juice market brought down less established juice franchises in 2006. By 'mid 2004 the juice bar industry, estimated to be worth more than $650 m by ACNielsen – had become saturated and recent arrivals [such as Pulp and Juice Station] were struggling under the weight of massive leases'.[42]

## *Trading While Insolvent*

The reasons an administrator was appointed can be found in reports to creditors. In order to maintain faith in franchising and in the integrity of franchisors, it has to be assumed that most franchisor insolvencies are triggered by a franchisor realising it is insolvent. If this is the case, it must immediately appoint an administrator to avoid breaching the corporations' legislation. To assume otherwise is to admit that corporate governance by franchisors flagrantly ignores consideration for the well-being and future of their franchisees.

## *Strategic Insolvency*

Franchisees depend on the continued sound operation of their franchisor, but as Doug Frazey suggests, this dependence does not necessarily bind franchisors 'to respect the reasonable expectation of the franchisee that, in return for its dependence, the franchisee can continue to operate as long as it [does not breach its

[41] Stephen Giles and Rod Young, 'The Rise and Fall of Stockmans Australian Cafes', FCA Visions Newsletter (Melbourne), August 2005

[42] Sue Mitchell, 'Signature Out of Pulp but Not Out of Juice', The Australian Financial Review (Sydney), 1–2 April 2006, 10

franchise] agreement'.[43] A financially troubled but not insolvent franchisor may want to exit the franchise business but not wish to or be able to exit by paying franchisees what their businesses should be worth. The revenue raising opportunities available to a franchisor include advertising for new franchisees, increasing costs to franchisees or avoiding liability by embarking on a course of strategic insolvency. Thus, insolvency may be part of a considered business strategy. According to US legal advisers, it provides 'an opportunity … to solve operational or financial problems and emerge as a more viable company'.[44] For franchisors, the operational or financial problems may include an inability to exit via a credible public offering, a wish to

> deleverage its balance sheet, accomplish a sale of assets, obtain new financing or improve its capital structure. For example, bankruptcy may assist a franchisor in addressing …; overexpansion in the market and the need to eliminate units, an unworkable equity structure, desire to sell or merge with another entity, threat of franchisee litigation, desire to refinance but the lender has expressed concern about financial or other issues.[45]

One US lawyer writes that '[f]ranchisors file for bankruptcy to escape or postpone the consequences of mass franchisee litigation, shareholder litigation, and lender enforcement activities'.[46]

An example of a strategic insolvency in Australia could be REDgroup. As shown in Fig. 8.1, REDgroup had a franchisee subsidiary Angus & Robertson with 170 bookstore outlets (including 53 franchised). It also had the Australian master licence for Borders. It operated 26 Borders stores, some of which had a Gloria Jean's coffee shop franchisee within the store. The administrators concluded '… it is difficult to maintain an argument that the [RED]Group was insolvent for any material period prior to 17 February 2011'.[47]

If the strategic insolvency was not of a franchisor, there would be no problems the law has not provided answers to. However, the law does not have satisfactory responses for franchisees in this situation. A franchisor's strategic insolvency suggests a lack of

---

[43] Doug Frazey, 'Case Note: When "Good Cause" Goes Bad: Minnesota Restricts Protection for Dealers under HUMEDA – River Valley Truck Ctr., Inc V. Interstate Cos' (2006–2007) 33(2) *William Mitchell Law Review* 711, 728 quoting David Hess, 'Comment, The Iowa Franchise Act: Towards Protecting Reasonable Expectations of Franchisees and Franchisors' (1995) 80 *Iowa Law Review* 333, 355

[44] Sarah B Foster and Carolyn Johnsen, 'The War of the Worlds: Bankruptcy Versus…' (Paper presented at the American Bar Association, 28th Annual Forum on Franchising, Florida, 19–21 October 2005) 1

[45] Sarah B Foster and Carolyn Johnsen, 'The War of the Worlds: Bankruptcy Versus…' (Paper presented at the American Bar Association, 28th Annual Forum on Franchising, Florida, 19–21 October 2005) 1

[46] Craig R Tractenberg, 'What the Franchise Lawyer Needs to Know About Bankruptcy' (2000–2001) (3)20 *Franchise Law Journal* 3

[47] REDgroup Retail Pty Limited and Associated Companies (administrators appointed) report by administrators pursuant to Section 439A(4)(a) of the Corporations Act 2001 S Sherman, J Melluish and J Lindholm, Ferrier Hodgson, 25 July 2011, 6. Fig 8.1 based on diagram in this report

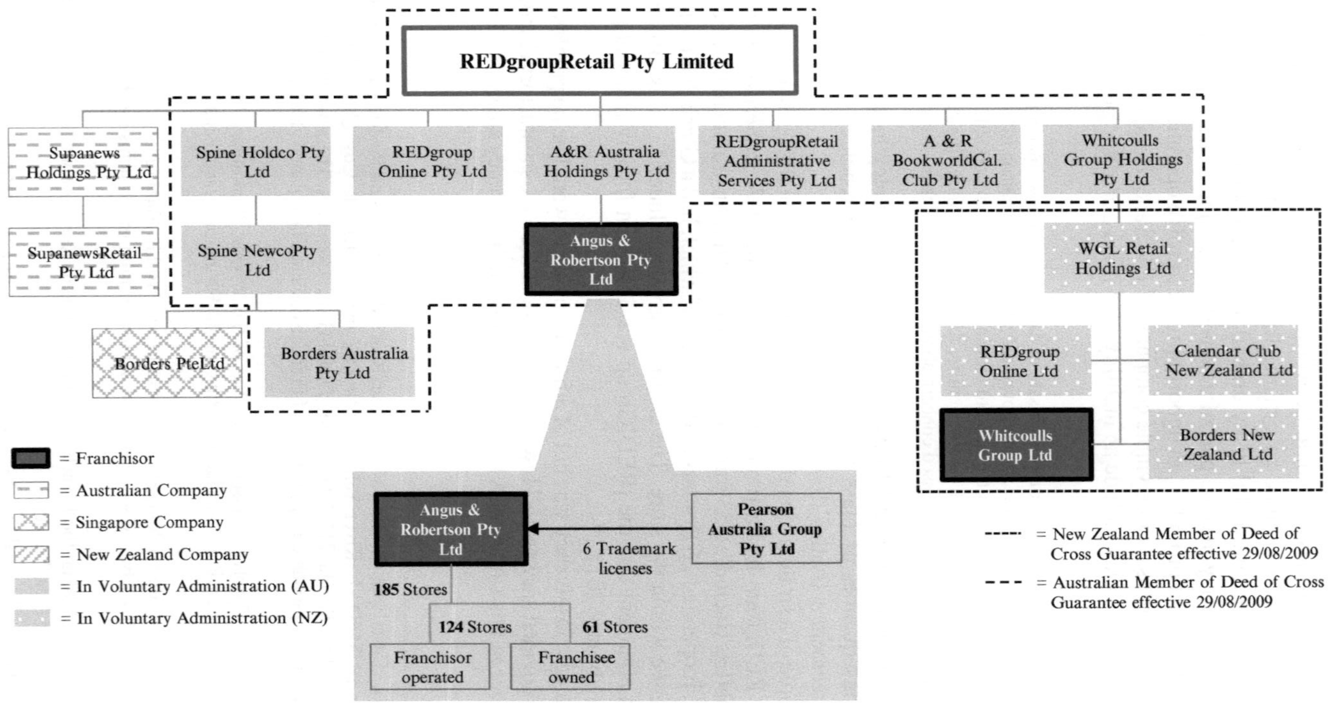


**Fig. 8.1** REDgroup: Adapted from diagram in REDgroup Retail Pty Limited and Associated Companies (administrators appointed) report by administrators pursuant to Section 439A(4)(a) of the Corporations Act 2001 S Sherman, J Melluish and J Lindholm, Ferrier Hodgson, 25 July 2011, 6

fairness and good faith towards franchisees. It is a variant of 'the "capricious termination" problem that was identified by Harold Brown in 1973 as the Achilles Heel of the entire franchising industry'.[48]

## Indicators of Impending Franchisor Insolvency

In the immediate pre-insolvency phase, the franchisor's own employees are likely to become aware of the precarious nature of the franchisor's business before the franchisees do because employees notice irregularities in their wages and hear 'in-house' whispers. Because the money flows from franchisee to franchisor in most cases, this unofficial early warning system of cash flow problems being exposed may not be available to franchisees. Franchisees may not become aware of the franchisor's position until:

- A supplier changes the terms of trade.[49] The flow-on effects of the franchisor not receiving previously favourable trading terms will be noticeable to franchisees that are required to source stock or other services through their franchisor.
- A landlord locks them out of their shop because the franchisor has not passed on the rent it has collected from the franchisee/licensee or franchisee/subtenant.
- The franchisor becomes unable to deliver on its contractual obligations to provide advertising support.[50]
- The franchisee learns of the franchisor's financial difficulty through the media.

However, as Canadian insolvency litigator Craig R Colraine points out, even though the signals that a franchisor's business is not trading solidly may be clear[51] to someone with full access to the franchisor's accounts, '[i]dentifying financial problems in non-publicly traded corporations is more difficult'.[52] Franchisees may

[48] Brown H, Franchising: Realities and Remedies (1973) 40 cited in Hunt SD, 'Franchising: Promises, Problems, Prospects' (1977) 53(3) *Journal of Retailing* 71, 77

[49] Michael C Jensen and William H Meckling, 'Theory of the Firm: Managerial Behavior, Agency Costs and Ownership Structure' (1976) 3(4) *Journal of Financial Economics* 305, 341 notes that '[a]s the probability of bankruptcy increases both the operating costs and the revenues of the firm are adversely affected'

[50] Craig Robin Colraine, 'Franchises: Insolvency and Restructuring' (Paper presented at the Distribution Law: Catch the Wave, Avoid the Rocks, Ontario Bar Association Continuing Legal Education, Toronto, Canada, 26 May 2003) 3

[51] Poor financial performance, including the accumulation of significant debt when the franchise system is not expanding, growing operating losses, the writing down of assets and refinancings, is an obvious indication [to the financially literate] that a franchise is in difficulty. In Craig Robin Colraine, 'Franchises: Insolvency and Restructuring' (Paper presented at the Distribution Law: Catch the Wave, Avoid the Rocks, Ontario Bar Association Continuing Legal Education, Toronto, Canada, 26 May 2003) 3

[52] Craig Robin Colraine, 'Franchises: Insolvency and Restructuring' (Paper presented at the Distribution Law: Catch the Wave, Avoid the Rocks, Ontario Bar Association Continuing Legal Education, Toronto, Canada, 26 May 2003) 3

suddenly find themselves having to pay cash on delivery for stock or managing hostile landlords where the franchisor has failed to pay costs incurred in relation to the franchisees' business – paid on time by franchisees to franchisor and then not on-paid to the suppliers on time. For example, a BHG franchisee discovered the franchisor had failed to pay the local advertiser, so the advertiser refused to deal with the franchisee until the franchisee got to the bottom of the problem and arranged direct payment from franchisee to supplier.

The significance of litigation as an early indicator of failure was identified in a Dun & Bradstreet Corporate Health Watch survey. It was concluded from the survey results that '[c]ompanies that have had legal action taken against them are nearly eight times more likely to fail than those that haven't'.[53] Further research would reveal whether the threat of franchisee litigation caused the franchisor to consider pre-emptive or strategic bankruptcy or whether the litigation caused the subsequent failure of the franchisor.

The number of franchisees at the time of the franchisor failure is not a true representation of franchisees affected by the failure as many may have already left the network, disenchanted at the lack of franchisor support, slow stock deliveries or other problems symptomatic of impending business failure. Hence, premature franchisee exits may also be an indicator of impending failure.

Consistent with Lafontaine and Shaw's conclusions,[54] franchise networks of any age and structure can fail. Failed franchisors in Australia include:

- Public companies and entities wholly owned by public companies (drive-in car wash business CarLovers, travel agent Traveland, retail gadget shop Danoz)
- Proprietary companies (retail mid-range jewellery franchise Kleins, Top Snack Foods)
- Groups of franchisors assembled by venture capitalists (REDgroup comprising Angus & Robertson)
- Long established businesses (Kleins Jewellery had been in business, for 25 years; Collins Booksellers, 76 years; Speeds Shoes, 94 years. None of these businesses had been franchising the entire time)
- Franchisors of short duration (A1 Mobile Radiator Repairs and Danoz Directions which ceased operations within 2 years of establishment)
- Franchisors with hundreds of franchisees (NoRegrets with 600, Traveland with 270)
- Businesses requiring franchisees to invest high sunk costs (Kleins, Kleenmaid ($400,000), Stockmans Australian Café, Cut Price Deli)
- Those requiring small sunk costs (Furniture Wizard, conducted from the franchisees' residential garages)

---

[53] 'Warning Signs of Failure', The Australian Financial Review (Sydney), 2 May 2006

[54] Francine Lafontaine and K L Shaw, 'Franchising Growth and Franchisor Entry and Exit in the US Market: Myth and Reality' (1998) 13(2) *Journal of Business Venturing* 95, in Frank Hoy and John Stanworth (eds), *Franchising: An International Perspective* (2003) 163

- Franchisors established before Australia's Code was introduced in 1998 (Cut Price Deli, Century 21, Great Australian Ice Creamery)
- Those established post the enactment of the Code (Kleins, Danoz, Trimit)
- Franchisors with franchisees operating as commission agents (gym business Beach House Group, Kleenmaid)
- Franchisees who pay royalties to their franchisor (the usual franchise model)
- Australian master franchisees of overseas-based franchisors (Kernels Popcorn from Canada, Delifrance from Singapore, Midas and Hooters from the USA).

## Case Study: Angus & Robertson

Some of the problems that arise when an administrator is appointed will now be demonstrated through a case study of a franchisor failure that started in the USA and quickly spread to Australia, New Zealand and Singapore. David Angus and George Robertson started selling books together in Australia in 1886. Angus & Robertson began franchising in 1977. The progression of their bookselling business is demonstrated in Fig. 8.2. The administrator was appointed in 2011.

As Fig. 8.2 shows, Angus & Robertson traded for over 100 years before its first merger in 1990. Thereafter, it experienced continued development until being purchased by a venture capitalist Pacific Equity Partners in 2004. The venture capitalist formed REDgroup Retail Pty Ltd. ('REDgroup') in 2009 and loaned it $138 m, secured over five bookselling brands including franchisor Angus & Robertson. By August 2009, REDgroup had 20% of the Australian book market.

Mr and Mrs Appleby bought two A&R franchised bookstores on Queensland's Gold Coast in November 2010. This timing enabled them to capitalise on the peak pre-Christmas trading period for booksellers. Many customers would have chosen gift vouchers as Christmas gifts and would have expected these could be redeemed at any of the 185 Angus & Robertson stores. Unbeknown to the employees or franchisees of A&R, by late 2010, it was becoming clear to the shareholders that all was not well in the REDgroup. Little could the Applebys guess that at 3 p.m. on 17 February 2011, only 2 hours after completing their franchisee induction at REDgroup Retail network's head office in Melbourne, their bank manager would call to tell them their franchisor, A&R, a subsidiary of REDgroup Retail Pty Limited, had entered administration.[55]

'At the time REDgroup was placed into administration by majority owners Pacific Equity Partners ('PEP'), it had 260 Borders, Angus & Robertson[56] and Whitcoulls stores in Australia, New Zealand and Singapore'[57] and owed 'an

[55] Sunshine Coast Daily 'Good staff and family support see stores write another chapter: Light at end of the tunnel', 13 September 2011, 20

[56] 48 franchisee owned and 137 franchisor owned and operated

[57] Chris Zappone, Booksellers' woes worsen as franchisees seek to defect, Sydney Morning Herald, 5 April 2011

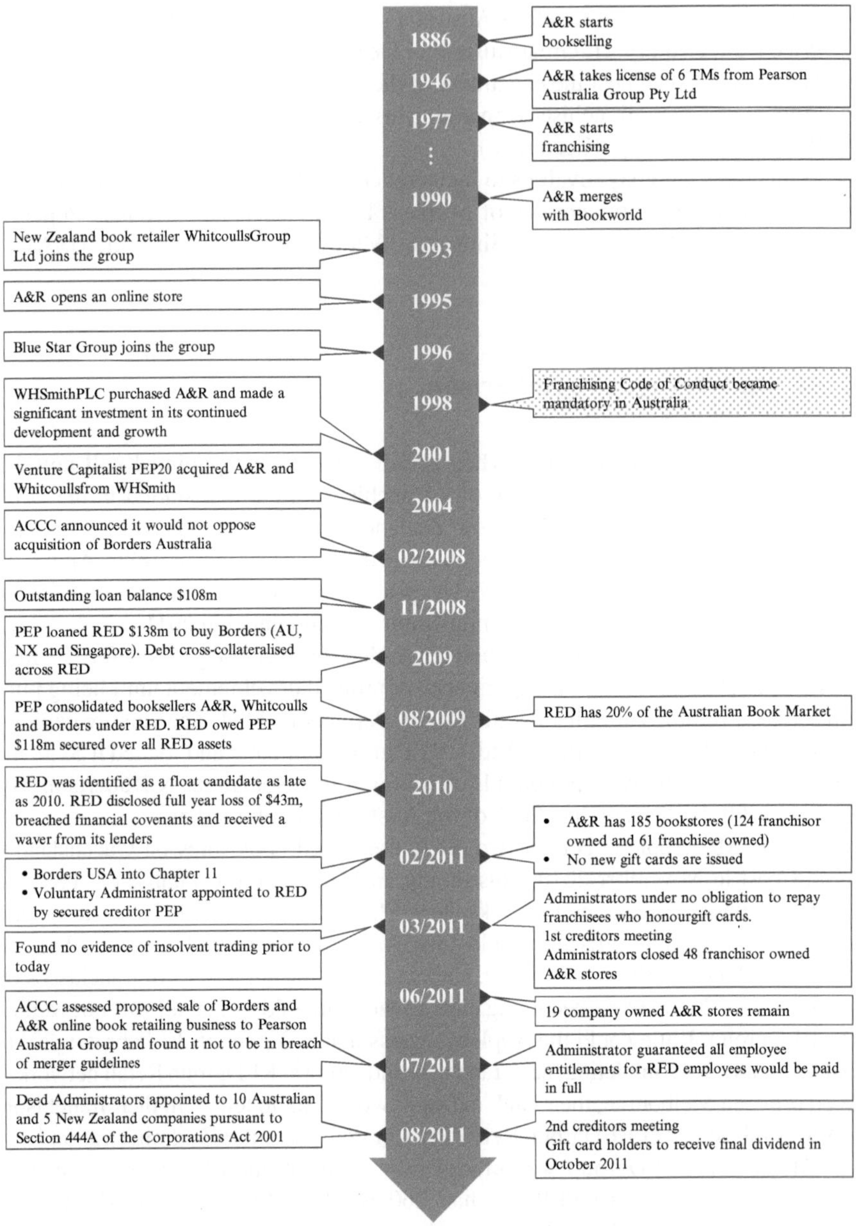


**Fig. 8.2** Rise and fall of Angus & Robertson

estimated $170 million'.[58] 'The REDgroup businesses in New Zealand [were] progressively sold down over the 4-month administration'[59] to three buyers separately interested in university campus, airport and shopping centre locations. The Australian online business was sold to the owner of the Angus & Robertson registered trademarks. The buyer had owned the marks since they were first registered.

In Australia, the administrators worked with the A&R franchisees and two potential buyers. By 17 June 2011, 4 months after the administrators had been appointed, a further 42 company-owned stores had been closed, leaving 19 company-owned stores and 48 franchisee-owned stores operating.[60] The administrators identified the A&R franchise agreements as saleable assets. Accordingly, the franchisees were required to continue trading while the administrators sought a buyer for the businesses or any of their component parts.

During the administration, the administrators were granted additional time by the court to hold the second meeting of creditors.[61] This is common in a franchisor administration and enables administrators to identify and negotiate with parties possibly interested in purchasing parts of the troubled business. It places the franchisees in limbo for several months.

Franchisees continued to follow the administrators' directions and await their fate while trading as well as they could. From the administrators' perspective, franchisees 'continue[d] to trade as normal'[62] during the administration. Following the appointment of the administrator, franchisees were told the administrators would not be responsible for redeemed gift certificates, and the franchisees experienced a 50% decline in sales. Despite the lack of ongoing support by the franchisor, post-administration royalties and marketing contributions payable by franchisees contributed $226,518 to the administrators' pool of funds available to pay REDgroup's employees and the costs of the administration. The company-owned stores were used as outlets to sell books at heavy discounts to the public. Ultimately, 'stock realisations [by the administrators were] sufficient to pay in full all employee entitlements, totalling approximately $11.7 million'.[63] Unsecured creditors who ranked below employees in the insolvency priorities, including franchisees, by implication received little or nothing.

---

[58] http://www.franchiseadvice.com.au/index.php?option=com_content&task=view&id=247&Itemid=1 Accessed 2011

[59] Ferrier Hodgson press release 'REDgroup redundancies' 30 May 2011

[60] Meeting on potential sale of Angus & Robertson underway, Smartcompany, 17 June 2011

[61] Australia: *Corporations Regulations* 5.6.12, the first creditors meeting must be held within 5 business days of the administrator's appointment. The second creditors meeting is generally required to be held within 21 days of the appointment of the administrator, but the court has discretion to delay this meeting if the administrators provide compelling reasons

[62] Ferrier Hodgson Press Release, 'Negotiations underway for sale of Angus & Robertson bookstores' 15 June 2011

[63] Ferrier Hodgson press release 'Second Meeting of REDgroup creditors', 27 July 2011

## *Collateral Damage: Gloria Jean's Within Borders Stores*

> When it comes to companies going bust, the insolvency of a franchise is usually about as shambolic as you can get. Of all insolvency matters, the most difficult is the failure of a franchise group… There are always problems with the Franchise Code, always leasing problems and unforeseen third party issues.[64]

A new unforseen dimension unfolded when Borders failed in Australia. Media reported that '14 [solvent] in-store Gloria Jean's coffee houses will be forced to shut after Borders stores were forced to cease trading by administrators'.[65] The superstore idea Borders had pursued led to Gloria Jean's (GJs) cafes co-branding with some Borders stores. A GJs franchisee pays (in 2008) $59,000 to secure licence to use TMs, $12,000 initial training and $300–$500,000 to fit out and start running a GJ's café. The GJ's franchisor assists franchisees by sourcing sites or assisting in the selection process of site; it secures the location and negotiates basic lease terms. By early 2011, 30% of the Borders US stores were unprofitable, losing $US2m/day. When problems in the USA spread to Australia, the G's franchisees located within the Borders stores were affected.

Fourteen franchisees bore the brunt of the problem. They would not have been involved in establishing the co-branding; that is a strategic decision made franchisor to franchisor. Although Gloria Jean's franchisor worked hard to try to ensure the 14 affected cafes would not have to close, they were fighting an uphill battle. There were already several G's in locations near to the Borders stores. This meant there were limited territories available for affected franchisees to relocate to. If the head lease is held by Borders, with a licence to GJs to occupy space within the Borders store, that right to occupy is lost when the Borders lease is disclaimed. Even if the GJs franchisee was able to remain in its site, the location is not attractive without the captive clientele of book buyers. Anecdotal evidence is that 12 of the 14 affected cafes closed, one remained in its location without Borders and one stayed in business in a new location. Co-branded franchisees have no claim on the Borders insolvent estate.

## Franchisees in the Franchisors Insolvency

Regulatory action against the franchisor in particular may give adverse publicity to the franchise that in itself will impact on the franchisee and its customers. The public will not distinguish between the franchisor and the franchisees.

The inability of franchisees to protect themselves as individuals from franchisor-created risks arises through the complexity of the twenty-first-century franchise network.

---

[64] D. Binning, Code Wars – a liquidator's worst fears, Australian Financial Review, 29 June 2006. Special Report, at 13, quoting David Cowling, insolvency partner with law firm Clayton Utz

[65] Gloria Jean's storm brews, 8 April 2011, News Ltd

For example, 'the franchisor' in Angus & Robertson Pty Ltd., a proprietary company, is one of 18 companies and trusts operating in three countries and controlled by parent REDgroup Retail Pty Ltd. A second example of a franchisor being part of a complex network of entities is Kleenmaid. Administrators were appointed to Kleenmaid in 2009. Kleenmaid operated through 15 companies structured as two corporate groups of which all but one company were placed into administration. Kleenmaid's administrator concluded that the groups had been insolvent since June 2007, possibly earlier.[66]

The franchisor's insolvency does not give franchisees the ability to walk away from the franchise or terminate contracts with third parties unless the contracts contain appropriate *ipso facto* clauses. Unlike an employee or supplier, franchisees have few choices except to ride the administration out with their fingers crossed. They must continue to honour their obligations under the franchise agreement and also continue to meet upstream and downstream contractual obligations.

As Jensen and Meckling point out, 'in certain kinds of durable goods industries the demand function for the firm's product will not be independent of the probability of bankruptcy.'[67] In franchising, the demand for the early morning take-away coffee sold by a franchisee where payment and supply is completed within a minute will be unaffected by the franchisor's impending or actual financial woes as long as the franchisee is able to retain its premises. Customers will continue to patronise the franchisee so long as they like the coffee. Only if the franchisee's business closes, will the customers patronise another cafe. By contrast, the demand for expensive items supported by long-term warranties, such as motor vehicles or white ware that will be bailed by the franchisor or franchisee until a builder needs to take delivery or products and services like travel, hotel or rental car bookings made and paid for now with delivery in the future, will be adversely affected as consumers prefer to deal with solvent suppliers.

Logically, given the issues of the franchisor not being an entity that necessarily has control over its own destiny, the franchisees' relationships with owners of trademarks and landlords, the franchise agreement's inability to be negotiated and the resulting contract imbalance, other asymmetrical features of the franchise relationship, and the positioning of franchisees outside the corporate governance concerns of franchisors, it is not surprising that franchisees are awkwardly positioned if the franchisor fails.

For the bulk of the franchisee's investment, it is not a creditor of the franchisor. Most of the franchisee's investment is in the form of the initial franchise fee, sunk costs and ongoing liabilities to third parties.

---

[66] Deloitte, The Kleenmaid Group (Administrators Appointed) Administrators' Report to Creditors Pursuant to Section 439A Corporations Act 2001, 14 May, 2009

[67] Michael C Jensen and William H Meckling, 'Theory of the Firm: Managerial Behavior, Agency Costs and Ownership Structure' (1976) 3(4) *Journal of Financial Economics* 305, 341

## What Would Make a Franchisee a Debtor?

Most franchisees will owe some money to their franchisor in the form of the current royalty payment. They are, thus, likely to be a debtor for small sums of money. In a typical case where the franchisor leases the premises from a landlord and then sub-leases to the franchisee, the franchisor's insolvency will be an event of default by the franchisor/head lessee. This would provide the landlord with a contractual right to terminate the lease. The consequences for the franchisee sub-lessee or licensee are potentially severe. The landlord would have the right to simultaneously evict the franchisee and call up the rental guarantee given by the franchisee.

## What Would Make a Franchisee a Creditor?

The franchisee is seldom in a position of being a secured creditor; bargaining power in franchise negotiations does not generally permit this outcome. The mechanics of each franchisor taking its own security over the assets of the franchisor would be impractical in any event. There may be more particular and quantifiable claims as creditor. Franchisees pay a fee on entry into a franchise. If this was, for the sake of example, $50,000 for a 5-year term and the franchisor failed 1 year into the franchisee's term, there is arguably $40,000 worth of unsupplied service by the franchisor. In the USA, a franchisee is an unsecured creditor in the franchisor's insolvency for the unexpired portion of the pro-rated royalty.

A&R franchisees became unsecured creditors for the face value of any unredeemed gift cards. Franchisees would also be creditors, probably unsecured, if they had engaged in mediation with the franchisor, and the resulting contract stipulated that the franchisor would pay the franchisee.

The opportunity to recover sunk costs following the franchisor's insolvency varies greatly – a franchisee establishing a retail outlet will not be able to recover sunk costs if the franchisor fails and the premises lease is disclaimed, whereas a franchisee will find a market for a second-hand vehicle or lawn mower more readily. A franchisee with low exposure to fixed premises or other purpose-built branded assets will be in a better position to mitigate its losses in relation to sunk costs.

One consequence of franchisees being commission agencies of an insolvent franchisor is demonstrated by the customers and franchisee of Beach House Group. One franchisee had 1,400 gym members when the administrators were appointed to its franchisor. Over time, the franchisee's customers had paid their membership levys of around $445 each direct to the franchisor. This provided the franchisor with approximately $620,000 from which it was bound to pay the franchisee a commission. The franchisee 'had no choice but to close as his cash flow dried up and debts hit more than $70,000....[He had been] ripped off, ...and ...can't even walk the streets "cause there are so many angry members".[68] Each of the 1,400 members would have been an unsecured creditor in the franchisor's administration. As the franchisor failed owing $20million, the members' chances of recovery looked bad.

Kleenmaid was another franchise arrangement structured as a commission agency. In this situation, franchisees are creditors for commission they are owed. Franchisees would also be creditors if they had purchased stock through the franchisor and items had been returned under warranty. Traveland franchisees were creditors for small sums because of the structure of travel insurance products. The franchisor may owe refunds to the franchisee that the franchisee itself has had to refund to its customers.

## What Franchisee Expenses Cannot Be Recovered?

Perhaps the most debilitating consequences for the franchisee are rights that may be exercised by the landlord or by the franchisor's administrator or liquidator. Franchisees vary in quality and potential value to an administrator. Franchisees that are new to the system and 'needy', or average performers, or those with another unattractive attribute may be seen as liabilities in the insolvency; for example, a franchisee may be a tenant in a retail shop whose head lease the franchisor has breached by becoming insolvent.

## Ongoing Rights and Obligations of Franchisees

It is difficult for franchisees to be proactive if they believe their franchisor is operating precariously. The franchise agreement and consequential contracts must be adhered to. 'Pending assumption or rejection [by the liquidator] the debtor [franchisor] is technically not required to perform the obligations under the executory contract, whereas the non-debtor party [the franchisee] is still required to perform'.[69]

A circular sent by the administrators to A&R franchisees headed 'Frequently Asked Questions' stated that the appointment of the administrators did not automatically terminate the franchise and that royalties should continue to be paid by direct debit from franchisees' banks, as usual. It advised of immediate operational changes such as reducing the value of existing gift cards and ceasing sale of new gift cards, advising franchisees not to replace faulty purchases [70] as company-owned stores are not accepting refunds. If a franchisee was owed money by the group of

---

[68] Julia Adler, Fury as Beach House gym at Northland shuts down, Preston leader, 3 March 2009

[69] Craig R Tractenberg, 'What the Franchise Lawyer Needs to Know About Bankruptcy' (2000–2001) (3)20 *Franchise Law Journal* 3, end note 22–5

[70] Although this refusal would constitute a breach of the warranties provisions of the *Competition and Consumer Act 2010* (Cth), no claimant could take action while the moratorium permitted under ss 444D and 444E of the *Corporations Act* was effective

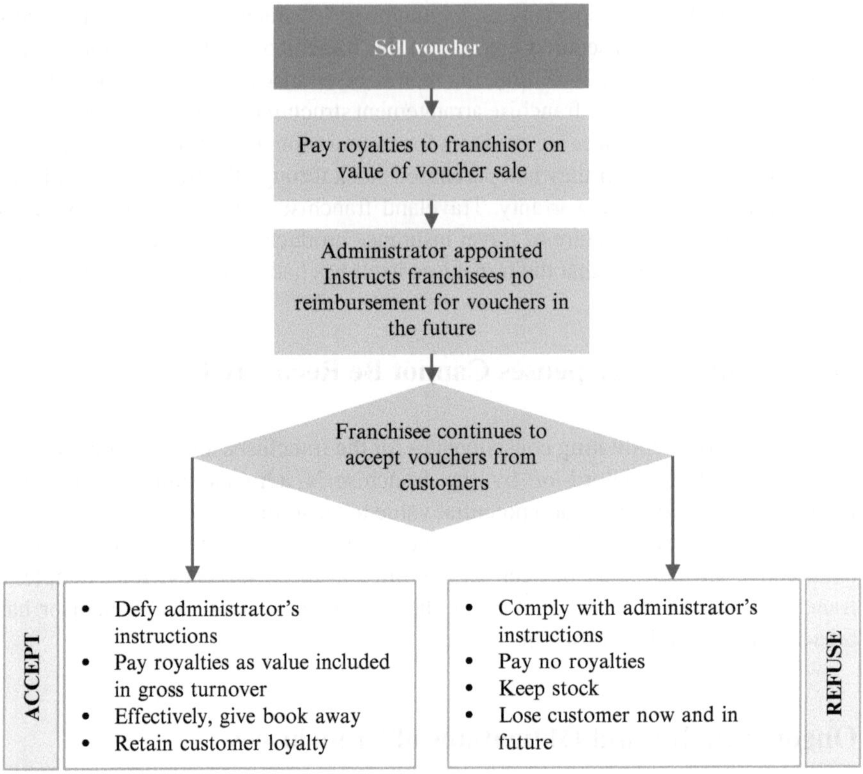


**Fig. 8.3** Gift card dilemma

entities in administration (including the franchisor), it would be an unsecured creditor for the amount owed and would be entitled to attend creditors meetings. Otherwise, franchisees had to continue to meet their contractual obligations but had no rights in the administration process.

Franchisee Mrs Appleby said, 'Not many people were aware we were privately-owned and they didn't understand the gift card situation. When we sold a gift card, A&R took that money off us straight away. We didn't get that money back until someone used that gift card and then we had to claim it back'.[71] Following the appointment of the administrators, '[t]he Applebys honoured A&R gift cards for as long as they could, despite the fact that they were not legally bound to and despite making a loss on them'.[72] Their dilemma in relation to gift cards is shown in Fig. 8.3.

Once the franchisor is in administration, the franchisee becomes an unsecured creditor for the value of any redeemed gift cards. The franchisor has already received

[71] Light at end of the tunnel: Good staff and family support see stores write another chapter, 13 September 2011, Sunshine Coast Daily, 20

[72] Light at end of the tunnel: Good staff and family support see stores write another chapter, 13 September 2011, Sunshine Coast Daily, 20

a royalty on the value of the gift card when it was originally sold and is now arguably unjustly enriched by the amount of that royalty.

## *Why Franchisor Angus & Robertson Failed*

Naturally there are differing views of what brought about Angus & Robertson's failure. The group's directors blamed everyone but themselves in attributing the failure of the REDgroup to '[s]ubdued discretionary consumer spending; the legislative framework in relation to the sale of books in Australia which limit[s] the ability of Australian booksellers to compete with overseas retailers due to

> [n]o Goods and Services Tax ('GST') … being added for Australian online consumers or overseas book purchases – whilst stores operating in Australia must add GST; Parallel importation restrictions …; The strong Australian dollar which had appreciated against the US dollar and the pound sterling by 20 per cent since September 2009 …; and Deep discounting and increased advertising … by discount department stores.[73]

The administrators agreed with the directors but added

> management buying decisions [with] more emphasis on 'buying' rather than 'selecting' stock resulting in overstocking with aged, poor stock; failure to recognize and promptly address loss making stores; under-utilisation of space in stores and poor organisation with no logical grouping and general lack of consistent business processes with little use and reference to signed off critical paths and event management cycles.[74]

A commentator offered a different perspective, suggesting that PEP saw:

> [v]oluntary administration … as a cost-effective way… to exit its ill-fated foray into book retailing. They knew what they were doing and they used the law to the maximum possible extent to extract everything they could out of it. … this was a staged exit.[75]

The likelihood that this was a strategic administration is given weight by the administrators' conclusion that there was no evidence of trading while insolvent, and that

> [d]espite preparing the company for a float or trade sale, last October … the company unveiled a full-year loss of $43 million for the 2009-10 year. The company, which is owned by private equity group PEP, was also forced to get a waiver from its lenders after breaching some of its financial covenants.[76]

---

[73] Ferrier Hodgson, REDgroup Retail Pty Limited and Associated Companies (Administrators Appointed) –Report by Administrators Pursuant to Section 439A(4)(a) of the *Corporations Act 2001*, 25 July 2011, 13–14

[74] Ferrier Hodgson, REDgroup Retail Pty Limited and Associated Companies (Administrators Appointed) –Report by Administrators Pursuant to Section 439A(4)(a) of the *Corporations Act 2001*, 25 July 2011, 13–14

[75] Jamie Gray, 4 August 2011, The New Zealand Herald

[76] Patrick Stafford, Borders Australia and Angus & Robertson Chains Collapse, Thursday, 17 February 2011 15:47 http://Www.Smartcompany.Com.Au/Retail/20110217-Borders-Australia-And-Angus-Robertson-Chains-Collapse.Html viewed 6 October, 2011

Voluntary administration thus provided an opportunity for the venture capitalist PEP to exit its investment when the financial climate did not permit it to exit by floating the REDgroup.

## *Should Franchisees Have Anticipated Insolvency?*

The front page of the disclosure every Australian franchisee receives warns

> franchising is a business and, like any business, the franchise (or franchisor) could fail during the franchise term. [In a masterful understatement it continues with the words,] [t]his could have consequences for the franchisee.

A short warning at the point in the relationship when the franchisee is psychologically committed to proceeding is unlikely to ring alarm bells. By analogy to a contract situation,

> [t]he more unreasonable a clause is, the greater the notice which must be given of it. Some clauses … would need to be printed in red ink on the fact of the document with a red hand pointing to it before the notice could be held to be sufficient.[77]

The Australian franchisor is not required to reinforce the statutory caution by identifying the possible consequences of its entering administration or becoming insolvent for the individual franchisee. Those consequences differ for each franchise network depending on the role of the franchisor in supplying premises, stock and on whether the franchisor/franchisee relationship is based on the franchisee paying royalties to or receiving commission from the franchisor. A franchisor is the only party that knows how it structures its own business, which risks it passes to franchisees and what the consequences of its failure might be for each franchisee. These cannot be foreseen by an inexperienced franchisee or an inexperienced adviser. The existing cursory warning may encourage a franchisee to shelter some of its personal assets from the business debts, but a franchisee's ability to do so would depend on the amount of debt needed to purchase the business and the amount of security other than personal assets that was available.

Rod Sims, chair of the ACCC, observes that 'franchisees are often couples [like the Applebys] or individuals, many of whom enter the franchising relationship without a great deal of business experience but nevertheless invest large sums of money – and sometimes their nest egg … without doing sufficient due-diligence checks'.[78] While these observations are well founded, no amount of due diligence

---

[77] *J Spurling Ltd v. Bradshaw*, 2 ALL ER 121, 125 (PC) 1956 referred to in Steinberg, Paul and Lescatre, Gerald, 'Beguiling Heresy: Regulating the Franchise Relationship' (2004) 109(1) *Pennsylvania State Law Review* 1, 299

[78] Lesley Parker, Do the numbers stack up? Sydney Morning Herald *November 2, 2011* quoting Rode Sims, chair of the Australian Competition and Consumer Commission http://www.smh.com.au/small-business/franchising/do-the-numbers-stack-up-20111102-1muio.html#ixzz1flnN2HE5 viewed 7 December 2011

can anticipate the events that precede some franchisor administrations, as discussed in Chaps. 2, 3, 4 and 5.

Buyers of A&R franchises, for example, would be forgiven for believing A&R knew the book trade and knew franchising. After all, A&R began franchising 34 years ago. Many franchisees would have entered the A&R system before PEP became the owner and before the existence of REDgroup. Those that knew of the involvement of the PEP might have been reassured to read that PEP was described as 'a leading Australasian private equity firm focusing on buyouts and late stage expansion capital in Australia and New Zealand that assists businesses move closer to their 'full potential'. [79]

REDgroup took out a loan with Pacific Equity Partners Fund IV, LP, for $138 million to complete the acquisition of Borders. 'The debt due to PEP is cross-collateralised across the group. PEP has lodged a Proof of Debt in the Administration of each company for $118,547,419'.[80] The franchisees would have had no knowledge of this debt or the manner in which it was secured. Because of the absence of corporate governance obligations between franchisees and franchisors, the franchisees have no role in deciding who owns the franchisor or what debt burden the franchise network assumes.

At a personal level, the Applebys 'had done a tour of the office [the same day the administrator was appointed], [the REDgroup] had welcomed us, the CEO had been in to talk to us the day before,' … 'And [Mrs Appleby said] call me naive, but I can't believe that any of the staff in that building on that day knew. Not the day-to-day workers'.[81] Neither the Applebys nor any of the other franchisees could have anticipated the financial state of the owner of the franchisor or the appointment of the administrator.

## *Retail Lease Issues*

In exercising his or her statutory duty, the liquidator will determine whether each contract is a liability or an asset. If the franchisor holds the head lease, the liquidator's right to disclaim onerous property has implications for the franchisee. The franchisees lost their right to trade from the premises.

The parties to a retail lease are free to negotiate and include a response to franchisor insolvency in their lease contract. Privity of contract may not exist between the owner of the premises and the tenant franchisee. This increases the franchisees' vulnerability if the franchisor becomes insolvent in three ways: (1) franchisees will

---

[79] https://www.pep.com.au/pages/default.asp Accessed 3 November 2011

[80] Ferrier Hodgson, REDgroup Retail Pty Limited and Associated Companies (Administrators Appointed) –Report by Administrators Pursuant to Section 439A(4)(a) of the *Corporations Act 2001*, 25 July 2011, 7

[81] Sunshine Coast Daily 'Good staff and family support see stores write another chapter: Light at end of the tunnel', 13 September 2011, 20

not be recognised as creditors in relation to their lost premises interests as there will be no contractual rights to connect their loss to the insolvency; (2) if they were a guarantor, the landlord will have made a legitimate call on the guarantee when the franchisor breached the lease, thereby depleting the franchisees' financial resources; and (3) they have lost the right to trade from the premises as result of the franchisor breaching the lease. For example, following the appointment of the administrator, one Beach House Group gym manager arrived at work following the appointment of the administrator and 'was greeted by … a sign on the door stating "Owner has repossessed the site under section 3D of the *Tenancy Act*. Closed until further notice"'.[82]

Returning to the franchisee premises occupancy models discussed in Chap. 3, it is worth considering the implications for franchisees' right to remain in their retail premises when their franchisor fails. The franchisee would have the best claim to retain the premises if it occupied its premises pursuant to the arrangements in Figs. 3.1, 3.2, 3.10 or 3.11. Under all other models, the franchisee would have, at best, a tenuous right to remain in the premises.

Registering ones interest under a lease on the title under the arrangements in Figs. 3.1 and 3.2 would preserve a franchisee's occupancy right while the franchisor was solvent. It would not do so if the franchisee's leasehold interest, if a liquidator decided the premises would fetch a better return for creditors if sold with vacant possession. In that case, the liquidator of an insolvent franchisor-premises owner could disclaim the lease.

In the Figs. 3.2, 3.4 and 3.6 arrangements, the implications for the franchisee if the franchisor entity fails depend on whether the related entity was in the pool of failed companies or survives the franchisor's insolvency without being wound up. If the franchisee still has a valid lease, but the franchise agreement has been disclaimed, the franchisee may find itself with a liability to pay rent to the end of the term, but no right to operate the business.

In the situation depicted in Fig. 3.10, while the benefits of leasing direct from the landlord are obvious for the franchisee, there may be a significant disadvantage. If the franchisor becomes insolvent, the franchisee has ongoing legal obligations under the lease, but the liquidator may disclaim the franchise agreement. If that were to occur, the franchisee would no longer be entitled to trade under the former franchisor's brand and would have to refit the premises. Disclaiming disentitles the franchisee to any benefits it was entitled to under the contract.

Even if the franchisee under Fig. 3.10 or 3.11 is not evicted as a consequence of the franchisor's failure, they can still suffer financially. Having renovated the premises to accommodate the franchisor's specific fit-out requirements, if the franchise agreement is disclaimed by the liquidator, the premises would have to be de-identified before the franchisee could continue trading from them.

---

[82] Nicole Jackson Patrons stunned by gym closure, La Trobe Valley Express 17 April 2008

In the worst-case scenario, a franchise may have recently bought into a franchise network that requires it make a significant investment sunk in the premises. It may also have provided a personal guarantee for the franchisor's head lease. The failing franchisor is likely to have used the franchisee's rent payments as a line of credit to prefer creditors other than the landlord. The landlord will simultaneously call on the franchisee's guarantee and terminate the head lease on two grounds – arrears of rent and outgoings (owed by the franchisor, paid to the franchisor by the franchisee but not passed on to the landlord) and administration or insolvency of the tenant (the franchisor).

Franchisees are not the only parties to suffer if they are unable to retain premises. From an administrator's perspective:

> [w]hilst a formal lease may exist over a property, if the mortgagee has not consented to the lease, the administrators issuing of rent redirection notices could be construed as giving consent. This may not be a desirable outcome [for the mortgagee] particularly where the preferred realisation strategy is to sell with vacant possession. In such a situation [short term] alternatives such as agreeing to a licence to occupy may be appropriate'.[83] 'It is common to find tenants in occupation that are either unknown to the mortgagee, or do not have the mortgagee's consent ... the existence of these tenants can negatively impact the potential value of the property ... the property might have greater value if marketed with vacant possession.[84]

## *Trademark Issues*

Trademarks are assets available to a franchisor's liquidators to sell to fund payments to creditors. They must attempt to obtain the highest possible price. A buyer of the trademarks may elect not to purchase the franchise agreements.

If the trademarks are not owned by the failed franchisor but by a third party, the franchisor's administration or insolvency may be an event of default under the trademark licence agreement. A third-party owner of the franchised trademarks may not wish to continue licensing to a franchisor that is demonstrably in financial difficulty.

'Much of a company's goodwill is associated with its name, which may be the subject of trade mark protection.[85] When the searches of the trademark registry were conducted, 2% of the franchisors had failed. Franchisees assume that they will continue to have the right to use the franchisors' trademarks so long as they adhere to

[83] Michael Fung and Melissa Humann 'Practical issues for controllers when dealing with occupied premises' 24(1) *Australian Insolvency Journal* 2012, 16, 17

[84] Michael Fung and Melissa Humann 'Practical issues for controllers when dealing with occupied premises' 24(1) *Australian Insolvency Journal* 2012, 16,18

[85] See Paul McGuinness, *Intellectual Property Commercialisation: a Business Manager's Companion* (LexisNexis Butterworths, 2003) 328

their contractual obligations. In the case of franchisor insolvency, this assumption is incorrect. If the trademark was owned by the failed franchisor company, it is a task of the liquidator to sell that trademark or maintain the goodwill of the name, if possible, in order to realise value for creditors. Trademarks provide an example of the difficulties liquidators face when trying to retain the franchise network as a cohesive trading entity. If franchisors own their trademarks and become insolvent, the trademark is an asset the liquidator could sell without needing to consult co-owners or franchisees.

The franchisor's intellectual property becomes an asset in the franchisor's liquidation. It is an asset, in the same way as franchise agreements are an asset – both are available to be sold by the liquidator for the best possible price, but they need not be sold to the same buyer. For example, the liquidator of Kleenmaid sold the name 'Kleenmaid' to an entity that did not buy any other part of the former Kleenmaid business.

> Compass Capital will now set up a new kitchen and laundry goods business using the Kleenmaid name. The Kleenmaid website will be updated by early next week with details about how people can buy products… Compass Capital acquired the right to Kleenmaid's brand and logo following [Kleenmaid's] collapse last year.[86]

An asset is only available for sale if it belongs to the debtor or another pooled entity controlled by the franchisor. If it is merely licensed to the debtor, then the act of bankruptcy will trigger a default in the licence agreement and entitle the trademark owner to terminate the licence. A third-party owner of the franchised trademarks may not wish to continue licensing to a franchisor that is demonstrably in financial difficulty. This leaves the liquidator in a position of having to decide whether to negotiate with the trademark owner for the right to continue using the trademarks. Where trademark owners live in foreign jurisdictions, it is expensive for liquidators to negotiate ongoing use rights for franchisees and only worth considering if a buyer wanted to keep the network together.

The implication of using trademarks as securities for loans is that they might be repossessed and on-sold to a new owner if the franchisor defaults on the loan. When I conducted searches of the trademark registry in 2006, 2.38% (8 franchisors) of the franchisor trademark owners had failed. Kleins, which failed since my research on trademarks was conducted, owed the National Australia Bank $20 million at the time it failed. The administrator said the Kleins trademark was part of the loan security by way of a fixed and floating charge. Only three of the 337 franchisors in the research sample had security interests registered against their trademarks.[87] This would mean the secured party would be a priority creditor in the franchisor's insolvency.

Even if the administrator or liquidator is able to retain the right for the franchisees to use the trademarks, 'the greatest difficulty for a financier in taking a security interest over a trademark is whether the trademark will retain its value once it has

[86] AAP, 'Compass Deal a Fresh Start for Kleenmaid', The Australian Financial Review (Sydney), 7 January 2010, 7

[87] The Athlete's Foot Australia P/L; Coldwell Banker Corporation (USA); Rams Home Loans P/L

ceased to be associated with the original business or company'.[88] If the crystallising event for the transfer of the trademark is insolvency, then it is likely that the value of the trademark will be severely damaged.[89]

For a master franchisee that has not registered its interest as an authorised user under the procedures established in the Trade Marks Act, the process of defending the trademarks that they in turn are licensing franchisees to use is more cumbersome. A greater degree of initiative will be required from the liquidator wishing to negotiate the right to ongoing use of the trademarks.

Unregistered trademarks are more difficult, expensive and time consuming than registered trademarks for liquidators to value, assert ownership over and sell.

## *International Dimensions*

Franchise relationships and agreements often contain international dimensions. This was identified in the pattern of trademark ownership at Chap. 3 and in Subway's standard franchise agreement referred to earlier. International law may have an impact on the jurisdiction and forum in which a franchise agreement is judged. Twenty-seven per cent of Australian-based franchisors[90] and 29% of French franchisors[91] reported they were franchising overseas in 2010. Although being exposed to more than one economy is a sound risk management strategy for a franchisor, operating across national borders does not guarantee the franchisor will remain solvent. Cross-border insolvency issues arise if the franchisor or a national master franchisor or the owner of the trademarks becomes insolvent. This leaves individual franchisees vulnerable. They are potentially unable to protect their investment and without rights under the franchise agreement.

Additional complications arise if the insolvent franchisor is actually the national master franchisee of an overseas-based franchisor. For example, the insolvency of the Kernels Popcorn Australian master franchisee in 2005 provided the opportunity for the Canadian franchisor to terminate the master licence. In the report to creditors in the Kernel's Popcorn insolvency, the administrators reported:

> [t]here were 24 Kernel's Extraordinary Popcorn stores [operating retail premises through model 7] of which 20 operated pursuant to franchise agreements. The company was also lessor of the following franchisee stores. … I was without funds … it was necessary for me to disclaim all of the company's leases on 24 March 2005.[92]

[88] See Paul McGuinness, *Intellectual Property Commercialisation: a Business Manager's Companion* (LexisNexis Butterworths, 2003) 328

[89] See Paul McGuinness, *Intellectual Property Commercialisation: a Business Manager's Companion* (LexisNexis Butterworths, 2003) 328

[90] L Frazer, S Weaven and K Bodey, *Franchising Australia 2010*, Griffith University

[91] Enquette Annuelle sur la franchise, Résultats 2010 Francais, 37

[92] 11 April 2005, ASIC Form 535 formal proof of debt or claim filed by the administrators pursuant to s 439A Corporations Act 2001 re Jatora Pty Ltd, formerly trading as Kernels Extraordinary Popcorn

So long as the master franchisee abides by the terms of its master franchise agreement and the head lease, the franchisee is not at risk of losing the premises unless the franchisee itself breaches the sublease. If the national master becomes insolvent, that is a breach of its master licence. This entitles the franchisor to terminate the agreement, thereby breaking the contractual nexus between the domestic franchisees and the overseas franchisor. The franchise agreement between the franchisee and the national master franchisee does not have to be novated to the overseas franchisor. Once the national master franchisee is insolvent, only a profound commitment to the brand would then motivate a replacement master franchisee to assume responsibility for all existing individual franchise agreements.

## Effectiveness of Current Law

Franchise agreements are executory contracts. In some jurisdictions, like Australia, this is irrelevant in the insolvency process. In others, like Canada, it can be relevant. A US lawyer writes that:

> [p]ending assumption or rejection [by the liquidator] the debtor [here, franchisor] is technically not required to perform the obligations under the executory contract, whereas the non-debtor party [here, the franchisee] is still required to perform.[93]

Securing meaningful remedies for breach of contract requires the breaching party to be solvent. We will see now how franchisor failure plays out through franchisees' contractual rights and remedies.

### Franchise Agreement Wording

The US website FreeFranchiseDocs[94] contains numerous standard franchise agreements and is a rich source of data. Seventy US franchise agreements were analysed to determine what a typical franchise agreement might say about insolvency. 'None of these agreements mentioned franchisor bankruptcy … In the same agreements, 23.5% were silent on the right for franchisors to terminate the agreement if the franchisee became bankrupt. Seventy-six per cent permitted the franchisor to terminate the franchise agreement, usually with no notice and no right to cure if the

[93] Craig R Tractenberg, 'What the Franchise Lawyer Needs to Know About Bankruptcy' (2000–2001) (3)20 *Franchise Law Journal* 3, end note 22–5

[94] Free Franchise Docs <http://www.freefranchisedocs.com/index.html> Accessed 5 June 2008

franchisee became bankrupt'.[95] In Australia, the *ex post* experience of a Traveland travel agency franchisee is consistent with the US findings:

> We'd just renewed the franchise agreements on our 4 [Traveland] outlets for 5 years when the franchisor's administrator was appointed. We went to see a QC to see if we could get out of the agreements and there was no way.[96]

The ideal world where 'negotiations between two … parties, … are designed to advance the wants and needs of each of those contracting parties'[97] does not describe the experience of franchisees. This failure to provide for an event which is demonstrably common is inexcusable. Common law contract theory lets franchisees down. In civil law countries however (for instance Germany), the bankruptcy of one party to a contract may constitute a 'good cause'[98] to immediately terminate the ongoing contract unless this is not permitted under the applicable insolvency law.

## Contract Law Actions

In theory, franchisees being parties to a contract have contract law available as a tool to challenge the administrators. In practice, it is difficult for a franchisor to breach a franchise agreement as the agreement imposes so few concrete obligations on franchisors. Franchisees without the appropriate *ipso facto* termination trigger in their franchise agreements have to decide whether to adopt the high-risk strategy of terminating their agreements or remaining bound to the failed franchisor in a legal 'holding pattern'. To pursue any litigated responses to breach of contract by the franchisor would tax an individual franchisee's resources. Litigation would be best undertaken by a group of franchisees.

In the absence of a breach of a term of the contract, a contract-based claim against a franchisor could be founded on anticipatory breach, the doctrine of frustration or on unjust enrichment. These possibilities are discussed below.

### Anticipatory Breach

Depending on the specific facts of each situation, some franchisees choose to plead 'anticipatory breach'. Franchisees may claim the franchisor has breached or will necessarily breach the franchise agreements in the future. Pleading anticipatory breach is a high-risk strategy that may require franchisees to tough it out in the face of vigorous opposition by administrators who would lose any right to claim ongoing

[95] J Buchan and B Butcher, 'Premises Occupancy Models for Franchised Retail Businesses in Australia: Factors for Consideration', (2009) 17(2) *Australian Property Law Journal* 143, 170

[96] Jenny Buchan and Lorelle Frazer, 'The Domino Effect – How Ansett's Failure Impacted on Traveland Academy of World Business' (Paper presented at the Marketing & Management Development Conference, Paris, 10–13 July 2006) 1901, 1906

[97] Lindy Willmott, Sharon Christensen, Des Butler, Bill Dixon, *Contract Law* (Oxford 3rd ed, 2009) 16

[98] http://www.iuscomp.org/gla/statutes/BGB.htm

royalties due under the franchise agreements if the franchisees were successful. The franchisees must be certain the administrator will not find a buyer for their agreements as that buyer might have been able to make good any breaches by the franchisor.

Anticipatory breach is a form of repudiation of contract that

> ...occurs where a party, prior to the time for performance under the contract, evinces an intention no longer to be bound by the contract. ... [I]f the anticipatory breach relates to a breach of an essential term or the repudiation goes to the root of the contract, the promisee [in this case, franchisee] may terminate prior to the time for actual performance.[99]

Consideration of anticipatory breach raises the issues of exactly what terms the franchisor breached. Typically, the franchisor has few contractual obligations, while the franchisee has many. It can be difficult to identify an actual contract term on which to found the claim of anticipatory breach following the appointment of an administrator. During the A&R administration, a group of 25 franchisees alleged the franchisor and the administrator had breached the franchise agreement by

> changing the terms on which franchisees could honour customers' gift cards issued up to 2 April, halting all gift card redemptions on 3 April, and, more generally, Angus & Robertson's failure to provide the services and benefits it is obliged to provide pursuant to the franchise agreement.[100]

The 25 were sued by the administrator. The matter was settled before trial. Because the matter was settled, it is unclear what specific breach of contract action the A&R franchisees relied on in making their decision to treat their franchise agreements as terminated by the franchisor.

### Frustration

Events may occur after a contract has been made which makes its performance pointless, more difficult or more costly or even impossible. Such events may result in the termination of the contract by operation of law, on the basis that it has been frustrated.

Frustration of a contract can only arise if the following conditions are met:

(a) The supervening event must cause a fundamental or radical change to the nature of the contractual rights and obligations.
(b) Neither party should have caused or brought about the supervening event.
(c) The supervening event must be such that it was not contemplated by the parties when they entered the contract. It follows, therefore, that there should be no provision in the contract designed to deal with it.

---

[99] Lindy Willmott, Sharon Christensen, Des Butler, Bill Dixon, *Contract Law* (Oxford University Press 3rd ed, 2009) 677

[100] Chris Zappone, Booksellers' woes worsen as franchisees seek to defect, Sydney Morning Herald, 5 April 2011

(d) It must be unjust to hold the parties to the contract to its terms as originally agreed upon.[101]

The failure of the franchisor will meet the first condition. The fundamental change from the franchisees' perspective is that the franchisor becomes unable to deliver on its side of the bargain. It may have lost the right to grant licences to franchisees to use the trademarks. It may have breached head leases that, in turn, deprive franchisees of their premises.

The franchise agreement is re-categorised as an asset or a liability. Whereas prior to the franchisor's liquidator being appointed, the franchisee was entitled to rely on the franchise agreement as a source of franchisor's obligations; from the time the liquidator is appointed, the franchisee has no right of access to remedies for breach of contract, and the liquidator is entitled to disclaim the franchise agreement as an onerous contract.

Condition (b) may preclude franchisees of some failed franchisors from accessing frustration as a cause of action. If, for example, the franchisor brought about its own failure by acting strategically or caused it by failing to manage its finances prudently, it is possible that franchisees may be prevented from claiming frustration.

Condition (c) is met in almost all franchise agreements. Solutions proposed in Chap. 9 would lead to franchisees being unable to access the remedy of frustration because all franchise agreements would address franchisor failure.

Whether condition (d) is met will depend on whose perspective is taken into account. From the administrator's perspective, it would be reasonable for the franchisee to be held to the contract, whereas for the franchisee, it may be unjust.

It is suggested that an Australian franchisee could not successfully argue frustration while the franchisor was under administration because the franchise agreement is between the franchisor or its assigns (which includes the administrator) and the franchisee.

It is also possible that the sale of the franchise network by a liquidator to an unsuitable buyer could frustrate the contract if *Penrith District Rugby League Football Club Ltd. v. Bradley Scott Fittler*[102] is applied. In that case, competition under a new league was found to be radically different from that contemplated by the contracts signed by Bradley Fittler and Matthew Sing ('the players'). A proposal to enter into new competitions and to transfer club's assets to new competition licensee discharged parties from further performance of contracts, and the innocent party (in this case the players) were not responsible for bringing about circumstances frustrating the contract. The contracts were held to have been frustrated.

[101] D Khoury and YS Yamouni, *Understanding Contract Law* (LexisNexis Butterworths 7th ed, 2007) 419

[102] BC9600163 NSWSC

Frustration has only been raised unsuccessfully in an Australian franchise case.[103] In Canada, a franchisee

> … sought rescission of its franchise agreement based upon fundamental breach. It also sought the return of the franchise fee, royalty fees and advertising fees paid to the franchisor. In considering the issue of fundamental breach and the numerous alleged breaches of the franchise agreement by the franchisor, the [British Columbia Supreme] Court found that the franchisee had obtained substantially what it bargained for under the franchise agreement and accordingly found that there was no fundamental breach of the agreement.[104]

Goldman explains this particular decision stating

> [w]hether a fundamental breach argument has any chance of success is fact dependent. The greater the benefit that the franchisee has already received from being part of the franchised system, the less likely that the franchisor's bankruptcy will be found to have fundamentally breached the franchise agreement.[105]

### Unjust Enrichment

Alternatively, franchisees could make out a claim in quasi-contract against the franchisee or its administrator or liquidator for unjust enrichment. This action would theoretically be available to franchisees in Australia, though it has not been tested in the context of insolvency in Australian courts. It depends firstly on the court granting consent to franchisees to embark on litigation against the administrator or liquidator or against the directors or solvent-related entities of the failed franchisor. Success in a restitutionary claim based on unjust enrichment depends on the plaintiff establishing the following elements:

(a) Benefit or enrichment [defendant has been enriched by the receipt of a benefit – in the case of the franchisor, upfront fee that was charged for the right to conduct a franchise for, say, 5 years, but the franchisor became insolvent after 2 years – 3/5 of the initial franchise fee could be the starting point].
(b) The benefit or enrichment has been obtained at the plaintiff's expense.
(c) Unjust factor (unjust to allow the defendant to retain the benefit).
(d) No bars exist to the restitutionary claim.

To succeed in a restitutionary claim, all these elements must be satisfied. In the first instance, the plaintiff must prove elements (a–c) on the balance of probabilities. In many cases, this would be sufficient. Generally speaking, it is up to the defendant [liquidator] to raise the issue of a bar to restitution. Then the plaintiff must prove

---

[103] *Otrava Pty Ltd v. Mail Boxes Etc (Australia) Pty Ltd* [2004] NSWSC 1066

[104] Steven H Goldman, *Tackling Troublesome Insolvency Issues for Franchisees* (2003) Unpublished 3–6 <http://www.goldmanrosen.com/pdf/franchiseesinsolvency1.pdf> Accessed 29 April 2007. Goldman's paper outlines 10 specific strategies franchisees may attempt to put in place, 11

[105] Steven H Goldman, *Tackling Troublesome Insolvency Issues for Franchisees* (2003) Unpublished 3–6 <http://www.goldmanrosen.com/pdf/franchiseesinsolvency1.pdf> Accessed 29 April 2007. Goldman's paper outlines 10 specific strategies franchisees may attempt to put in place, 12

element (d). If, on the balance of probabilities, the court is not satisfied that there is no bar to a restitutionary claim, then the plaintiff fails.[106]

The use of an unjust enrichment action could be considered by franchisees that recently paid a franchise fee but derived very little benefit prior to the franchisor's failure. The pool of money available to the liquidator to pay creditors is artificially expanded by the franchise fee; thus, the liquidator is 'unjustly enriched'. This was pleaded by a group of franchisees in Ontario, Canada, in one of the Country Style Food Services cases.[107] There, while the franchisees did not act quickly or cohesively enough to succeed, the court did not rule out unjust enrichment as a possible cause of action for future franchisor insolvency cases.

Both the action for frustration and the action for unjust enrichment may have the best chance of success where the franchise term has only just begun, as the franchisee will have paid all upfront costs but derived minimal benefit from the investment.

## Contract and Quasi-Contract Remedies

Franchisees' access to remedies for breach of contract brought about by the failure of the franchisor is hindered by a number of factors.

First, contract law relies on the doctrine of privity of contract. The law presumes that franchisees and franchisors have a contractual relationship with each other and that this contract is the source of the breach. This does not acknowledge the complex matrix of contracts and entities that comprise the franchise network and the franchise system. The commitments that a franchisee has under third-party contracts are not contingent on the franchisors' remaining solvent.

Second, Hadfield observes, the contract law is of limited effectiveness 'when [it] is limited to the awarding of damages, a remedy that may be inadequate to deter deliberate fraud and that may be no deterrence at all against those who have no assets'.[108] An award of damages is a costly pyrrhic victory if the other party is insolvent. Where the franchisor is insolvent, there is not enough money available to meet a judgment debt to put the 'innocent' party back into their pre-contractual situation.

---

[106] Philip Davenport and Christina Harris, *Unjust Enrichment* (Federation Press, 1997) 34

[107] *Country Style Food Services Cases: Country Style Food Services Inc v. 1304271 Ontario Ltd* Ontario Superior Court of Justice Chapnik J, Judgement: 11 February 2003; in the matter of the Companies Creditors Arrangement Act, RSC 1985 C c-36, as amended and in the matter of the Courts of Justice Act RSO 1990 c-43, as amended and in the matter of a plan of compromise or arrangement of Country Style Food Services Inc, Country Style Food Services Holdings Inc, Country Style Realty Limited, Melody Farms Specialty Foods and Equipment Limited, Buns Master Bakery Systems Inc. and Buns Master Bakery Realty Inc. 15 April 2002 Court of Appeal for Ontario Docket M28458 (unreported decision)

[108] Gillian K Hadfield, 'The Many Legal Institutions that Support Contractual Commitment' in Claude Menard and Mary Shirley (eds), *Handbook of New Institutional Economics* (2004) 175, 194

The problems are exacerbated when the number of franchisees affected by one franchisor insolvency is counted; the 'innocent parties' may include tens of franchisees. Any litigated or mediated victory by the franchisees will be hollow.

Third, the powers given to administrators and liquidators under the *Corporations Act* render franchisees' consumer protection and contract law rights impotent. This is explored in the remainder of Chap. 8.

Fourth, the franchisees' situation under any of the contracts signed as a consequence of becoming a franchisee will be impacted by the franchisor's failure in different ways to the impact on the franchise agreement. These contracts are likely to stand alone, with the franchisor's failure not providing justification to vary or terminate them.

The costs to franchisee consumers of a failed franchisor are often catastrophic, extending beyond loss of the franchised business to loss of their home (because of personal guarantees and loans secured over the franchisee's personal assets) and relationships. This is a strong example of Trebilcock's fourth characteristic introduced in Chap. 4 as the franchisor's administrator or liquidator is not appointed until after the franchisee has made the whole of its sunk investment. Satisfactory *ex post* relief is not available from an insolvent, asset-poor, debt-burdened franchisor.

## *Litigation Embargo During Administration*

In Australia, any action taken by any party other than the administrator needs to overcome the hurdle posed by *Corporations Act 2001* (Cth), section 440D, which imposes a limited stay of proceedings:

> (1) During the administration of a company, a proceeding in a court against the company or in relation to any of its property cannot be begun or proceeded with, except:
> (a) with the administrator's written consent; or
> (b) with the leave of the Court and in accordance with such terms (if any) as the Court imposes.

Nor are franchisees able to initiate proceedings without the consent of the court if a liquidator is appointed.

But, '[w]hile legal proceedings against the company are stayed, existing proceedings by the company are not stayed'.[109] Thus, the franchisees are vulnerable if they decide, for example, to stop paying franchise fees following the appointment of the administrator. The administrator may issue proceedings against franchisees without seeking leave of the court. Against this background, the effectiveness of statutory protection of franchisees in the face of misleading and deceptive conduct and protection through precontract disclosure requirement in the face of a franchisor's administration will now be considered.

---

[109] Michael Murray, *Keay's Insolvency: Personal and Corporate Law and Practice,* (Thomson Reuters 6th ed, 2008), 318

## Statutory Prohibition Against Misleading and Deceptive Conduct

Some franchisors sell franchises knowing the franchisor is financially distressed. Examples include retail jewellery franchisor Kleins sold franchises while it was clear that it was 'in trouble',[110] gym franchisor Beach House Group (BHG)[111] and white goods franchisor Kleenmaid that was said to be 'hopelessly insolvent'.[112] Kleenmaid's administrators reported '…each of the companies traded whilst insolvent prior to our appointment as Administrators. We are of the opinion that each of the companies in the group has been insolvent since March 2008'[113] and had thus been trading while insolvent for 13 months.

It is arguably misleading and deceptive conduct on the part of all involved in the sale and in breach of the *Australian Consumer Law* to continue to sell franchises when a franchisor suspects or knows it is insolvent or in financial difficulty. In an analogous case concerning an employee *Moss v. Lowe Hunt & Partners*,[114] Katzmann J held that it was misleading or deceptive to describe a business as 'successful' when, without the continued support of its parent company (which itself had difficulties), it would be insolvent. In the circumstances, the silence of defendant, its failure to disclose its financial predicament amounted to misleading and deceptive conduct.[115]

Like Mr. Moss's employer, the REDgroup continued selling franchises while the parent juggled finances at a high level until the administrators were appointed in February 2011. The REDgroup had the appearance of being a very well-organised, well-capitalised, geographically diversified, robust and focussed player in the retail bookselling world. Any franchisee joining the group prior to PEP's involvement in 2004 would have received a disclosure document that could not have mentioned PEP. Any joining before 2009 would have preceded the existence of the REDgroup.

Solvency information cannot be discovered other than through the level of due diligence no franchisee could be expected to conduct. An action for misleading and deceptive conduct could arguably be pursued against the franchisor's directors in

[110] 'Kleins collapse turns nasty' available at http://www.smartcompany.com.au/retail/cleins-collapse-turns-nasty.html. See also 'What happens if a franchisor fails' at http://www.birkettlong.co.uk/site/library/legalnews/what_happens_if_a_franchisor_fails.html.

[111] Cor Cordis Liquidators Report (19 October 2009) 13. In the opinion of BHG's liquidator, the franchisor was insolvent in 2005 and remained so from that time. BHG was still accepting franchise fees from new franchisees in the third quarter of 2006

[112] Richard Hughes, Liquidator, Deloittes, verbal observation at Griffith University franchising seminar

[113] Deloitte, Kleenmaid Group Report to Creditors pursuant to Section 508 of the *Corporations Act* 2001, 25 August 2010

[114] [2010] FCA 1181

[115] *Moss v. Lowe Hunt & Partners* [2010] FCA 1181, Katzmann J

person, the franchisor's bank if it was also the lender and the accountants that prepared the franchisor's disclosure document even if the franchisor was insolvent. Each of these people led the franchisee to believe the franchisor was solvent, and each had the power to discover that it was not.

## Disclosure Under Franchising Code of Conduct

In *Beer v. Personal Service Coffee Corp.*,[116] MacFarland J.A. observed

> [t]he focus of the [Arthur Wishart] Act is on protecting the interests of franchisees. The mechanism for doing so is the imposition of rigorous disclosure requirements and strict penalties for non-compliance. For that reason, any suggestion that these disclosure requirements or the penalties imposed for non-disclosure should be narrowly construed, must be met with scepticism.

McFarland went on to cite Winkler C.J.O in 'the recent case of *Salah v. Timothy's Coffees of the World Inc.*,[117] who wrote

> The Wishart Act is sui generis remedial legislation. It deserves a broad and generous interpretation. The purpose of the statute is clear: it is intended to redress the imbalance of power as between franchisor and franchisee; it is also intended to provide a remedy for abuses stemming from this imbalance. An interpretation of the statute which restricts damages to compensatory damages related solely to proven pecuniary losses would fly in the face of this policy initiative.[118]

Merely enacting situation-specific legislation is insufficient. The approach above reveals that at least in Ontario, the court recognises that protecting franchisees and their investments from the opportunities franchisor have to wilfully exploit or inadvertently mismanage a franchise system requires the courts to take a wide view in interpreting that legislation to ensure it fulfils its purpose.

Turning to a specific example, Angus & Robertson's disclosure in Australia would have disclosed over 250 items of information under 23 major headings. The disclosure items with the potential to reveal information about the franchisor, its plans and its apportioning of risk are the following: items (2) franchisor's details ('franchisor' and 'associate' identified here are defined terms), (3) franchisors' business experience, (4) litigation, (7) intellectual property (A&R would have revealed the existence of six registered trademarks used by Angus & Robertson), (9) supply of goods or services to a franchisee, (15) franchisor's obligations, and (18) obligation to sign related agreements. In short, a significant amount of information about

---

[116] (2005), 256 D.L.R. (4th) 466, [2005] O.J. No. 3043 (Ont. C.A.), at para. 28

[117] Ibid at para 32 citing 2010 ONCA 673, [2010] O.J. No. 4336 (Ont. C.A.) at para 26

[118] Trillium Motor World Ltd v. General Motors of Canada Ltd Trillium Motor World Ltd (plaintiff/moving party) and General Motors of Canada Limited and Cassels Brock & Blackwell LLP (defendants/respondents) Ontario Superior Court of Justice G.R. Strathy J. Heard: December 15–16, 2010, Judgement: March 1, 2011, Docket: CV-10-397096CP

the franchisor, its directors, the operational and physical environment the franchisee will become part of and the financial outlay required of the franchisee is disclosed. The franchisor was A&R. Under the heading (2), the franchisor must disclose as associates, any who

(i) is a director or related body corporate, or a director of a related body corporate, of the franchisor; or
(ii) for a franchisor that is a proprietary company — directly or indirectly owns, controls, or holds with power to vote, at least 15 per cent of the issued voting shares in the franchisor; or
(iii) is a partner of the franchisor; and

whose relationship with the franchisor is relevant to the franchise system, including supplying goods, real property or services to a franchisee.[119]

Without access to the A&R disclosure document provided to the A&R franchisees, it is not clear whether the existence of PEP would have been disclosed. PEP would not have been supplying goods, real property or services to the franchisees as it was too distant and had a finance role superficially unrelated to franchisees. But, '[d]ata volume is not as important as the manner of data presentation and the disclosure process … needs to reflect that common-sense reality'.[120] There are eight PEP entities. To have conducted a search on each of these entities would have been ultimately pointless. The administrator's conclusion that there was no evidence of the REDgroup having traded while insolvent suggests that the most diligent franchisee would have found nothing to cause alarm in the corporation's records. Franchisee due diligence would not reveal that

> [b]y the time the businesses [Borders, Angus & Robertson and Whitcoulls] were fully acquired in June 2008, … [REDgroup] experienced declining sales and coupled with significant debt repayments was, until the appointment of Administrators, struggling to meet its financial obligations.[121]

Or that

> [o]n 22 June 2010 the directors [of REDgroup] sought legal advice regarding the risk of insolvent trading.[122]

These actions by the directors however helped establish to the administrators that there was no evidence of insolvent trading – directors had been proactive about the possibility of becoming insolvent.

---

[119] Code, Part 1, 3(1), with specific identity details about both corporate and noncorporate 'associates' required to be disclosed under the disclosure document

[120] Steinberg, Paul and Lescatre, Gerald, 'Beguiling Heresy: Regulating the Franchise Relationship' (2004) 109(1) *Pennsylvania State Law Review* 1, 298

[121] REDgroup Retail Pty Limited and Associated Companies (Administrators Appointed) report by administrators pursuant to Section 439A(4)(a) of the Corporations Act 2001 S Sherman, J Melluish and J Lindholm, Ferrier Hodgson, 25 July 2011, 8.

[122] REDgroup Retail Pty Limited and Associated Companies (Administrators Appointed) Report by Administrators Pursuant to Section 439A(4)(a) of the Corporations Act 2001 S Sherman, J Melluish and J Lindholm, Ferrier Hodgson, 25 July 2011, 9

The franchisor makes disclosure as a single legal entity, but the franchisor seldom stands alone. For example, the REDgroup operated through 18 separate corporations and trusts in three countries (Australia, New Zealand and Singapore). While it is relatively easy and inexpensive to conduct a search of one proprietary company, conducting meaningful due diligence on more than one is expensive. Conducting due diligence on a trust is impossible. The more entities there are, the more expensive and difficult it becomes for franchisees to conduct meaningful due diligence or to interpret what they see. A franchisor does not provide prospective franchisees with an organisation chart of the franchisor's entire network, with roles of each entity the franchisee will depend on named and the flow of money between franchisee and the network clearly stated. It is thus impossible for advisers to assess the franchise offering in its true context.

The next problem is that franchisees are encouraged to ask existing franchisees what it is like being a franchisee. Intuitively, they should be a great source of reliable information, but they may be loyal to their own investment, thinking of how adverse report card could affect the resale possibility, and not prepared to expose its problems. Worse, existing franchisees might be bound by confidentiality agreements they have signed to resolve disputes, or they simply may be intimidated and not brave enough to speak their truth until they are out of the system.

Franchisors are not obliged to disclose the debt load that they, or the ultimate owner, is carrying unless that debt has triggered litigation that needs to be disclosed under the 'Litigation' heading (4) in the disclosure. One of the items under 'Litigation' identifying information to be provided to an incoming franchisee is item 4.1(a) (iii) contravention of the *Corporations Act 2001* (Cth). Trading while insolvent would be a contravention of the Corporations Act, but as already noted, the franchisor A&R was not trading while insolvent. The nearest the parent appears to have come to financial difficulty is, as identified after the administrator had been appointed, that 'REDgroup … was also forced to get a waiver from its lenders after breaching some of its financial covenants'.[123] A breach of a contract with a third party may be a warning bell about impending insolvency, but it does not need to be disclosed under 'Litigation'. In this case, the breach was not by the franchisor but by the parent and thus more remote and not requiring disclosure.

The disclosure discloses a considerable amount of information about the franchise, but the risk is that the franchisor will come from a bad family. In the case of A&R, the 'bad family' element was not the franchisor that made disclosure. It was the venture capitalist that bought the network, married it to other businesses and then failed to nurture it. Franchisees enter a complex network severely under-informed.

The Australian Government's Office of Best Practice Regulation writes in terms of 'desired objectives'.[124] This is interpreted as objectives that meet appropriate

---

[123] Patrick Stafford, Borders Australia and Angus & Robertson Chains Collapse, Thursday, 17 February 2011 15:47 at http://Www.Smartcompany.Com.Au/Retail/20110217-Borders-Australia-And-Angus-Robertson-Chains-Collapse.Html Accessed 6 October, 2011

[124] Australian Government, *Best Practice Regulation Handbook* (2007) Department of Finance and Deregulation A.2 <http://www.finance.gov.au/obpr/docs/handbook.pdf> Accessed 30 May 2010

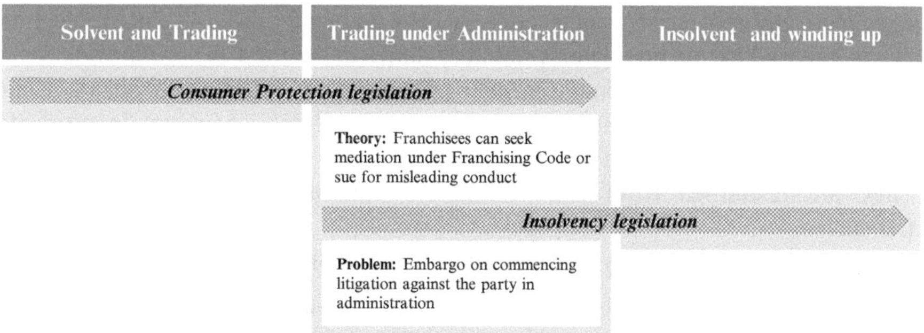


**Fig. 8.4** During administration insolvency legislation trumps consumer protection legislation

benchmarks. There are several problems to be considered when mandating disclosure. It is difficult for a franchisee to test the accuracy of the material supplied in the disclosure for a host of reasons.

Where disclosure is effective, it is as a tool to balance the positions of contracting parties during the formation of the contract. Disclosure has never been proven to be effective in redressing imbalance of power in performance.

## *Attitude of Administrators of Insolvent Franchisors to Code*

Accepting that franchisors may fail, it is important to ask whether the precontract disclosure and franchise agreement could have had a role in protecting the franchisees' investment. The first occasion when precontract disclosure's ability to protect franchisees is really tested is when the franchisor's administrator is appointed. Administrators generally treat the Code as not applying to them. As a possible outcome of administration is that the business under administration may be handed back to its directors then there is no invariable argument for denying franchisees the right to mediate with the administrator. In some cases, such where the franchisor is insolvent and the franchisees' supply chain for both stock and premises was directly through the franchisor's group, mediation may be pointless, but in other situations where the franchisees and their franchisor's businesses are not so intermeshed, it may be valid (Fig. 8.4).

## Responses Available to Franchisees

In Australia, from the time the administrator is appointed up until a recommendation to wind the company up is accepted, both the *Competition and Consumer Act* and the *Corporations Act* regulate the franchise relationship. Once the liquidator is appointed, any protection franchisees may have had under the consumer protection law is replaced by the liquidator's statutory duties under the *Corporations Act*.

The *Corporations Act* does not help franchisees of failing franchisors. Their franchise agreements are categorised as assets or liabilities. Their sunk investments are losses to themselves but are not the source of any possible claim as a creditor. They are restrained from commencing or continuing litigation against the franchisor.

New York franchise lawyer Craig Tractenberg recommends

> [t]he best protection [for franchisors] against the risks inherent in the bankruptcy process is to terminate the franchise agreement before bankruptcy is filed. If the franchise agreement is terminated before bankruptcy is filed, it is not protected by the automatic stay and the franchise is not property of the estate.[125]

Tractenberg also advises that '[c]omplete termination is required'.[126] Similarly, the best protection for franchisees is for them to be legally entitled to terminate the franchise agreement during the period of administration before the franchisor's liquidator is appointed. If they purchase into a second franchise network after the first franchisor fails, they are likely to insist on the franchise agreement containing an *ipso facto* clause.

As a practical matter, where the franchisor is in administration, franchisee associations may collectively attempt to negotiate an arrangement with all interested parties, including landlords, franchisees and creditors – both secured and unsecured. This can be a difficult exercise. Franchisees may be widely geographically dispersed. In practical terms, their personal resources are spread very thinly. Generally, any such collectively negotiated agreements will have to be binding upon all franchisees to be effective.

## Stepping Back to Make Progress

> 'We can distinguish four broad theoretical approaches to the legal regulation of consumer overindebtedness. First, insolvency law focuses on the problem of distribution of assets and the enforcement of debts from the creditor's point of view. Secondly, the inability to pay constitutes a breach of contractual relationship that is a problem of private law. Thirdly, sociolegal scholarship looks at overindebtedness as a social problem and asks what the reasons for overindebtedness are and what kinds of persons become overindebted. Fourth, an economic approach focuses on the signals that the system gives to the actors by asking

[125] Craig R Tractenberg, 'What the Franchise Lawyer Needs to Know About Bankruptcy' (2000–2001) (3)20 Franchise Law Journal 3, end note 8; See, for example, *Moody v. Amoco Oil Company* 734 F 2d 1200 (7th Cir) cert denied, 469 US 982 (1984). Tractenberg is writing for an audience of lawyers whose clients are franchisors whose franchisees are becoming bankrupt, but the same applies to franchisees.

[126] Craig R Tractenberg, 'What the Franchise Lawyer Needs to Know About Bankruptcy' (2000–2001) (3)20 Franchise Law Journal 3, end note 9

> what kinds of incentives and disincentives the system gives to the debtors and, to a lesser extent, to the creditors'.

Johanna Niemi's[127] identification of four theoretical approaches highlights the franchisees predicament. All four need to be addressed with the franchisee correctly located within the frame in order to produce a workable solution to the consequences for franchisees of their franchisor's failure. Firstly, while insolvency law does focus on assets and creditors, it identifies franchisees as simply parties to contracts (assets or liabilities) that are a potential source of royalty revenue for the administration, and thus franchisees are also unsecured creditors and debtors. Franchisees' creditor status is separately acknowledged in jurisdictions where parties to executory contract (franchise agreements) have rights (e.g. the USA) as unsecured creditors to claim for the unexpired portion of what they have contracted for. How to assess an accurate value for that unexpired portion is a task for accountants.

Secondly, the contractual relationship is a problem as the franchisees' predicament has evolved out of contagion, by the franchisor not being able to meet its financial obligations. The contracts the franchisee signs do not recognise that the franchisor might become insolvent; thus, franchisees are left looking for statutory exit strategies.

Thirdly, overindebtedness was an easy situation for a franchisor to arrive at prior to the Global Financial Crisis when banks were willing lenders. However, once the GFC hit and franchisors had difficulty borrowing from traditional lenders and venture capitalists were less bullish, they still had a free line of credit available to them – the fees paid by new franchisees. Franchisees themselves had the bank of mum and dad. As Jason Gherke points out,

> BOMAD will become an increasingly common feature on the franchise financing landscape as more borrowers fail to meet bank servicing and securitisation requirements.[128]

The situation outlined and the thinking attributed to these particular franchisees can equally be shifted to the franchisor, funded by selling franchises even when it would not be able to satisfy a scrupulous lender that it could meet its own debts. The timing reinforces the categorisation of franchisees as consumers, unable to test whether the product (franchisor) they are investing in is financially fit and not entitled to a refund if it is not fit.

Dispute resolution provisions in Franchising Code of Conduct were ignored in administrators dispute with Angus & R franchisees; the administrators went straight to court.

Instances of franchisor failure are increasingly well publicised. Media attention tends to highlight the plight of customers and the franchisor's employees, paying scant attention to franchisees. For example, the Mercury made no mention of failed

---

[127] Johanna Niemi, 'Personal insolvency' chapter 14 in Geraint Howells, Iain Ramsay and Thomas Wilhelmsson with David Kraft (eds) Handbook of Research on International Consumer Law Edward Elgar, 2010, 415

[128] Jason Gherke, Why BOMAD funding is critical to franchisee and franchisor growth 27 March 2012, http://www.smartcompany.com.au/franchise-tips-and-trends/why-bomad-funding-is-critical-to-franchisee-and-franchisor-growth.html

franchisor Speeds Shoes' franchisees who had each invested $180,000–$300,000 on their outlets, rather focussing on employees, writing '[m]ore than 60 workers face losing up to $200,000 in wages, superannuation and holiday pay after the collapse of a discount shoe chain'.[129] This failure of the media to include franchisees in the franchisor failure stories tends to enforce the franchisees' invisibility and reinforce the mantra that franchising is a safe entry point into small business.

The lessons to be learned from Barbara's House & Garden litigation seem forgotten 20 years later:

> [w]hen Mrs. Bateman had been working for the company for some two years, the company became involved in the vigorous promotion of franchises to operate 'Barbara's House and Garden' stores .... The promotion was portrayed as the natural expansion of an outstandingly successful business, but financial statements tendered in evidence suggest it was in fact an attempt to keep a foundering business afloat by getting in substantial franchise fees.[130]

History repeats itself. Strathfield Car Radio replicated the Barbara's House and Garden strategy in 2009, going one step further and embracing franchising as a way of resurrecting itself out of administration. Strathfield Car Radio's administrator adopted a strategy of

> selling franchises in order to rid themselves of unprofitable assets and to raise capital. [For example] mobile phone and electronics retailer Strathfield, ... collapsed into administration earlier this year but emerged after a major shareholder injected fresh capital. Strathfield has announced it will pursue a franchise strategy as it attempts to turn its fortunes around.[131]

A clear theme running through the examples of failure are that the franchisor and its related entities, not the franchisees, are the authors of the system's fate.

---

[129] Tim Martin and Catherine Hockley The Mercury (Hobart), 2 April 2004, 11

[130] *Re Richard Vincent Bateman and Georgina Gay Bateman v. Barbara Jean Slatyer; Harvey John Slatyer; Graham Walter Tiekle and Barbara's House & Garden (Retail) Pty Limited* [1987] FCA 58, para 3

[131] Jacqui Walker, Franchising Under Pressure (2009) Smartcompany <http://www.smartcompany.com.au/franchising/20090505-will-franchising-survive-the-recession.html> Accessed 20 August 2009; and see James Thomson, Retail Chain Strathfield Collapses into Administration (2009) Smartcompany <http://www.smartcompany.com.au/retail/retail-chain-strathfield-collapses-into-administration.html> Accessed 31 May 2010

# Chapter 9
# Solutions to Risks Franchisees Face

**Abstract** Franchisor insolvency is identified as a 'known/unknown' with potentially dire results when the Australian Risk Standard is applied. The rationale for protecting consumers, and in particular franchisees, is thus presented in Chap. 9. Consumer protection benchmarks from Australia, New Zealand and the European Union are introduced, and their utility tested in the context of franchisor failure. The EU Consumer Policy Strategy 2007–2013 is selected as the benchmark most able to address the problem of protecting franchisees from the consequences of their franchisor's failure. A range of non-legislative and legislative solutions are explored, and some solutions are proposed.

Franchise lawyers Rupert Barkoff and Andrew Selden identify 'the risk that "your franchisor goes bankrupt"[1] as an "uncontrollable risk"' in their practitioner guide on franchise law. Chapter 8 revealed that franchisors fail in greater numbers and with more serious consequences for franchisees than the rhetoric suggests. If we accept the truism that failing to plan is planning to fail how should a known but uncontrollable risk be proactively managed? In this chapter, three consumer protection benchmarks will be discussed. They will be put forward as more appropriate than the current 'fair and in good faith' Australian benchmark for evaluating consumer protection laws for franchisees. I will then consider non-regulatory responses before moving to look at a range of possible regulatory responses.

[1] Rupert M Barkoff and Andrew C Selden, *Fundamentals of Franchising* (3rd ed, 2008) 278


DOI 10.1007/978-1-4614-5614-8_9, 

[T]here are three fundamental questions surrounding the debate about consumer protection:

- Why do consumers need protection?
- When ought the state intervene to protect them?
- How ought the government to intervene?[2]

The law in its current form cannot deliver consumer protection to franchisees in the event of franchisor failure. Rather, it lulls franchisees, as well as financiers and franchisee advisers, into a potentially false belief that the franchisee's future is secure in the franchise model. Warnings built into the contracting process enable franchisees to factor the possibility of the franchisor failing into their own financial models and to make a more accurate evaluation of how much risk they are taking. However, this is not sufficient. An important further component of consumer protection is for the business consumer of a failed product, the franchise business, to have rights in the insolvency process. This is what is currently missing.

Andromachi Georgosouli adds that

> consumer protection policies have as an overarching objective to improve economic efficiency by remedying market failures and preserving the fairness of the process and outcomes of the transactions.[3]

Consumer protection does not exist in a regulatory vacuum. Thus, a fourth fundamental question should be added:

## What Is the Context in Which Consumer Protection Functions?

This leads to the question, why do consumer protection inquiries,[4] economic models created by franchise academics and regulatory responses assume that the supplier, in this case the franchisor, will be solvent at the time the product or service, the franchise business support, is supplied?

'[C]onsumer protection has an ancient genesis, dating back at least to Roman times with the adoption in Roman law of various implied warranties against latent defects in the sale of goods'.[5] Trebilcock identifies two sources of pressure on traditional consumer protection regulation, being

---

[2] Iain D C Ramsey, 'Rationales for Intervention in the Consumer Marketplace' (1984) *Occasional Paper for the Office of Fair Trading* 1, of Andromachi Georgosouli, 'Investor Protection Regulation: Economically Rational?' (2006) *Working Paper Series, University of London, Centre for Commercial Law Studies* 10, fn 24 <http://ssrn.com/abstract=893451> Accessed 4 June 2010

[3] Andromachi Georgosouli, 'Investor Protection Regulation: Economically Rational?' (2006) *Working Paper Series, University of London, Centre for Commercial Law Studies* 7 <http://ssrn.com/abstract=893451> Accessed 4 June 2010

[4] For example, Australian Government Productivity Commission, *Review of Australia's Consumer Policy Framework*, Report No 45 (2008)

[5] Michael J Trebilcock, 'Rethinking Consumer Protection Policy' in Charles E F Rickett and Thomas G W Telfer (eds), *International Perspectives on Consumers' Access to Justice* (Edward Elgar, 2003), 68

> the rapidity of technological change, globalisation and deregulation of formerly regulated monopolies have dramatically expanded the range of consumer products and services available in any given jurisdiction, making product and service-specific regulation increasingly problematic and intensifying the informational challenges faced by consumers.[6] and

> a veritable revolution in industrial organisation theory … particularly as it relates to market structure, bargaining power and information, has rendered simplistic structure-conduct-performance paradigms that keyed on a small number of variables and that underpin many aspects of contemporary consumer protection policy also increasingly problematic.[7]

Trebilcock's conclusion that the true focus of consumer protection is in the quality and cost of information falls short. He concludes, by implication, that with the right amount of the right information provided at the right time and the right price, the consumer can be adequately protected. This may be true where goods and services are not designed to last for decades or where ongoing servicing can readily be provided by replacement suppliers. It does not apply when the business of the franchisor supplier fails.

Further, Trebilcock's analysis starts with the assumption that the consumer market is competitive and, by implication, that it remains competitive even once a consumer has made a purchase. He suggests that 'where a market is very imperfectly competitive or non-competitive, problems of consumer protection may have to be addressed through competition policy or economic regulation'[8] rather than through consumer protection.

The sale of franchises is a hybrid. Before the franchise agreement is executed, the market is competitive. Once the agreement has been executed, the franchisee is committed to dealing with a monopoly. Franchisees have purchased a bundle of products, services and use rights from the franchisor. If the franchisor's business fails, there is no alternative franchisor to step into the insolvent franchisor's shoes. A competitor may potentially take over the company-owned and franchisee-owned sites but may not wish to enter contracts with the existing franchisees. A purchaser purchasing even an expensive item such as a car is not obliged to return to the manufacturer for driving lessons, servicing, all routine future suppliers of parts, petrol and oil and ultimately to sell the vehicle only through the manufacturer. The purchaser of the vehicle may get it serviced anywhere, buy petrol anywhere and can sell it on the open market long after the manufacturer has ceased to exist. The insolvency of the manufacturer is not going to prevent the consumer from gaining full use and enjoyment out of the car. Franchisees are a *sui generis* category of consumer because the purchased bundle of products, services and use rights only stays intact while the franchisor is solvent.

---

[6] Michael J Trebilcock, 'Rethinking Consumer Protection Policy' in Charles E F Rickett and Thomas G W Telfer (eds), *International Perspectives on Consumers' Access to Justice* (2003), 68

[7] Michael J Trebilcock, 'Rethinking Consumer Protection Policy' in Charles E F Rickett and Thomas G W Telfer (eds), *International Perspectives on Consumers' Access to Justice* (2003), 68

[8] Michael J Trebilcock, 'Rethinking Consumer Protection Policy' in Charles E F Rickett and Thomas G W Telfer (eds), *International Perspectives on Consumers' Access to Justice* (2003) 69

## Benchmarks

A benchmark is 'a means of evaluating by comparison with a standard or point of reference'.[9] Following its review of Australia's consumer protection laws, Australia's Productivity Commission ('PC')[10] recommended that the

> Australian Government should adopt a common overarching objective for consumer policy, being: To improve consumer wellbeing by fostering effective competition and enabling the confident participation of consumers in markets in which both consumers and suppliers trade fairly and in good faith.[11]

The PC concluded that 'fairness' and 'good faith' are the appropriate benchmarks for measuring markets in which consumers can participate confidently. The PC's recommendation led to the drafting of the *Competition and Consumer Act 2010 (Australian Consumer Law)* (ACL). The ACL does not include consumer protection for franchisees whose franchisor fails because the PC confined its inquiry to consumers that currently fell under a long-standing definition of consumers that excluded consumers buying for resale – as franchisees hope they are doing. The PC did not appreciate that while there may be effective competition, confident participation in the market by franchisee consumers and good faith on the part of both parties; nonetheless, franchisors will fail, and franchisees will suffer without access to recourse. In franchisor failure situations, there is not necessarily any absence of good faith. Good faith is not a suitable benchmark in this context. Until the problem of franchisor failure is addressed, an acceptable level of fairness will not have been achieved.

Concluding that fairness and good faith are inappropriate benchmarks for evaluating the adequacy of the response of consumer protection regulation to franchisor failure, meaningful benchmarks need to be identified. Three robust consumer protection benchmarks ('the Benchmarks') for measuring the utility and the success of regulation to protect franchisees as consumers are the following:

1. B1: Regulation should provide effective protection from serious risks and threats that [franchisees as business] consumers cannot tackle as individuals.[12]
2. B2: There should be accessible, timely[13] and meaningful redress where consumer detriment has occurred.
3. B3: The cost of meeting B1 and B2 should be less than the benefits.

---

[9] Bruce Moore (ed), *The Australian Oxford Dictionary* (2nd ed, 2010) 117

[10] http://pc.gov.au/

[11] Australian Government Productivity Commission, *Review of Australia's Consumer Policy Framework*, Report No 45 (2008) Volume 2, ix

[12] Commission of the European Communities, *EU Consumer Policy Strategy 2007–2013 Empowering Consumers, Enhancing their Welfare, Effectively Protecting them* (2007) European Commission 5 <http://ec.europa.eu/consumers/overview/cons_policy/doc/cps_0713_en.pdf> Accessed 5 March 2010

[13] Australian Government Productivity Commission, *Review of Australia's Consumer Policy Framework*, Productivity Commission Report No 45 (2008) vol 2, xv

## *B1: Regulation Should Provide Effective Protection from Serious Risks and Threats That Franchisees as Consumers Cannot Tackle as Individuals*

Of the national consumer policy objectives identified by Australia's Productivity Commission,[14] following a review of those of New Zealand,[15] the United States,[16] the United Kingdom and[17] Canada,[18] an objective espoused by the European Union '[t]o protect consumers effectively from the serious risks and threats that they cannot tackle as individuals'[19] best articulates one of the specific issues that confronts franchisees. The risk of franchisor failure is a serious risk and threat that even groups of franchisees cannot tackle effectively by themselves. This inability of franchisees to address the risks or threats of franchisor failure as individuals is the core of their problem.

The Australian Risk Standard, AS/NZ 4360/2004, provides a methodology for identifying and managing risk in a business that could be used by both franchisors

[14] Summarised in the Australian Government Productivity Commission, *Review of Australia's Consumer Policy Framework*, Productivity Commission Report No 45 (2008) vol 2, xv., 52

[15] To create an environment that is conducive to good and accurate information flows between suppliers and consumers so that consumers can transact with confidence. New Zealand Ministry of Economic Development 2003, *Creating Confident Consumers – the Role of the Ministry of Consumer Affairs in a Dynamic Modern Economy*, (2003) 7. Australian Government Productivity Commission, *Review of Australia's Consumer Policy Framework*, Productivity Commission Report No 45 (2008) vol 2, 29

[16] To prevent business practices that are anticompetitive or deceptive or unfair to consumers, to enhance informed consumer choice and public understanding of the competitive process and to accomplish these missions without unduly burdening legitimate business activity. Federal Trade Commission (2006) 'Strategic Plan Fiscal Years 2006–2011', Washington, 1. Australian Government Productivity Commission, *Review of Australia's Consumer Policy Framework*, Productivity Commission Report No 45 (2008) vol 2, 29

[17] To place empowered consumers at the heart of an effective competition regime, bringing UK levels of competition, consumer empowerment and protection up to the level of the best by 2006. UK Competition Commission 2007, 'The roles of the Competition Commission and Department of Trade and Industry in promoting competition', from www.competition-commission.org.uk

[18] Building trust in the marketplace so that consumers can protect themselves and be able to confidently and knowledgeably drive demand for innovative products and services at competitive prices. (Office of Consumer Affairs, Canada 2007). www.ic.gc.ca

[19] (1) To empower EU consumers: Putting consumers in the driving seat benefits citizens but also boost competition significantly; Empowered consumers need real choices, accurate information, market transparency and the confidence that comes from effective protection and solid rights; (2) To enhance consumer's welfare in terms of price, choice, quality, diversity, affordability and safety. Consumer welfare is at the heart of well-functioning markets; (3) To protect consumers effectively from the serious risks and threats that they cannot tackle as individuals. A high level of protection against these threats is essential to consumer confidence. Commission of the European Communities Commission of the European Communities, *EU Consumer Policy Strategy 2007–2013*, (2007) 5–6 <http://ec.europa.eu/consumers/overview/cons_policy/doc/EN_99.pdf>

**Table 9.1** Risk analysis template

| | Event | Solution |
|---|---|---|
| Known knowns | Day-to-day events | Address in contract |
| Known unknowns | Franchisor might fail | If impact would be severe on either party, include, if not, leave to future negotiation |
| | Franchisor might pursue strategic insolvency | Weight with respect to impact on network and on individual franchisee |
| | Parent company might decide to close franchise division/strategic insolvency | Provide contract-based strategy |
| Unknowns | Far-fetched events that are never likely to impact on the network | Address through 'motherhood' clauses, that is, general obligations such as to cooperate, act reasonably, act in good faith |

and franchisees to determine whether a given franchise agreement addresses the key risk items. An aspect of the methodology is to categorise events in tabular form as in Table 9.1 as 'known knowns', events which will occur, such as the franchise agreement will terminate at the end of the term; 'known unknown' events which are known to be possible but their effect is not fully knowable; and 'unknowns'. The category each event is placed determines its treatment in the franchise agreement.

In the context of the Risk Standard, franchisor insolvency is a risk that should be evaluated and planned for as a 'known/unknown', that is, it is known that it could occur, but unknown if or when it will occur.

## Why Franchisees Are Unable to Tackle These Risks and Threats as Individuals

The Australian Government argues that 'the parties to the contract are best placed to determine commercial matters'.[20] There are reasons why franchisees are unable to accurately measure and factor in the commercial risk of franchisor failure. Even if they do identify it as a possibility, they are then unable to tackle the consequences with any certainty. In summary:

1. The franchise network is a complex set of legal structures. Every franchise network is configured differently, and the configuration changes over time without the franchisees having any control over the franchisor, its direction or the company it keeps.

[20] Commonwealth Government Response to the Report of the Parliamentary Joint Committee on Corporations and Financial Services, Australian Senate, *Opportunity Not Opportunism: Improving Conduct in Australian Franchising* (2008), 21

2. Pre-contract disclosure fails to adequately put franchisees on notice about the significant threat which is beyond their ability to research and beyond their control – the franchisor's survival. Franchisees have always accepted that their own business might fail. It is franchisor failure that is the more unthinkable and less manageable risk. 'On signing the franchise agreement, most of the franchisee's rights to receive consumer protection are derived from pre-contractual conduct by the franchisor. At that point the franchisor was probably, though not invariably, solvent'.[21] Disclosure is made of current and past events, not future plans. It also fails to disclose specific information about the players in the network and the direction of money flows within the network and the risks and threats thus accepted by franchisees operating as commission agents.
3. Franchisees are unable to conduct affordable and effective due diligence.
4. The franchise agreement is drafted by the franchisor. Because it is not negotiable, the information provided in the disclosure and acquired through due diligence is of limited value.
5. Asymmetries contribute to the franchisees' inability to evaluate the risk of franchisor failure or plan for it.
6. The consumer protection legislation offers no rights and no meaningful protection to franchisees following the appointment of an administrator.
7. The winding up process provides liquidators with rights that are the antithesis of franchisees' needs. Franchisees have no right to negotiate with the receiver or administrator. When the administrator is appointed, they have no franchisee-specific rights in the creditors' pool except in jurisdictions where unexpired rights under executory contracts are recognised.
8. There is no sufficiently funded representative of the interests of all franchisees, whereas franchisors interests are strongly represented by well-funded national and international industry lobby groups.
9. In practical terms, however, none of the remedies available in Australia's CCA or Code are applicable to the franchisor administration/insolvency situation. Damages, injunctions, deleting the offending words of a contract, enforceable undertakings and advertisements are all remedies based on the assumption that the breaching party is still solvent. Administrators reject franchisees' requests that they attend mandatory mediation under the Code, and the Code does not apply to liquidators.
10. Even if remedies were available to franchisees, the stay of proceedings under *Corporations Act*s 440D means they are not able to pursue any remedies through the courts while the franchisor entity is in administration.
11. If the franchisee successfully navigates the minefield, it arrives at a regulatory vacuum in relation to its rights in the administration or the insolvency. This is not satisfactory.

[21] JM Buchan, Franchisor failure: An assessment of the adequacy of regulatory response. PhD thesis, 2010, Queensland University of Technology, 76. (Franchisors Beach House Group, Kleins Jewellery and Kleenmaid were insolvent for up to 13 months, and selling franchises during those months, prior to entering administration)

## *B2: There Should Be Accessible, Timely and Meaningful Redress Where Consumer Detriment Has Occurred*

> The implementation of consumer policy, and the vindication of consumer rights, are each dependent on the existence of mechanisms to secure alignment of the conduct of business with the applicable legal norms set through legislation and/or judicial decision making.[22]

### Accessible Redress

Hadfield writes:

> [c]ontract law makes its own promises to contracting parties: it promises to be available to accurately interpret the agreement the contracting parties have made, to impartially judge the performances rendered, and to reliably implement the appropriate remedies. … Courts must be accessible at relatively low cost in geographic and linguistic terms to contracting parties.[23]

Hadfield also states that

> [d]elay in the resolution of contract disputes is an important impediment to the effectiveness of contract law – not only does the value of payment decrease with time but so too does the probability of recovery diminish as the potential for assets to be dissipated increases and circumstances change to make performance more difficult and/or less valuable.[24]

As was demonstrated on the next page justice extracted from a solvent franchisor through the courts is very expensive and very slow. The Hoys alternative to litigation was to have their franchise terminated by their franchisor. Hadfield's thoughts are also valid when the redress is to come from the diminishing assets of an insolvent estate. Accessing redress through an administrator or liquidator is far more problematic at any cost.

### Timely Redress

The possibility of timely redress is particularly significant where the parties to the dispute are in an ongoing contractual relationship. This is recognised and addressed through the opportunity to mediation disputes if the franchisor is solvent. Timeliness is especially important for the franchisee whose right to profit from the relationship ends on the termination date of the franchise agreement. Examples of lack of timeliness are common where one party has an interest in not settling a dispute. The

---

22 Colin Scott, 'Enforcing consumer protection laws', in Geraint Howells, Iain Ramsay and Thomas Wilhelmsson with David Kraft (eds) *Handbook of Research on International Consumer Law* (Edward Elgar, 2010)

23 Gillian K Hadfield, 'The Many Legal Institutions that Support Contractual Commitment' in Claude Menard and Mary Shirley (eds), *Handbook of New Institutional Economics* (2004) 175, 181

24 Gillian K Hadfield, 'The Many Legal Institutions that Support Contractual Commitment' in Claude Menard and Mary Shirley (eds), *Handbook of New Institutional Economics* (2004) 175, 182

franchisor may be reluctant to settle for fear of setting a precedent. For example, in Hoy, following the franchisor's refusal to mediate, the franchisee had to litigate or accept defeat. The franchisee said:

> I was told the proceeding were likely to cost me around [A]$300,000 ... and that my matter stood a good chance of succeeding ... but more importantly there was no other way of restraining the franchisor from acting upon the termination notice without an injunction. ... At the time we thought it was commercially sensible to begin proceedings to prevent the termination and to protect our asset. By ... the end of 2006 the costs had reached $140,000. The court ordered mediation which we attended to no avail in November 2006. The franchisor had made it clear from the beginning that they were going to fight us all the way ...We had to subpoena [telecommunications] carriers to obtain the evidence we required and even this process was not easy and cheap. We had to provide an undertaking to the court that we would not disclose the information we read before we were allowed to view the documents. Once I viewed the documents I was certain our issue ... was an issue that affected every [Allphones] franchisee and I was not allowed to tell my fellow franchisees or the ACCC. The carriers each charged between [A] $1000 to over $3000 for producing the documents. [25]

In the failed Danoz Directions franchise network, one franchisee signed a franchise agreement for a 5-year term with a 5-year renewal in February 2004, the franchisor failed in October 2004. The franchisee instituted proceedings against the franchisor's directors alleging unconscionable conduct and misleading and deceptive conduct. In September 2009, 2 days of hearing time were allocated, and in April 2010 a further 2 weeks of hearing time were allocated for the litigation initiated by the franchisee in the Federal Court of Australia. This is not timely. Timely redress is also important where franchisees are required by the administrator to continue operating. Continuing also involves paying staff, meeting commitments under premises agreements and meeting franchise agreement commitments while the administrator and then the liquidator decide on the future of the franchisor.

Accessible and timely are not sufficient measures of redress where one party is insolvent. Meaningful redress is also vitally important.

## Meaningful Redress

Meaningful redress leaves the franchisee able to move ahead with his/her life unencumbered by debts and bad relationships accumulated because of the conduct of the franchisor; contaminated through contagion. Franchisor-transmitted debt and franchisor-transmitted poor supplier relationships should not be a consequence of being a franchisee. As was demonstrated by the Angus & Robertson franchisee gift card choices, loss of customers is also a risk of franchisor administration.

Meaningful redress is also cost effective. Few franchisees can afford protracted litigation. An example of one routine trial demonstrates the resources required to

---

[25] Evidence to Parliament of Australia Joint Committee on Corporations and Financial Services, Senate of Australia, *Inquiry into Franchising Code of Conduct*, undated, 4 (Nicole Hoy) <http://www.aph.gov.au/SENATE/COMMITTEE/corporations_ctte/franchising/submissions/sub08.pdf> Accessed 17 January 2010

litigate. In the courtroom on each of the 12 hearing days, in *Danoz*,[26] were one senior counsel, one junior barrister, one solicitor for each party plus the judge, the judge's associate and a court officer plus the parties and expert witnesses.

Legal options should extend beyond the theoretical and should be meaningful, accessible and timely. The current situation fails against these measures.

## *B3: The Cost to the Franchisor and the Legal System of Meeting B1 and B2 Should Be Less Than the Benefit to Franchisees Whose Franchisor Fails*

Benchmark B3 requires that a cost-benefit analysis[27] ('CBA') be conducted to justify any proposed solutions. 'Cost-benefit tells us the menu of trade-offs which policymakers face'.[28] As part of the Best Practice Regulation preliminary assessment, Australian Government policy requires that a CBA should be conducted, and identified that

> [f]or a Regulation Impact Statement (RIS) to be assessed as adequate, it should demonstrate that: the benefits of the proposal to the community outweigh the costs; and the preferred option has the greatest net benefit for the community, taking into account all the impacts.[29]

The Australian Government evaluates projects by assessing their benefit-cost ratio (BCR).[30] Currently it would be badly hampered in a BCR assessment by the lack of data on the real cost of franchisor failure.

---

[26] *Morris v. Danoz Directions Pty Ltd (No 1)* [2009] FCA 134; *Morris v Danoz Directions Pty Ltd (in Liq) (No 2)* [2010] FCA 836

[27] Government, Department of Finance and Deregulation, *Cost Benefit Analysis* <http://www.finance.gov.au/obpr/cost-benefit-analysis.html> at 7 March 2010. [Cost-benefit analysis] CBA is an analytical tool that can be used to assess the benefits and costs of regulatory proposals. CBA involves examining costs and benefits from the perspective of the community as a whole to help identify the proposal with the highest net benefit. Where regulation is designed to reduce the risk of physical or economic harm, a CBA should include a risk analysis detailing how the regulation will change the likelihood, frequency or consequences of an adverse event occurring

[28] Tyler Cowen, Using Cost-Benefit Analysis to Review Regulation (1998) George Mason University Draft 2. <http://www.gmu.edu/centers/publicchoice/faculty%20pages/Tyler/Cowen%20on%20cost%20benefit.pdf> Accessed 8 March 2010

[29] Government, Department of Finance and Regulation, *Best Practice Regulation Guidance Note: Decision Rules in Regulatory Cost-Benefit Analysis* 1 <http://www.finance.gov.au/obpr/cost-benefit-analysis.html> at 7 March 2010

[30] Australian Government, Department of Finance and Regulation, *Best Practice Regulation Guidance Note: Decision Rules in Regulatory Cost-Benefit Analysis* 1 The benefit-cost ratio (BCR) of a project or regulation is the present value of the estimated benefits divided by the present value of the estimated costs. In mathematical terms, it is expressed as

$$BCR = \sum_{t=1}^{n} B_t / (1+r)^t / \sum_{t=1}^{n} C_t / (1+r)^t$$

The decision rule when using BCR is accept a policy only if BCR > 1; and in deciding between alternative policies, select the one with the highest BCR

Traditionally non-regulatory solutions are preferred to regulatory solutions, so we will now examine the range of possible non-regulatory solutions.

## Non-regulatory Solutions

### *Status Quo*

The 'do nothing' solution requires all franchisors to continue preparing, updating and delivering extensive Code compliant disclosure that fails to enable franchisees to understand or evaluate commercial or legal risk. Franchisees will continue to pay for legal and financial advice provided on the basis of inadequate information. They will continue to be unable to objectively verify much of that information. Most franchisees will not negotiate *ipso facto* clauses into their agreements and will not be able to protect their own assets as well as franchisors can. Franchisees will continue to be unnecessarily vulnerable to the franchisor's failure.

### *Education*

It has been acknowledged that more education is needed for prospective and incumbent franchisees and also for franchisors. Australian Government-sponsored reports on franchising have identified education as an essential part of the solution to shortcomings of the franchise model. Australia's Reid Report identified 'the inadequacy of advice and education for small businesses'[31] as a matter for concern. The Matthews Review's Report[32] contained 15 references to education. The South Australian Parliament Report[33] in 2008 contained 42 references to education. It did not directly identify education as a solution to franchisor failure.

The West Australian report, also in 2008, referred to education 38 times, including the following well-intentioned but gratuitous observation about franchisee failure:

> The risk of business failure [impliedly a franchisee's business, not a franchisor's] will always exist. This risk can be reduced by undertaking thorough business feasibility assessment and planning prior to entering into any commercial arrangement. …The importance of pre-entry education for franchisees has emerged as a key issue.

---

[31] Committee on Industry, Science and Technology (Reid Committee), *Finding a balance; Towards fair trading in Australia* (1997) 1. <http://www.aph.gov.au/house/committee/isr/fairtrad/report/CHAP1.PDF > Accessed 22 June 2010

[32] Graeme Matthews, *Review of the Disclosure Provisions of the Franchising Code of Conduct* (2006)

[33] Economic and Finance Committee, South Australian Parliament, *Franchises* (2008)

Thorough pre-purchase due diligence is impossible to conduct in franchising and becomes meaningless when the franchisor entity subsequently merges, is taken over or becomes insolvent.

## *Make Franchise Agreements Accessible*

One tool for self-education is reading franchise documents. Every franchisor should be required to post all versions of their standard pro forma franchise agreements and disclosure documents on a publicly accessible, free, website. This would mean that franchisees and their advisors could compare the document they have been asked to sign with the franchisor's pro forma agreement and with other offerings in the market sector. This would enable them to identify differences that may then require explanation. It would also enable them to identify how the agreement has changed over time. This will be particularly helpful to a franchisee purchasing in a resale. They will be able to identify how the agreement they are required to sign differs from the one the current franchisee operate under. Accessibility would also assist advisers who are not familiar with the nuances of franchising.

## *Franchisee Union*

Franchisees face significant impediments to self-representation as lobbyists or as litigants. Franchisees do not join trade unions in Australia. As individuals they do not have resources to involve themselves personally in politics at a national level in addition to running their own business and in some cases participating in their own franchise network's advisory council. They risk alienating their franchisor if they express views that the franchisor or the FCA find threatening or inconvenient. Franchisees may fear that if, hypothetically, they were seen to be devoting time to union affairs, their franchisor would build a case to terminate for breach of a term of the franchise agreement that requires the franchisee to devote all time and energy to its business.

In Europe, recognising the difficulties of finding time and money for consumers to self-represent effectively:

> [t]he EU has subsidised consumer group representation through the European Consumers' Organisation (BEUC) and the European Consumer Law Group (ECLG) as well as specialised groups such as European Association for the coordination of Consumer Representation in Standardisation (ANEC).[34]

[34] Ramsay, Iain 'Consumer Law, Regulatory Capitalism and the 'New Learning' in Regulation' (2006) 28(1) *Sydney Law Review* 9, 18

While franchisors and franchisees do have matters of common interest where the franchise industry groups such as the International Franchise Association and the Franchise Council of Australia can provide adequate representation. The areas where their interests are in conflict should not rely on academics or individual franchisees with sufficient motivation and courage to make a submission to a government inquiry to be aired.

Alternatively, although the idea ignites dissent from franchisor-focused groups, governments could support franchisee union membership as a policy initiative to enable the franchisees' voice to be accessed. For example, in Japan the problem of whether a franchisee union could be established and how it would be funded has been overcome in Japan. There, individual owners of franchised convenience stores were permitted to become members of an existing union in 2009.[35] It is easy to dismiss one franchisee's voice as being non-representative but difficult to dismiss those of unions representing the tens of thousands of franchisees the world over.

Governments could subsidise the establishment of representation channels for franchisees whose most persistent outlets currently in Australia and the United States are writing blogs and lobbying politicians and the media.

## *Insurance*

It should be possible for franchisees to insure against the consequences of their franchisor failing. In a submission to a senate inquiry, a director of a supplier adversely affected by the insolvency of a mining company wrote:

> [s]uppliers to industry have few options … Take out their own insurance [debtor insurance] at rates that are up there with the insolvency practitioners themselves. …The cost of this insurance is … becoming even more out of reach as the risk to the insurers book escalates as insolvencies are becoming more and more common. There is no way that suppliers can be secured … they have no choice but to be unsecured creditors.[36]

He proposes that:

> ASIC's charter should be to ensure protection for all stakeholders and this could be achieved by writing into AS 4000 that there should be reciprocal insurance rights for all stakeholders. If premiums were gathered by the insurance industry on every contract then the overall premium would be drastically reduced.[37]

---

[35] Anderson Mori and Tomotsune, Formation of Labour Union by Convenience Store Franchisees (2009) <https://www.internationallawoffice.com per cent2fNewsletters per cent2fDetail.aspx per cent3fg per cent3d4ca4add7-f8bd-4530-a6eb-82b0fa183729> Accessed 5 January 2010

[36] Submission to Economics Committee, Australian Commonwealth Senate, *Inquiry into Liquidators and Administrators*, 3 December 2009, Submission Number 1 (Greg Crook)

[37] Submission to Economics Committee, Australian Commonwealth Senate, *Inquiry into Liquidators and Administrators*, 3 December 2009, Submission Number 1 (Greg Crook)

The insurance solution is appealing, but in the franchising sector, the absence of reliable comprehensive data about franchisor failure would make it difficult for actuaries to assess the likelihood of failure or the magnitude of loss and therefore to set premiums accurately. Further, the absence of a mandatory requirement that franchisors register would make it extremely difficult to achieve widespread compliance with any requirement to pay into an insurance fund.

## *Reconfigure Some Obligations*

Requiring franchisors to provide their own security deposits for retail premises could help mitigate the effects of their failure on their franchisees. This would mean that if the franchisor head tenant failed, a franchisee would not be called on to meet the franchisor's liability for unpaid rent or outgoings.

Requiring franchisors that operate through the commission agency model to supply personal guarantees from the franchisor's directors to franchisees is also possible, though *ad hoc* and seldom agreed to by franchisors. Personal guarantees would remain actionable if the principal debtor, the franchisor, became insolvent.

## *Deem Franchisors to Be Trustees*

Franchisors hold money paid by franchisees in trust in a range of situations. For example, the sums like the $60,000 option fees charged to its franchisee by Danoz for the rights to three future sites are currently treated as general revenue and are not traceable in the franchisor's insolvency. The moneys franchisees pay to a central advertising fund is another example of funds that could easily be held in a separate account until the moneys are spent for legitimate advertising purposes. Obviously where a franchisor is the head tenant, it receives franchisees' rent and outgoings and is required to pass these to the landlord and statutory agencies. All funds received by franchisors for third parties should be deemed to be held on trust for the franchisees.

## *Standard Form Franchise Agreements to Address Risks*

It is reasonable to expect that the major legal and commercial risks that a franchisee faces as a consequence of signing the contract could be addressed in the standard contract. Intuitively, it would seem that franchisors and franchisees should be able to incorporate provisions such as *ipso facto* clauses into their contracts to address the possibility of the franchisor's business failing. The legal profession itself needs to wake up to the power imbalance created by franchise agreements. As noted in

Chap. 5, in its submission to The Australian Consumer Law Consultation on Draft Provisions on Unfair Contract Terms, the Law Society of New South Wales provides examples of 'standard form contracts' frequently used in conveyancing transactions and states that:

> the Committee believes that the use of these forms has significant consumer benefits: [being] familiarity, comprehensiveness, compliance with legislative provisions, frequently updates, flexibility, efficiency, risk management, balance between the parties to the transactions.[38]

Whilst these points hold true for standard form contracts drafted by an impartial party, standard form commercial agreements such as franchise agreements are drafted by the overwhelmingly more powerful party in a relationship. The Law Society's thinking about standard form contracts is inaccurate in the context of standard form franchise agreements.

In answer to Ramsey, Georgosouli and Trebilcock, providing franchisees with protection from the consequences of franchisor failure is a situation when the state ought to intervene to protect consumers. The forces of the competitive marketplace have failed franchisees. Only consumer protection and insolvency policy and regulation working together can correct this market failure. The problems will not go away, and they will not be resolved without parliamentary intervention. A range of possible regulatory interventions are now identified.

## Regulatory Solutions

Private contract law is unable to provide solutions to the franchisees' problem of franchisor failure. And, whilst a franchisee whose franchise agreement or premises lease has been disclaimed has a right to lodge a proof of debt in the liquidation as an unsecured creditor for its loss, this is a deficient form of consumer protection. Regulatory solutions should:

1. Provide franchisees and their advisers with more meaningful pre-contract disclosure.
2. Level the playing field for franchisees before they sign a franchise agreement, during the franchisor's administration and after the franchisor's business is wound up.
3. Keep the franchise network intact long enough to determine whether it may be sold as a viable network rather than being dismantled.

The supply of a franchise business to the franchisee business consumer is similar, theoretically, to any other product that is supplied with a standard form contract, and with a projected fixed life span denoted in the sale agreement.

[38] Law Society of New South Wales, *Australian Consumer Law – Consultation on Draft Provisions on Unfair Contract Terms* (2009) Australian Government, The Treasury <http://www.treasury.gov.au/contentitem.asp?NavId=037&ContentID=1537> Accessed 4 June 2010

> Franchisors need franchisees to make significant investments of both time and [equity and borrowed] money in their businesses. But, of course, such investments are only worth making if the franchisee can expect to earn some reasonable return on these investments over a sufficiently long period of time. If it takes five years, for example, to fully recoup ones investment in a franchise, then no franchisee should invest unless the relationship is expected to last for at least five years.[39]

When a consumer purchases a product or service in Australia and the product or service does not meet standards, the person has rights to claim against the supplier or manufacturer. 'We don't have to worry if a product doesn't work because if it doesn't you can take the product back and it will be replaced. The [*Competition and Consumer Act 2010*] has... lifted the standard of retail trader behaviour in Australia'.[40] These options are currently not available to franchisees that purchase into a franchise network that turns out to be faulty and to fail.

## Consumer Protection Legislation

Currently in Australia consumer protection takes the form of general prohibitions on particular conduct: unconscionable, misleading, deceptive, threatening and discriminatory to name a few. It also provides specific franchisee protection through the Code.

## Unconscionable Conduct s 22 ACL under the CCA

Eric Posner writes:

> [a] simple model of the consumer goods market implies that courts should not use the unconscionability doctrine to strike down contracts. More complex models that take account of asymmetric information and bargaining power imply that such contracts should be struck down only in particular circumstances, when courts have information about variables that are intrinsically difficult to measure.[41]

Franchising is replete with asymmetries whose variables are difficult to measure. For example, a franchisor's future intentions are intrinsically impossible for a franchisee to measure. If a court were to follow Posner's thinking the way would be open for it to strike down franchise agreements if the franchisor behaved unconscionably by pursuing unmeasurable damaging strategies or those inconsistent with selling a long-term licence, such as voluntary administration or strategic insolvency.

Bigwood recognises limitations of arguments based on unconscionability, albeit in the context of common law, as being that

---

[39] Roger D Blair and Francine Lafontaine, *The Economics of Franchising* (Cambridge University Press, 2005) 272, 264

[40] Louise Sylvan, 'The development of a modern Australian consumer movement' ACCC update issue 16, 2004, 12 at 13

[41] Eric A Posner, Economic Analysis of Contract Law after Three Decades: Success or Failure (Working Paper No 146, (2d series) (2002)) 15

> No matter how attractive the precept of unconscionability is as a judicial matter, the number of transactions that can be reached and controlled is too small to have a social impact, and the reluctance of courts to review countless agreements is too strong.[42]

Australia responded to the challenge of unconscionable conduct in business (franchisor) to business (franchisee) transactions in 1998. The *Trade Practices Act* was amended in by the addition of s 51AC (now s 22 ACL). This was statutory acknowledgement of the particular vulnerability of business consumers. The phrase 'business consumers' is used in s 22 (formerly s 51AC of the TPA), but the term is not defined. In announcing [the introduction of s 51AC], the government accepted the principle that small business people are entitled to a legal protection against unfair business conduct comparable with that which consumers already have against corporations.[43] In practice, however, an action against the franchisor for unconscionable conduct that led to the franchisor becoming insolvent would only result in meaningful relief to the franchisees if they included the failed franchisor's solvent directors as defendants.

The unconscionable conduct provisions of the CC Act have not been widely used by franchisees. The Hoy cases[44] provide a clear example of why franchisees are reluctant to litigate. The franchisee spent $650,000 on legal fees, and the term of their franchise agreement had expired by the time the litigation concluded.

One option to see if s 51AC could be made to work better would be to shift the burden of proof to the party that has the evidence to establish that the conduct is not unconscionable, the franchisor.

## *Imply Terms into All Franchise Agreements via a Franchise Contracts Act*

The Australian Government has stated that:

> [i]f potential franchisees can identify and access the information needed for informed business decision, they should have a better basis with which to negotiate a contract that meets their requirements. Parties engaged in trade and commerce should have a high degree of freedom to contract.[45]

Two aspects of this statement are fundamentally flawed. Firstly, the paragraph starts with the powerful little word 'if'. It has been shown that franchisees cannot

---

[42] Rick Bigwood, *Exploitative Contracts* (Oxford, 2003), 277, citing R A Epstein, 'The Social Consequences of Common Law Rules' (1982) 95 *Harvard Law Review* 1717, 1750

[43] Peter Reith, *New Deal: Fair Deal – Giving Small Business a Fair Go* (1997)

[44] *Hoy Mobile Pty Ltd v. Allphones Retail Pty Ltd (No 2)* [2008] FCA 810. In *Allphones Retail Pty Ltd v. Hoy Mobile Pty Ltd* [2009] FCAFC 85, Allphones unsuccessfully appealed the decision, *Allphones Retail Pty Ltd v. Hoy Mobile Pty Ltd* [2009] FCAFC 85 and in *Australian Competition and Consumer Commission v. Allphones Retail Pty Ltd (No 2)* [2009] FCA 17 the regulator then prosecuted successfully on behalf of some franchisees who were damaged by the same unconscionable conduct that Hoy had uncovered.

[45] Commonwealth Government Response to the Report of the Parliamentary Joint Committee on Corporations and Financial Services, 21

identify the information needed to make an informed business decision. When they can identify it, accessing it becomes an insurmountable hurdle.

Secondly, the notion of franchisees being able 'to negotiate a contract' is flawed. At best the franchisee can understand it as a legal document. Even this understanding will leave them without context. It is like buying a sports car to drive through Australia's outback, never having been there before. You might be lucky, and it might not rain and the grader might have graded the road the day before you drive on it – or you might realise too late that the car is woefully ill-suited to the task.

A solution is to protect franchisees from the worst results of franchisor failure through new legislation. The idea of specific franchising legislation is not new. It was proposed in 1997 in the Reid Report.[46]

The purpose of a Franchise Contracts Act would be to reform the law relating to franchise agreements so that a fair balance is struck between the interests of franchisors, franchisees and other stakeholders. A wide range of implied terms are proposed below. A secondary benefit of legislation over all obligations being contained in individual franchise agreements as is the case now is that franchise agreements would be shorter. This would help reduce the time and expense devoted to generating agreements and consequently would save both franchisors' and franchisees' money. In proposing that terms be implied into all franchise agreements, it must be acknowledged that franchise agreements can be disclaimed as onerous contracts by liquidators. They would, however, apply to the franchisor and the administrator prior to disclaimer.

## Product or Service Warranty

When a consumer purchases a product or service in Australia and the product or service does not meet standards, the person has statute-based rights to claim against the supplier or manufacturer. These avenues are currently not available to franchisees that purchase a franchise that turns out to be faulty and to fail – not fit for its purpose. The *Competition and Consumer Act 2010* (Cth) ('CCA') does not provide redress if a manufacturer becomes insolvent, but the *Corporations Act* classifies consumers of defective products as unsecured creditors. The franchisor failing before the end of the franchise term is arguably analogous to a product or service failing.

Under the CCA, protection is provided for 'consumers' from manufacturing defects, acknowledging that one defectively manufactured product can cause damage to hundreds of consumers. Franchisees do not fit the definition of 'consumer' in the CCA s 4B.

Consumer warranties could be incorporated into a Franchise Contracts Act and become implied terms in all franchise agreements so a franchisee could claim the failed franchisor had breached. This would include, for example, terms:

[46] Committee on Industry, Science and Technology (the Reid Committee) *Finding a balance; Towards fair trading in Australia* (1997)

1. Implying undertakings as to title, encumbrances and quiet possession. These would become relevant where the franchisor has not secured premises leasing rights but requires the franchisee to commence trading, such as in *Shakespeare's* case[47].
2. Concerning supply of franchise by description or supply of goods by sample. It would apply, for example, to protect the franchisee purchasing a greenfields business based on its description and the franchisor's evaluation of its potential.
3. Importantly for franchisees whose franchisor fails, undertakings as to quality and fitness would be implied.
4. A term which addresses supply of services should be implied. This would extend to both those services that have not been supplied with the requisite due care and skill and services that are not fit for their purpose.
5. A term that achieves the same result as the current s 37 CCA would provide consumer protection in respect of false descriptions and could be applied to franchises that are sold as licences and thereby avoid complying with the Code.
6. A term addressing franchises of unmerchantable quality which turns out to be the case with franchise businesses sold by franchisors that were already insolvent when the franchisee paid its franchise fee.

## Franchisor Duties

The franchisor currently has a duty under Disclosure item 18(2) of the Code to tell franchisees about a breach of the *Corporations Act* within 14 days of becoming aware of it. There is no evidence as to whether they do so. However, even if they do, the moment the franchisee has executed the franchise agreement and any cooling off period has expired, it is too late to protect itself from a franchisor's breach of the *Corporations Act*. The franchisor's breach of the *Corporations Act* is not a breach of the franchise agreement and does not give the franchisees the right to terminate the franchise agreement and all ancillary commitments.

Where the franchisor is a corporation, the franchisor directors' duties [48] should be expanded so the directors owe to franchisees the same duties as directors currently have to a company. The rationale behind this is that franchisees provide a significant amount of the operational infrastructure that, absent franchisees, the franchisor would have to supply, and franchisees assume a significant amount of the franchisor's business risk. The issue of franchisor's duties to franchisees could usefully be pursued in the future.

---

[47] *Shakespeares Pie Co v Multipye* [2006] NSWSC 930

[48] Directors have statutory duties under *Corporations Act 2001* (Cth) ss 180 (care and diligence), 181 (good faith), 182 (use of position), 183 (use of information), 184 (good faith, use of position and use of information – criminal offences), 190 (responsibility for actions of a delegate), 191 (disclosure of material personal interests) and 588G (insolvent trading)

## Specific Fiduciary Duties

A further future inquiry is whether the directors of the franchisor do or should owe any fiduciary duty to franchisees. The issue of franchisors as fiduciaries was addressed in Germany where guidelines have been developed by the German Franchise Association to interpret Article 3.3 of the European Franchise Federation ('EFF') Code of Ethics:

> [Article] 3.3 [states] In order to allow prospective Individual Franchisees to enter into any binding document with full knowledge, they shall be given a copy of the present Code of Ethics as well as full and accurate written disclosure of all information material to the franchise relationship, within a reasonable time prior to the execution of these binding documents.[49]

By way of contrast, in the United States '[f]ranchisors owe no fiduciary duty to franchisees,[50] and no other duty to honor the franchisee's expectations is likely to come from the franchise agreement itself[51] or from contract law governing it'.[52] The issue was raised but not resolved in Australia in the context of a solvent franchisor Australia in *Hoy Mobile Pty Ltd v. Allphones Retail Pty Ltd* (No 2).[53]

## Duty of Care

A statutory duty of care should be imposed on administrators and liquidators dealing with a failed franchisor towards franchisees. Under the expanded duty, administrators and liquidators would owe a duty of care to the franchisees to consider their legitimate needs as stakeholders. This includes the possibility for franchisees to continue operating their businesses if the cause of the failure is not related to the viability of the individual franchisee businesses. It would also mean that any purchaser of the franchisees' business would be required to satisfy the administrator or liquidator that it was competent to run the franchise system.

---

49 European Franchise Federation, *European Code of Ethics for Franchising* <http://www.eff-franchise.com/spip.php?rubrique13> Accessed 6 March 2010

50 Doug Frazey, 'Case Note: When 'Good Cause' Goes Bad: Minnesota Restricts Protection for Dealers under HUMEDA – River Valley Truck Ctr., Inc V. Interstate Cos' (2006–2007) 33(2) *William Mitchell Law Review* 711, 728 quoting Paul Steinberg and Gerald Lescatre, 'Beguiling Heresy: Regulating the Franchise Relationship' (2004) 109 *Pennsylvania State Law Review* 105, 174 and fn 133. See also *Broussard v Meineke Discount Mufflers Shops, Inc* 155 F.3d 331 (4th Cir. 1988)

51 Doug Frazey, 'Case Note: When 'Good Cause' Goes Bad: Minnesota Restricts Protection for Dealers under HUMEDA – River Valley Truck Ctr., Inc V. Interstate Cos' (2006–2007) 33(2) *William Mitchell Law Review* 711,728 quoting Robert W Emerson, 'Franchising and the Collective Rights of Franchisees' (1990) 43 *Vanerbildt Law Review* 1503, 1509, n 21 (noting the franchisor usually drafts the franchise agreement and that most obligations fall on the franchisee)

52 Doug Frazey, 'Case Note: When 'Good Cause' Goes Bad: Minnesota Restricts Protection for Dealers under HUMEDA – River Valley Truck Ctr., Inc V. Interstate Cos' (2006–2007) 33(2) *William Mitchell Law Review* 711, 729

53 [2008] FCA 810

## Franchisor to Obey All Relevant Law

The franchisor should have an implied contractual obligation consistent with the franchisees' current obligation to carry on business activities in compliance with all laws, regulations and codes of conduct. A statutory obligation should exist to require the franchisor to meet all contractual and statutory obligations between itself and each franchisee, itself and third parties and itself and ASIC, the ATO and other levels and arms of government relevant to the franchise network, where a breach would cause harm to the franchisee. A breach of this implied term, depending on its seriousness, could give rise to a right for the franchisee to terminate the franchise agreement and sue for damages for breach of contract. The term would need to be drafted widely enough to acknowledge that it might not be the franchisor that fails – it might be another entity in a franchisor's network that fails, taking the franchisor and franchisees with it.

## Franchisor to Comply with All Obligations Towards Third Parties

The franchisor should be required to comply with all collateral contract obligations and all obligations that arise under statute. A breach of any of the third party or collateral contractual obligations that impacted detrimentally on franchisees would enable the affected franchisees to terminate their agreements and seek damages from the franchisor. This term would be used by franchisees whose franchisor did not pay the rent, outgoings or other third-party payments that it had received from the franchisee in a timely way. In failing to do so, the franchisor has put the franchisees' businesses and reputation at risk.

## Franchisee Representative on Franchisor's Board and Franchisee Committee During Administration

In the United States,

> [t]he [United States Trustee] may also appoint additional committees of creditors or equity security holders as the UST 'deems appropriate.' (11 U.S.C. 1102(a)(1)). This is important in a franchisor bankruptcy if franchisees believe their interests are not adequately represented on the Committee. Because franchisees may not have an actual liquidated claim against the franchisor at the time of filing, they may not be included on the list of twenty largest creditors and may not be solicited to serve on the Committee. Yet, they have a large stake in the bankruptcy. Franchisees may urge the UST to appoint a separate committee or petition the court to allow the formation of a franchisee committee.[54]

[54] Sarah B Foster and Carolyn Johnsen, 'The War of the Worlds: Bankruptcy Versus…' (Paper presented at the American Bar Association, 28th Annual Forum on Franchising, Florida, 19–21 October 2005), 20. Cases in which franchisee committees have been appointed: *In re Nutri/System, Inc*, 169 BR 854 (Bankr EDPa 1994); *In re First International Services Corp*, 25 BR 66 (Bankr D Conn 1982); *In re Rusty Jones, Inc*, 128 BR 1001 (Bankr ND Ill 1991)

The merits of all franchisees being officially recognised and represented in creditors' meetings, whether they are creditors or debtors, should be considered.

## Implied Term to Take Effect on Appointment of Administrator

A term should be implied into all franchise agreements that if an administrator is appointed to the franchisor or to any of the entities in the franchisor's network that threaten the viability of the franchisee's business, a two-step process will be triggered:

Step 1: when an administrator is appointed to their franchisor, any franchisee may give notice to the administrator that if a satisfactory resolution (restructuring that takes into account the franchisee's interests as well as those of the franchisor's creditors or sale to appropriate buyer) is not found within x days, it will terminate the agreement.

Step 2: if the administrator does not meet the requirements in x days, the franchisee has the right to terminate the franchise agreement, without this being a deemed breach and without it compromising any other rights the franchisee may pursue. The franchisees may express their losses as unsecured creditors for an amount of their initial investment, adjusted by depreciation and other appropriate considerations, plus any amounts currently owed in the franchisor's administration/subsequent insolvency.

This approach could be adopted in relation to both franchisor and franchisee failure. This would mean the current asymmetrical provisions in the Code and all franchise agreements favouring franchisors in the event of franchisee failure could be removed from franchise agreements, thus making them shorter. It would also eliminate the risk of franchisees being sued by the administrator or liquidator for anticipatory breach.

There is debate in insolvency law about the merits of *ipso facto* clauses. Step 1 above is a refined *ipso facto* clause. Currently franchisors give themselves, but not the franchisees *ipso facto* clauses in the franchise agreement. Franchisors (but not franchisees) are also given this power by the Code. For franchisee consumers to be given statutory protection in the form of a modified *ipso facto* clause would be consistent with the approach in jurisdictions such as Canada that recognise solvent parties to executory contracts merit special consideration in insolvency of the other party.

## Consequential Amendments as Additional Implied Terms

The franchisees' option to terminate their franchise agreement would have a secondary right attached to it – on the appointment of the administrator, all payments (e.g. royalties, advertising, rent) falling due from the franchisee to the franchisor or any franchisor-related entity that was also under administration would cease to be payable.

Payment obligations – without arrears – would resume if the franchise network was successfully revived. This would mean the vulnerable business consumers, the franchisees, were not funding the franchisor's administration.

The tenancy contract between the landlord and the franchisor would be novated:

> A novation occurs when two parties to a contract enter into an agreement with a third party under which, in consideration of the first party [the landlord] releasing the second party [the franchisor] from the contract, the third party [franchisee] undertakes to assume responsibility for performance in place of the second party. A transaction… is not effective as a novation unless an intention is clearly shown that the second party's obligations are to be extinguished.[55]

The franchisee would step into the shoes of the failed franchisor but would not take on the liabilities accrued by the underperforming franchisor. Premises rent formerly collected by the franchisor for on-payment to landlords would thus become payable direct to the landlord. This would not disadvantage the administrator or the franchisee's landlord but would enable the franchisee to demonstrate to the landlord whether the franchisee has a viable business as an independent operator.

These provisions would provide an incentive for the administrator to acknowledge franchisees as parties with rights, not merely to categorise franchise agreements and premises leases as assets or liabilities of the franchisor. They would enable the administrator to keep the franchise network together if a viable buyer was found quickly, but would not leave franchisees in limbo for extended periods while the administration proceeds.

The drafting would have to be done with careful attention to incentives. It is important not to incentivise the administrator from acting too hastily in proposing the administration proceed quickly to liquidation merely to prevent the franchisees from exercising their option to terminate.

## Amend Franchising Code of Conduct

Improved disclosure does not mean longer disclosure. It is disclosure that is differently structured and more meaningful. In economic terms, the duty to disclose is formulated on the following basis:

> [I]n general a person has a property right to information when it is costly to gain such information, but the person does not have a property right and therefore cannot take advantage of this information when the information is obtained at a very low cost.[56]

An application of this principle means franchisors would provide franchisees with less disclosure that is of greater value, information the franchisee could not

[55] NC Seddon and M F Ellinghaus, *Cheshire and Fifoot's Law of Contract* (LexisNexis, 8th Australian ed, 2002), 360

[56] Donlad Wittman, *Economic Foundations of Law and Organization* (Cambridge University Press, 2006) 194, 104

gain access to otherwise or only at great cost. This is also recognised in Opportunity not opportunism:

> Better disclosure does not necessarily mean more disclosure; disclosure documentation should be in line with Code requirements and should focus on the provision of information which is difficult and/or expensive for the franchisee to obtain through other means.[57]

Four aspects of the Code could usefully be amended. They are the Code's application to administrators, the scope of entities that the franchisor has to disclose, the form and content of the disclosure document and the public accessibility of the disclosure document.

## Application of Code to Administrators

The current, untested view held by some administrators in Australia that the Code does not apply to them results in administrators denying franchisees the right to require mediation during the administration. Mediation might not be the disastrous waste of time and resources that administrators claim – it may be opening a meaningful dialogue between administrators and franchisees and provide the administrators with a loyal franchisee base whose contracts can be sold. Franchisees may express an interest in buying the franchise system if they had a voice in the insolvency process.

Power and fund imbalances, the tight timelines surrounding all aspects of the winding up procedure, the embargo on commencing litigation against the party in administration mean it is unlikely that franchisees would ever be able to mount an effective challenge, so the incorrect view prevails. To resolve this, a statement should be inserted in the Code to clarify that it binds administrators.

## Entities Making Disclosure

The franchisee needs to base its purchasing decision on full and accurate information. The franchisee should be given information that is specific to its actual business. Even franchisors that have supposedly invariable policies about specific aspects of business do make exceptions for particular sites, so generic information is not necessarily accurate.

It was shown in Fig. 8.1 that 'the franchisor' may be one of a group of numerous corporate and trustee entities. It is not necessarily the entity whose failure will trigger

---

[57] Commonwealth Government Response to the Report of the Parliamentary Joint Committee on Corporations and Financial Services, Australian Senate, *Opportunity Not opportunism: Improving Conduct in Australian Franchising* (2008), xiii

the failure of the group. The fragmentation of ownership of vital assets (including trademarks and premises leases) means that disclosure by and of *the franchisor* exposes only part of the franchise network to scrutiny by the franchisees' advisers. To achieve fuller, more telling information, a credit rating agency report on the franchisor entity should be required to be provided by the franchisor. A credit rating agency provides context for the franchisor entity's operations. Such a report shows related entities and individual directors which are not presently a feature of disclosure. It reports on their credit history which, if one believes that history repeats itself, is significant information to an incoming franchisee interested in assessing risk. The information provided would enable an accountant to analyse the franchisor's attitude to risk, debt and creditors and would provide a far more comprehensive picture of the franchise network than is provided through the current disclosure.

It should be noted that credit rating agencies do obtain some of their information from the subject entity. To avoid this being misleading, the information that was supplied by franchisor or related entity should be identified so the franchisee will not be misled into believing the report is entirely objective.

## Form and Content of the Disclosure

Recommendation 1 of 'Opportunity not opportunism' proposed that the current absence of warnings about franchisor failure should be addressed thus:

> The … Code [should] be amended to require that disclosure documents include a clear statement by franchisors of the liabilities and consequences applying to franchisees in the event of franchisor failure.[58]

The government responded that

> individual franchisees, rather than franchisors, would be better placed to assess the liabilities and consequences applying to them in the event of their franchisor failing. In addition, such a statement may induce a belief among franchisees that, in the event of franchisor failure, they will not be exposed to any risks other than those noted in the disclosure document.[59]

A preference for generic information to be supplied by the regulator is problematic. It is impossible for a regulator delivering generic material to provide material that would alert a franchisee that their situation is materially different to that of

[58] Commonwealth Government Response to the Report of the Parliamentary Joint Committee on Corporations and Financial Services, (2007) xiii. This was also recommended in Graeme Matthews, *Review of the Disclosure Provisions of the Franchising Code of Conduct* (2006) 13, and agreed to in principle in the Australian Government Response (2007) 7–8 which placed the responsibility, inappropriately, with the ACCC

[59] Commonwealth Government Response to the Report of the Parliamentary Joint Committee on Corporations and Financial Services, Australian Senate, *Opportunity Not opportunism: Improving Conduct in Australian Franchising* (2008) 21

others in the network. Because of considerable variation of risk-shifting methods and outcomes both from franchise to franchise and within each franchise network, any risk statement should be tailored to each specific franchisee's situation. Take for example the fate of the 14 Gloria Jean's franchisees co-branded with Borders. Their risks were quite different to stand-alone Gloria Jean's cafes. Only the franchisor could identify this, and only in relation to assets/contracts to which the franchisor or a related entity was a party. A second example is if the franchisor usually takes the head lease but has selected one site whose lease contains a demolition clause, they might decide not to take the head lease as they do not want to retain the site long term. In this case, the franchisee takes the lease in their name. Only the franchisor will know this is a departure from its usual practice.

Franchisors should set out in plain language specific possible contractual and statutory consequences of their own failure for their franchisees. They would include information such as the following:

- The franchisor's liquidator may disclaim (i.e. terminate) your franchise agreement and lease without consulting you. This could result in you losing your business.
- If you guarantee the franchisor's head lease, you could lose the amount of the guarantee if the franchisor breaches the lease.
- If your lease was not disclaimed but the franchise agreement was disclaimed, you would have to continue paying rent and outgoings on your premises, but could not continue with the franchise.
- If the franchisor does not own the trademarks, patents or designs that you need access to for your business, you are likely to lose the right to use these if the franchisor becomes insolvent. You may also lose access to these if an administrator finds a buyer for the franchisor. That buyer may not want franchisees.
- This franchise is a commission agency. If the franchisor fails, you will not receive any commission from the administrator or liquidator. Please consider the impact of receiving no commission on your cash flow.

Over time, warnings may lead to franchisors amending their standard franchise contracts to level the failure part of the playing field. They may also lead to banks that fund both a franchisor and its franchisees, being more diligent about managing the franchisor side of the ledger. Of course even if enough information was supplied, franchisees would still be unable to self-protect if franchise agreements did not allow them to terminate the contract and deal satisfactorily with all of their collateral obligations when the franchisor failed.

### Consequential Amendments to Premises Legislation

After a franchisor fails, the franchisee's business may be viable on a stand-alone basis as long as the franchisee can retain its premises. A possible solution is to follow the Ontario, Canada, approach that affords franchisees in such situations the right to elect to become the lessee.[60] This situation is exemplified in the Canadian case, *Majdpour v. M & B Acquisition Corp*:[61]

As a franchisor's insolvency can cost the franchisee its tenancy, the Ontario solution should be adopted widely.

## Amendment to Corporations' Regulation

'Information and warnings are the traditional tools of consumer protection'.[62] The need to consider other policies to complement information rules should be stressed.[63] In considering the limitations of information as a consumer protection mechanism, Geraint Howells identifies the availability of time, the education level of the consumer, lack of alternatives, market impediments to swapping and the contributions of behavioural economists to our understanding of consumers and markets. Through demonstrating the limitations of each, he argues that whilst information and warnings do have an important role to play in consumer policy, we must not expect too much of these tools. There remains a need for 'some caution and respect for the

---

[60] Ontario, Canada: Commercial Tenancies Act, R.S.O. 1990, c. L.7

1. 'Tenant' includes a person who is lessee, occupant, sub-tenant, under-tenant, and the person's assigns and legal representatives. ('locataire') Commercial Tenancies Act, R.S.O. 1990, c. L.7, s. 1; 1994, c. 2, s. 1; 1994, c. 4, s. 1; 1997, c. 24, s. 213 (1, 2); 1999, c. 6, s. 9 (1); 2005, c. 5, s. 10 (1, 2)

39. (1) The person who is assignee, liquidator or trustee has the further right, at any time before so electing, by notice in writing to the landlord, to surrender possession or disclaim any such lease, and the person's entry into possession of the leased premises and their occupation by the person, while required for the purposes of the trust estate, shall not be deemed to be evidence of an intention on the person's part to elect to retain possession under section 38. R.S.O. 1990, c. L.7, s. 39 (1)

Rights of Sub-tenants

(2) Where the assignor, or person or firm against whom a receiving order has been made in bankruptcy, or a winding up order has been made, being a lessee, has, before the making of the assignment or such order demised any premises by way of under-lease, approved or consented to in writing by the landlord, and the assignee, liquidator or trustee surrenders, disclaims or elects to assign the lease, the under-lessee, if the under-lessee so elects in writing within 3 months of such assignment or order, stands in the same position with the landlord as though the under-lessee were a direct lessee from the landlord but subject, except as to rental payable, to the same liabilities and obligations as the assignor, bankrupt or insolvent company was subject to under the lease at the date of the assignment or order, but the under-lessee shall in such event be required to covenant to pay to the landlord a rental not less than that payable by the under-lessee to the debtor, and if such last mentioned rental was greater than that payable by the debtor to the said landlord, the under-lessee shall be required to covenant to pay to the landlord the like greater rental. R.S.O. 1990, c. L.7, s. 39 (2)

[61] 2001 CanLII 28457 (ON SC) <http://www.canlii.org/en/on/onsc/doc/2001/2001canlii28457/2001canlii28457.html> Accessed 6 June 2010

[62] Geraint Howells, Iain Ramsay and Thomas Wilhelmsson with David Kraft (eds) *Handbook of Research on International Consumer Law* (Edward Elgar, 2010)

[63] Geraint Howells, 'The Potential and Limits of Consumer Empowerment by Information' 22(3) *Journal of Law and Society* (2005) 349 at 362

limitation of the potential of information to empower consumers'[64]. There are limits to what can be achieved through pre-purchase disclosure, franchise agreements and retail leasing legislation.

Returning to nature where no element exists truly in isolation, similarly neither consumer protection, nor contract law nor insolvency are isolated concepts. UNCITRAL recognises the need to look beyond the boundaries of each legislative silo when addressing problems that cross boundaries. It

> raises [the challenge of] the relationship between insolvency and other law. [It] recommends that the relationship between insolvency law and other laws should be clear and, where possible, references to the other laws should be included in the insolvency law'.[65]

UNCITRAL has raised an important issue. The intended consumer protection and contract law responses are profoundly affected by the insolvency of the franchisor. It is unrealistic to expect consumer protection to do the entire job of protecting franchisees and their investments. Franchisees need to be accommodated far better than they currently are within insolvency regimes.

[64] Geraint Howells, 'The Potential and Limits of Consumer Empowerment by Information' 22(3) *Journal of Law and Society* (2005) 349 at 362

[65] UNICITRAL, *Legislative Guide on Insolvency Law* (2005) 19 <http://www.uncitral.org/pdf/english/texts/insolven/05-80722_Ebook.pdf> Accessed 15 December 2009

# Chapter 10
# Concluding Remarks

**Abstract** The fundamentals of franchising have changed dramatically in the 21st century. The complex new franchising world includes hitherto unknown stakeholders; venture capitalists, listed companies and liquidators. It positions franchisees as consumers to a greater extent than ever before, well removed from their franchisor and its corporate governance obligations. The low hanging legal fruit has been picked in franchising. This chapter is a call to re-examine assumptions and respond to the new franchising.

Franchising is a powerful business model that empowers people to become self-employed and to provide employment in their communities. But the model is far from perfect. Franchising is a relatively new form of business. It exploded into the dynamic, manipulable, attractive form that we see today only after the lengthy development of policy and regulation for the governance of corporate groups and the provision of rights to employees, consumers and creditors.

The stakeholders in a franchise network and in the franchise system have a mutual interest in profit, but beyond profit their needs and interests diverge and conflicts can arise.

Franchise agreements are not 'negotiated'; they are generally standard form contracts drafted by the franchisor. Not surprisingly, they protect the franchisor's interests. The law needs to mature along with the maturation of the franchise business model. Effective franchising policy requires an understanding of the risks and roles franchisees assume, and an acceptance of their present inability to accurately measure, or mitigate these risks.

As the franchise model is integrated into other models, franchisors increasingly operate within an environment that is more complex than many franchisees, financiers, regulators and franchisee advisers recognise. Today's franchisors are increasingly nested within public companies or owned by venture capitalists who assemble groups of franchised and non-franchised brands for the sole ultimate purpose of exiting (with a sizeable profit) via a public listing.

J. Buchan, *Franchisees as Consumers: Benchmarks, Perspectives and Consequences*,
DOI 10.1007/978-1-4614-5614-8_10, 

Consequently, franchisees often contract with undercapitalised and asset-poor franchisor subsidiaries that may, themselves, be expendable to their owners. The franchisor might not be a corporation; it may be, as Kleenmaid was, one of the 14 interdependent entities sitting alongside another related corporate group of ten corporations that dealt directly with the 'franchisees" customers, whose roles are not identified or explained to the franchisee. The franchisees' money, now controlled by the franchisor, may flow freely among the franchisors' entities; it may not be used for the purposes the franchisees paid it for. The cost of the due diligence may be prohibitive, or the franchisee may decide to save money on advisers and believe the layman's rhetoric that due diligence requires only that they have looked 'at the facts of [the] deal from all angles to make sure they stack up'.[1]

The franchisee's ongoing contractual liabilities to third parties assume, but are not contingent on, the franchisor's solvency. As we saw in Chap. 3, the franchisor may control the franchisees' premises. If the franchisor has breached head leases by failing to pay rent or committing an act of bankruptcy, landlords may terminate leases and evict the franchisees even though the franchisees are up to date with rental payments to the franchisor. At the level of state and territory legislation, if the franchisor breaches the head lease, even a franchisee sub-lessee or licensee that could trade strongly without the franchisor's brand has no statutory rights to become head lessee. Although the existence of the trademarks and other intellectual property used by franchisees will be identified in the disclosure document, they may not be owned by the franchisor. This was explored in Chap. 3.

Trebilcock points out that '[a] consumer protection problem is more likely to be present where there is no obvious reason for consumers to doubt their general expectation of safety, so their expectation can easily be exploited'.[2] This describes the problems identified here. It is widely assumed that disclosure protects franchisees in key risk areas, or that it at least provides them with the information they need to structure their affairs so as to protect themselves. The erroneous belief that franchisees are able to conduct adequate due diligence and that somehow this ability is adequate protection for them is a strong deterrent to more regulatory intervention. So also is the prevailing view, cultivated by franchisor interests, that current regulatory structures are adequate for franchising. Change will not come from franchisors; the status quo works for them and all of their stakeholders excluding franchisees. There is still no legal mechanism to impose meaningful checks and balances on franchisors, and this absence reproduces significant asymmetry at numerous junctures, leaving franchisees struggling to protect themselves from a franchisor's exploitative conduct and unable to deal with franchise system failure. Franchise agreements can last from as little as 1 year to, in some cases, 35 years and, in rare cases, indefinitely. It is unrealistic to expect a franchisee to conduct due diligence that sees into the future even if infinite resources were available for this task.

---

[1] Jason Gehrke, What is Due Diligence (2009) Smartcompany <http://www.smartcompany.com.au/franchise-tips-and-trends/20090929-what-is-due-diligence.html> Accessed 5 June 2010.

[2] Michael J Trebilcock, 'Rethinking Consumer Protection Policy' in Charles E F Rickett and Thomas G W Telfer (eds), *International Perspectives on Consumers' Access to Justice* (Cambridge University Press, 2003) 70

The protection and warnings delivered in pre-purchase disclosure are insufficient. There are many stakeholders in the franchise network whose conduct may impact on the network and ultimately on the franchisee. Problems can be hidden elsewhere in the network, where they incubate until they destroy the franchisor. Problems may not arise until after the franchisee has made its investment. When disclosure is stress-tested by exposing it to the common occurrence of a franchisor entering administration, it fails to protect franchisees. We expect too much of disclosure.

Current regulatory interventions based on the assumptions that only proven concepts are franchised, and they do not fail, are outdated. In economic terms, the current franchising model is a classic example of market failure. Franchisors pass the risk and consequences of franchisor failure onto franchisees. The externalities that manifest themselves when franchisors fail are not costed into the model. It fosters deficient research that leads to policy that fails to protect franchisees from the threats they cannot address as individuals.

Australia's Productivity Commission recommends that 'policy makers should have regard to the evidence on how consumers and businesses actually behave'.[3] It is impossible to make effective franchisee protection policy without understanding and addressing the risks and roles franchisees assume and accepting franchisees' inability to accurately measure or mitigate these risks. Some risks 'cannot be removed by simply informing the consumers of them … it may be unfair to expose individuals to the full burden when the risk materializes, and rules that share the risk may be a solution'.[4] In the past, lack of collated evidence on how failed franchisor suppliers and their liquidators behave towards franchisee consumers has meant that the regulators have not regarded the situation as one requiring attention. But awareness is growing that franchisors fail more often than previously believed, and that policy makers and regulators could play a role in alleviating adverse effects of franchisor insolvency. Where the failed firm is a franchisor, not only will the 'total value of the firm fall'[5] but as the insolvency law is currently structured franchisees will 'bear [a disproportionately high] wealth effect of the bankruptcy cost'.[6]

'What a franchisor should be selling is the experience that the franchisor has gained in operating a business successfully'.[7] This is not always done in good faith. Franchisors are able to manage risks; currency fluctuations by arranging futures contracts, supplier risk by making it a condition of giving suppliers supply contracts that suppliers provide a credible alternative backup supply line if a disaster befalls the original supplier and interrupts supply. Franchisors are able to mitigate

---

[3] Australian Government Productivity Commission, *Review of Australia's Consumer Policy Framework*, Productivity Commission Report No 45 (2008) vol 2, 42

[4] Geraint Howells, 'The Potential and Limits of Consumer Empowerment by Information' (2005) 22(3) *Journal of Law and Society* 349 at 365

[5] Michael C Jensen and William H Meckling, 'Theory of the Firm: Managerial Behavior, Agency Costs and Ownership Structure' (1976) 3(4) *Journal of Financial Economics* 305, 341

[6] Michael C Jensen and William H Meckling, 'Theory of the Firm: Managerial Behavior, Agency Costs and Ownership Structure' (1976) 3(4) *Journal of Financial Economics* 305, 341

[7] Ray Borradale, Some Heaven Some Hell, Blog on 2012-04-19 20:52 at http://www.bluemaumau.org/node/11500/talk

the consequences of the risk of a landlord implementing a 'demolition clause' in a lease before the end of the lease term by 'allowing' franchisees to take those leases in their own names. 'Parties to a relational contract are not expected to break the relational rules'.[8] These include the rule that 'a [franchisee] party to this type of [franchise] contract does not (rationally) intend to assume the risk of [the franchisor's] opportunistic behaviour'.[9] Franchisors currently break the relational rules with impunity by making risky decisions that may impact their franchisees without any contractual or corporate governance constraints.

It was shown, in Chap. 4, that franchisees occupy a unique space in the business world, being neither employees nor independent contractors/suppliers. Other players that would perform the roles in a non-franchised business that franchisees perform in the franchise network would negotiate appropriate protection from identified legal and business risks before signing contracts. In Chap. 5 I explored the franchise contract and demonstrated key aspects of franchise agreements: they are not traditional commercial contracts between two business people; a few individual franchise agreements may contain *ipso facto* clauses relating to the franchisor's insolvency, but most do not. Even if they did include clauses to protect franchisees, the remedies available for breach of contract are inappropriate as a means of compensating franchisees.

'Private law does matter to those who can use it effectively, for example businesses that incorporate judicial rulings in standard terms or that seek judicial [or regulator]'[10] rulings as a framework for structuring their business methods. Franchisors are such people. Consumers have rarely been able to harness private law to have such systemic effects. Private contract law is, however, unable to provide solutions to the problems franchisees experience when their franchisor fails.

A fundamental difficulty, identified by Rohrbacher in relation to the United States, in developing legal policies around contract-based property rights is that '[f]or executory contracts in bankruptcy, the debtor's (here, franchisor/liquidator) right to performance is treated as property, but the debtor's obligation to perform is treated as contract'. [11] Thus, the franchisee finds the liquidator can at the same time

[8] William Michael Dixon, 'An Examination of the Common Law Obligation of Good Faith in the Performance and Enforcement of Commercial Contracts in Australia' (Thesis (SJD), Queensland University of Technology, Brisbane, 2005) 77 citing NC Seddon, 'Australian Contract Law: Malestrom or Measured Mutation?' (1994) 7 *Journal of Contract Law* 93, 96

[9] William Michael Dixon, 'An Examination of the Common Law Obligation of Good Faith in the Performance and Enforcement of Commercial Contracts in Australia' (Thesis (SJD), Queensland University of Technology, Brisbane, 2005) 77, citing G Hadfield who has suggested an interpretation of 'good faith' as fidelity to an implicit obligation not to use discretion opportunistically: G K Hadfield, 'The Second Wave of Law and Economics: Learning to Surf' in M Richardson and G Hadfield (eds), *The Second Wave of Law and Economics* (1990) 60 as referred to by JM Paterson, 'Good Faith in Commercial Contracts? A Franchising Case Study' (2002) 29 *Australian Business Law Review* 270, 290

[10] For example, Bakers Delight's successful application under *Trade Practices Act 1974* (Cth) s 47

[11] B Rohrbacher, 'More Equal Than Others: Defending Property-Contract Parity in Bankruptcy' (2005) 114(5) *Yale Law Journal* 1099, 1101

have the right to exercise quasi-ownership rights over the franchisee's business and to disclaim the franchise agreement as an onerous contract. Regulators and the law will only succeed in providing adequate protection to franchisees as business consumers when it can be 'credibly demonstrate[d]' [12] that franchisees and master franchisees can enter a franchise agreement knowing that if their franchisor enters administration or is wound up, they will have had the opportunity to assess and prepare for this risk before they sign the franchise agreement and have access to a formal, legislated exit strategy rather than an ad hoc response.

In this book, broad issues have been explored: the increasingly complex corporate and risk environment in which franchisees operate, the roles of franchisees, the purpose and shortcomings of consumer protection, the corporate governance of franchise networks and systems and the franchisor insolvency. The reasons the law does not accommodate franchisees adequately have been explained, along with why franchisees are a special category of consumer that needs better ex ante protection and new recognition in insolvency regimes to ensure the franchise model prospers in the future.

In effect, the 'low-hanging fruit' has now been picked where laws have been created prohibiting misleading and deceptive conduct and requiring disclosure. But once-good law and policy need continuous revision to see if it is working. As Michael Webster observes, 'the current franchise legal model is not hospitable to risk capital. Proper balance between control and reward must be restored'.[13] Like the cost of the air we breathe, the impacts of a franchisor's risky decisions or disastrous failure on its franchisees are currently externalities in economic terms. Franchising does not neatly fit into existing legal frameworks. There are multiple gaps. The most urgent is the accommodation of franchisees if their franchisor fails. So long as the law treats franchising as a simple, two-party, contract-based, commercial relationship, it will miss the mark. Franchisors will continue to act in their own interests, relatively unchecked, and franchisees will continue to absorb the risks of their franchisors' insolvency, relatively unsupported.

[12] Commission of the European Communities, *EU Consumer Policy Strategy 2007–2013*, (2007) 2 <http://ec.europa.eu/consumers/overview/cons_policy/doc/EN_99.pdf> Accessed 5 March 2010

[13] http://www.bluemaumau.org/fair_franchising_bill_will_create_jobs_california

# Index



J. Buchan, *Franchisees as Consumers: Benchmarks, Perspectives and Consequences*,
DOI 10.1007/978-1-4614-5614-8_10, © Springer Science+Business Media New York 2013

## K



## L



## M

MIX
Papier aus verantwortungsvollen Quellen
Paper from responsible sources
FSC® C105338

If you have any concerns about our products,
you can contact us on
**ProductSafety@springernature.com**

In case Publisher is established outside the EU,
the EU authorized representative is:
**Springer Nature Customer Service Center GmbH**
**Europaplatz 3, 69115 Heidelberg, Germany**

Printed by Libri Plureos GmbH
in Hamburg, Germany